Modular Programming in COBOL

Business Data Processing: A WILEY SERIES

Editors: Richard G. Canning
Publisher, Canning Publications, Inc.

J. Daniel Couger
Professor Management and Computer Science
University of Colorado

Personnel Implications for Business Data Processing
Robert A. Dickmann

Design of Sequential File Systems
Thomas R. Gildersleeve

Management Reporting Systems
James M. McKeever in collaboration with Benedict Kruse

A Guide to Packaged Systems
Robert V. Head

Control of the Information System Development Cycle
Robert I. Benjamin

Decision Tables: Theory and Practice
Solomon L. Pollack, Harry T. Hicks, Jr., and William J. Harrison

An Introduction to Data Base Design
John K. Lyon

The Organization of the Data Processing Function
Frederic G. Withington

COBOL Support Packages: Programming and Productivity Aids
Stanley M. Naftaly, Bruce G. Johnson, and Michael C. Cohen

Modular Programming in COBOL
Russell M. Armstrong

Modular Programming in COBOL

Russell M. Armstrong

Principal Systems Analyst
HRB-Singer, Inc.

A WILEY-INTERSCIENCE PUBLICATION

JOHN WILEY & SONS
New York • London • Sydney • Toronto

Library of Congress Cataloging in Publication Data

Armstrong, Russell M
Modular programming in COBOL.

(Business data processing: a Wiley series, formerly the Wiley Communigraph series on business data processing)
"A Wiley-Interscience publication."
Includes bibliographical references.
1. COBOL (Computer program language) I. Title.
HF5548.5.C2A75 001.6'424 73-4030

ISBN 0-471-03325-1

Printed in the United States of America

10 9 8 7 6 5 4

In Memory of My Father

GEORGE RUSSELL ARMSTRONG

Acknowledgments

Many people have helped me in various ways in the course of preparing this book, and even the most hopefully exhaustive list would omit some. Professor Daniel Teichroew of the University of Michigan challenged me to make several improvements over the first draft and provided a number of useful references. Thanks are due my reviewers, particularly Howard Morgan of the Wharton School at the University of Pennsylvania, George Montillon of Procter and Gamble, Albert van Dureen of Phillips, and one other anonymous individual. At Weyerhaeuser I must acknowledge the continued interest and support of my long-time friend and former teacher, Emmett Platt. The early support and focus provided by my colleagues on the Weyerhaeuser Flexible Systems project should be noted: Don Bohlin, Bill MacDonald of Weyco and Ralph van Brunt of Honeywell.

The Weyerhaeuser document *System Transferability* by Ron D. Johnson and Jackie Knoll (now of the Boeing Company and the Canadian Defense, respectively) was an invaluable reference for Chapter 3.

Typing and proofing support was provided by several individuals, but particular thanks are due Miriam Briggs on the final draft and Kathy Caldwell on the preliminary draft.

Finally, I would probably not be finished yet but for the encouragement of my department director at HRB-Singer, Inc., Dr. Terry Heil.

RUSSELL M. ARMSTRONG

State College, Pennsylvania
December 1972

Contents

Introduction

The material in this book was developed as a result of my experience with numerous system development projects whose costs limits and/or deadlines were threatened or exceeded because programs did not run in a dependable manner. The difficulty could nearly always be traced to a few repetitive occurrences, for example:

1. Programs were too long and/or complex to be made reliable.
2. Even if the programs demonstrated some use of modularity, the interfaces among them were ill-defined.
3. The problem had not been properly defined in the beginning, and as change after change was introduced the system went out of control.
4. Frequently, to compound the above problems, the originators of important segments of the system (definitions, programs, and interfaces) had been transferred to other projects or were otherwise unavailable to follow through with their part of the system.

This book is about modular COBOL programming as a major way to deal with these problems in developing business applications systems. I hope to make the point that modular programming is good programming and good programming is modular. Good programming cannot save a bad problem definition and can have only limited success in saving a bad systems design, but bad programming can certainly wreck the best analysis and design. It is the program code that ultimately defines a system.

If an organization is to benefit fully from modular programming, there should be a commitment to it on all levels of system responsibility. The systems manager should say, "I want it," and ask the development project leaders to produce. Analysts and designers must understand modularity to the extent that they do not contradict it in their designs. For this reason I have arranged the chapters so that material also of interest to systems managers, project leaders, analysts, and designers appears in the first part of the book, followed by technical programming material. I recommend that readers delve as deeply into the book as their technical familiarity permits.

Chapter 1 defines, in very broad terms, those problems organizations face in systems development that can be greatly relieved if not actually cured by modular programming. The message to the system manager is essentially that modular programming is a good investment.

Since modular programming does not occur spontaneously, but requires at least a work environment that does not contradict it, Chapter 2 deals with programming quality control. I discuss those aspects of responsibility, and measurement related to initiating and reinforcing modular programming. The underlying premise is that it benefits everyone if the process of programming is well defined and controlled.

Chapter 3 discusses the additional problems of reusing, transferring, or converting programs to other systems, applications, or computer configurations.

The frequent transfer of personnel mentioned above implies, in part, the need to communicate the workings of a program to those unfamiliar with it. Chapter 4 is a discussion of program documentation and is concerned with basically two ideas: that documentation should truly aid communication, and how to make documentation as much as possible a by-product of the development process.

Chapter 5 establishes the basic definition and a perspective of the term *modularity* as it applies to systems. Modularity exists on several levels in systems development and has been ill-defined in computing literature to date.

Chapter 6 begins the technical COBOL portion of the book. From this point on the material becomes quite explicit and requires a reasonable working knowledge of COBOL. Chapter 6 explains how modularity is developed at the most detailed level of a single COBOL program.

Chapter 7 deals with multiprogram modularity, subprograms, linkages, and the interfaces they require.

Troublesome areas frequently encountered in COBOL and how to avoid them is the subject of Chapter 8. This is where the use of simple, standardized methods is introduced. Chapter 9 continues, elaborating on the material of Chapter 8, on the subject of developing reusable modules.

Chapter 10 contains a message of concern about the need for production-oriented language capability.

The Appendix contains sample coding, demonstrating recommendations for programming and documentation style.

CHAPTER 1

Change and Flexibility in Systems

THE MYTH OF SYSTEMUS

COBOL was designed, in part, to be a very readable language. It is one of the few languages in which a programmer can legitimately tell a computer to "GO TO HELL." It then becomes the programmer's responsibility to define the particular characteristics of the HELL that he has created. The nature of the damnation that claims many system development efforts could have been symbolized in Greek mythology as an individual who is given as his punishment what seems to be a simple task to perform only to find that, upon completion, something has changed so that the task must be started over, and so on into eternity.

In his penetrating study of the nature of our society, Alvin Toffler's *Future Shock*[1] describes the difficulties individuals and organizations have in adapting when the future comes too quickly, when change occurs too rapidly. The future often arrives too soon for many organizations that are developing information systems. A system may not yet be complete when a change occurs that affects it. The manager who requested the system may be promoted, transferred, or terminated. The staff that developed the system may similarly not be available to modify or maintain it. The scope or volume of the activities the system was designed to support may change. A new installation of computer hardware may require massive conversion and reprogramming.

The rapid changes that affect decision-making processes in organizations call for information systems that are highly responsive. Responsiveness means that a system is timely and accurate, and also that it is cost-effective, humane (adapts to its user's needs rather than vice versa), and flexible. This book deals primarily with achieving flexibility in systems.

A flexible system is designed for ease of reconstruction; the parts are modular and discrete and perform a visible and clear function. Replacement or addition of a capability is analogous to the same process in a component high fidelity sound system; one simply plugs it in or unplugs it. The greater the degree of modularity, the more flexible the system may become.

There is an occasional tendency to confuse flexibility with generality, but they are independent. "Generalized" implies that a system has been implemented to serve some perceived majority of requirements for some problem area. Thus there are many generalized systems for accounting, payroll, scheduling, and so on. Generalized systems usually contain a wider range of possibilities than a single user may require. This implies that each user must pay for unused capability, as well as for the overhead of choosing among the generalized alternatives. If a user wishes to perform some process or receive some output that varies from what a generalized system provides, modification of the system may prove difficult. This is where generality and flexibility may overlap.

Application systems can be made flexible by a strategy of design and program construction that minimizes the impact of change. Indeed, the philosophy of an organization developing systems should be that change is a normal and expected event. Methods need to be provided that allow systems to be developed and altered to meet changing requirements without the prohibitive time and cost that usually accompany this activity.

INFLEXIBILITY AND COSTS

The symptom of inflexibility in systems most visible to the user and to systems management is high cost. Change is the most costly item in data systems; this is a fact. The question involves the dimension of this cost, and where in the life of a system it occurs. Let us view the systems cycle as being roughly divided into four main categories[2]: (1) systems definition, (2) systems construction, (3) achieving operational status, and (4) operating. The lightly shaded portion of Figure 1 shows the expected cost distribution associated

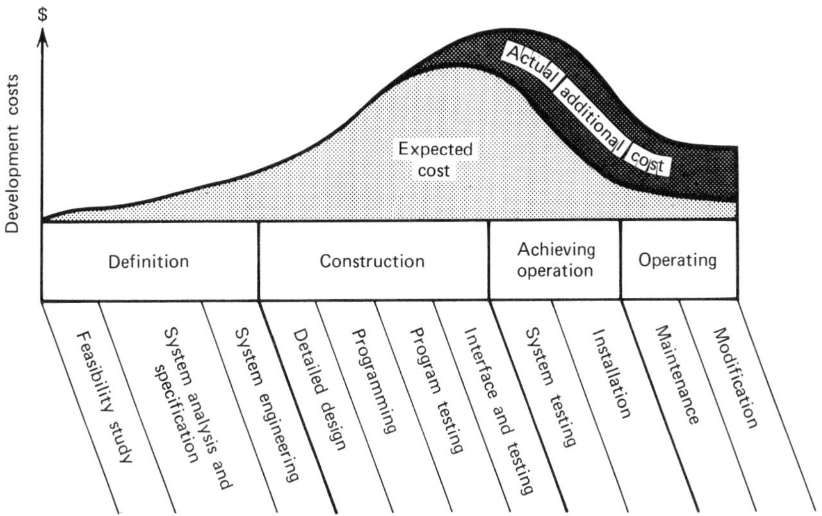

Figure 1 **Cost distribution over system development cycle.**

with system development. Costs are projected to begin rising through the definition phase, peak toward the end of the construction phase when program testing is complete, and fall off rapidly through installation to the time the system reaches operational status. The heavily shaded portion of the figure illustrates the more likely actual distribution. As programs defy efforts to make them reliable, or become resistant to change, or as interfaces do not interface, costs continue to rise in the construction phase. As a result, the construction phase spills over into the installation, and the same symptoms occur in system testing. As problems continue to occur and as the system becomes even harder to change in a reliable manner, the costs of operational maintenance and modification turn out higher than expected and may continue to rise. Most likely, at some phase relatively early in the operating life of the system, the whole process will be started over.

Higher costs and delayed delivery in the face of change mean a loss of responsiveness to the dynamics of an organization's needs. When a system cannot be adapted to changing conditions, its users frequently turn to some other source for information on which to base their operations. While their alternate source may be more responsive than a poor computer system, it may also be greatly less responsive than a good system would be. In addition, the rate at which organizations are being forced to respond and adapt is itself accelerating. If computer-based systems are to remain in or achieve a posture that an organization considers responsive, then methods that will produce more flexible systems must be used.

FLEXIBLE VERSUS "COMMON" SYSTEMS

Many organizations are large enough so that a given operational function is duplicated in one or more alternate locations. The organization may seek to soften the impact of change by establishing a policy that a given function will be performed in the same manner at all locations. If this is done, it is reasoned, the systems that support these functions should also be the same or "common." Typically, these functions are familiar basic operational systems such as general ledger, accounts receivable, accounts payable, inventory management, responsibility accounting, project and budget control, and payroll and manpower management systems.

This is an attempt to solve the problem by organizational methods, but is not likely to succeed, since even with common systems there may be legitimate variability from location to location. Input and reporting should be subject to the needs and wants of individuals, if we are to recognize the humane aspect of systems. Processing exceptions are easy to cite: local or state tax calculations in a payroll system; local costs incurred by state transportation tariffs; state laws regarding disbursement and payment (e.g., California rules on payment in certain categories of building contracts). Locations with different-sized computers may have to adopt different data base strategies. No matter how much commonality an organization may be able to define, that too may change. Present management may alter its ideas about how the organization operates, or a new management may take over. Even if a significant degree of commonality can be achieved in an organization, flexibility is still a most important attribute of a system. The same is true of an organization that seeks to create or buy some "final, definitive, generalized system" only to find that the future rushes in and erodes that definition.

THE FLEXIBLE SOLUTION

As discussed in the preceding paragraphs, the strategy of many organizations is to try to fix the requirements, to make time stand still, rather than to adopt a more flexible development strategy. So when a common or general system is not suitable, the frequent response is to create another inflexible common or general system. There is, however, a technical strategy that is largely independent of the definition of the requirements. In other words, no matter how rigid or volatile the requirements may seem to be, it is still good business to develop a system in a flexible manner.

The following chapters present a technical solution to many of the problems involving time and cost overruns in the development and maintenance of information systems. A large part of this solution involves modularity. Although there is a fair amount of literature available on modularity, much of it is devoted to describing the benefits rather than the techniques. Quickly reviewed these benefits are:

1. Problems can be more easily solved.
2. A modular system is more easily tested and debugged.
3. Modules may be reused, saving development time.
4. Programming tasks may be assigned more independently of the "critical path" in a project.
5. Estimates for the resources required for a project are improved for modular systems.
6. A system may be more easily changed.

Other benefits could be cited; the interested reader may refer to the references for additional justification.[3] The situation (for reasons stated later) is that these benefits are recognized by many but attained by few. This book provides information that will permit an organization to achieve these benefits. While the focus is on modular COBOL programming, in detail heretofore unobtainable, I have included other related issues which, if not properly considered, may contradict the benefits of modularity. Thus there is information on project control, program documentation, the design of program interfaces, and trouble areas in the COBOL language.

I did not invent modularity; many of the recommendations to be found here are scattered throughout computing literature. What I have tried to do is to bring many of these ideas together in a coherent package. I have also tried to avoid the formalism that places a barrier between much of the good theoretical work taking place and the implementation of that theory in a productive environment. My philosophy is that the test of good theory is good practice. A systems organization can write its COBOL programming standards directly from this book.

REFERENCES

1. Toffler, Alvin, *Future Shock*, Random House, New York, 1970.
2. Benjamin, Robert, *Control of the Information System Development Cycle,* John Wiley, New York, 1971. The categories have been borrowed from this book.
3. Consult especially the following references: Jackson, Michael, and Swanwick, Anthony B., "Segmented Level Programming," *Computers and Automation,* February 1969. Canning, Richard, "Modular Cobol Programming," *EDP Analyzer,* July 1972.

CHAPTER 2

Program Quality Control

This chapter is basically about quality control as it applies to programming, with additional attention to some of the broader aspects of a benign environment for systems development.

The keys to creating an environment where clean, modular, and flexible coding is practiced lie in definition and measurement. Definition involves identifying what is desirable, communicating it to a staff, and assigning definite responsibilities. Specifications are made as to what is to be done, and any necessary instruction is provided to explain how it is to be done. Since all is not perfect in the world, some measurements must be made to insure that the "what" is being followed and that the "how" has been understood.

The responsibility for implementing and sustaining an environment in which a high quality of modular code is produced involves to some degree most of a systems development staff. I have chosen to describe this environment as a series of discussions outlining the responsibilities of systems management, project leaders, system designers, and programmers.

RESPONSIBILITIES: THE SYSTEMS MANAGER

The manager of a systems function is the one who should make the initial commitment to implement modular, clean programming and the quality control procedures required to insure its continued use. Although such a program might be adopted by a technical staff independently of systems management's concern, making it clear that management is watching and measuring greatly accelerates the staff's learning curve.

The manager is also responsible for the quality of the work environment, and in some organizations there is a serious need for reform. My experience to date has been that those who are the most enthusiastic about modularity and clean code are individuals in small software service organizations, or free-lance programmers. In small organizations a programmer is strongly motivated to help increase efficiency, reduce costs, and improve profit. A small organization just cannot afford, and will not retain, an individual who performs otherwise. Also, the contract orientation of many small shops helps to improve the definition of each project; more careful planning is done because a contract involves a specified and fixed amount of cold hard cash. In some small service companies, profit sharing, which extends down to the project staff level, is a strong motivational factor.

A typical large organization emphasizes precisely the opposite type of motivation. There is a much denser proportion of managers to technicians in a large organization. Communications are more formal and time-consuming, and individuals may be evaluated more on the quality of their communication (status reports, etc.) than on the product. In large organizations in which the systems function is essentially subsidized (either provided out and out as a "free" service to divisions, or subject only to "memo-billing" charges), the profit role of the systems organization may not be clear. Indeed, there may be no motivation to be efficient or capable in a "profitable" sense, and resources are wasted. While a contractual relationship can be used to focus on issues of definition, communications, and responsibility, this is also in contradiction to the informal relationship between service functions and line functions in many large organizations. Often neither the client's nor the provider's roles are made explicit, and after a project history of miscommunication each can blame the other for failure.

All this serves to point out that a systems manager in pursuit of efficiency, who wishes to achieve lower systems costs and increased capability, must make sure that these aims are supported in the working environment.

CODE IS TO BE SEEN AND NOT HEARD ABOUT

The manager should also understand how the programming effort should be measured. The most current, during-the-fact way to evaluate a systems project and to obtain modular, flexible, clear code is to read the code itself. We can insure that the concerns of flexibility (maintainability, adaptability, and higher reliability) can be met by maximizing the cleanliness, modularity, and intelligibility of the code. It is the fault of many systems organizations that only the programmers read any code—either what they themselves write, or what they are charged with maintaining. For various reasons project leaders and system managers seldom read the code produced by their projects or departments.[1]

Part of this is due to our definition of responsibility for the various systems jobs, and our system of rewards. In many organizations (user organizations are worse offenders than service or vendor organizations), the job of programmer is considered to be entry-level and transitory. When a certain level of competency, seniority, or favorable visibility has been obtained, a promotion is awarded. As long as an individual has the basic title of programmer and the promotion involves appending a new modifier (senior, lead, staff, associate), the individual continues to be involved with code. However, if the salary structure for programmers is not parallel and equal to that of systems designers or information analysts, a problem arises. At a certain level of competency, an individual may have to be promoted to the title of systems designer or analyst merely to justify a higher salary. A situation of this kind has a very strongly implied message, a hidden syllogism, that: (1) programming is not the path to success; (2) programmers work with and understand code; therefore (3) to work with and understand code is not the path to success. The entire stretch of the systems career ladder from designer to system management is occupied by people who seem to regard program code as anathema. Perhaps they have unpleasant memories of coding difficulties, which are best forgotten.

An analogy may be made to the effect that this situation constitutes a lack of literacy. A systems project leader who cannot read code is at the same disadvantage as a publisher of French novels who cannot read French. One person may call the novels trash and another may praise them as works of great literary merit. The point is that anyone in the systems project hierarchy who cannot read code must depend absolutely on someone else to do programming quality control. Since in many systems organizations this dependence is defaulted to the programmers themselves, the result is no quality control. A systems department's code may be "trashy," but the systems manager's only information may be that projects exhibit frequent cost overruns, deadline difficulties, and similar symptoms of "dirty" code.

Realistically, in all but the smallest organizations, the systems manager will assign one or more individuals with primary quality control responsibility. This is not to imply, however, that the manager abdicate all contact with the code produced by his staff.

Unfortunately, one cannot look at code and decide easily if it is doing its job correctly. That is the role of rigorous test procedures and is beyond the scope of this volume. All code appears formidably potent, but not all code appears clean and simple. The "boss" should expect that the technical staff can demonstrate the cleanliness and orderliness of its code, and that the better the job they are doing the easier it should be.

I have discussed measurement seemingly in terms of aesthetics rather than dollars and cents. Take it as a matter of faith that experience will show that a well-written, well-documented program is a good investment. Two more usual ways in which one might measure the results of modularity involve watching for reductions in programming and system maintenance costs.

Measuring whether programming time has been reduced presumes that a systems group has kept track of the time it has spent in the past and therefore has a basis for comparison. One problem in the early stages of implementing flexible practices is that a fair amount of time is expended in changing programmers' habits. If programmers are unfamiliar with modularity and clean constructs, they will have some difficulty in trying to think about solving their programming problems this way. Some false starts are to be expected.

The maintenance costs of a system will not show up for some time. Here again, the maintenance costs presume a basis of comparison. One possible contradiction is that a flexible system may receive more maintenance because of its greater alterability. If each change in a system improves its responsiveness and increases user satisfaction, and if changes are easy to make, everyone wins.

The trouble with both of these two measurements is that they are after the fact. If the code has been badly written, the organization is stuck with it, and the programmers who wrote it are also the only ones who will want to maintain it (the maternal instinct is strong enough for the creator of a system to tolerate continually "changing its diaper"). It is far better to insure that clean code is being written while it is being written. The issues of development and maintenance time and costs tend to take care of themselves.

Maintenance falls into two general categories: (1) postimplementation debugging, correcting a system that is faulty in relation to the orginal requirements, and (2) alterations in the system as a result of requirement changes. Systems tend to be inflexible in both of these situations for the same reason.

THE QUALITY CONTROL FUNCTION

If a systems department has not already assigned quality control responsibilities, the systems manager may want to assign a senior technician to this job. There may not be a continued full-time need for a quality control advisor, certainly not in small organizations, but it may be appropriate during the initial phases of a quality control program to make this a temporary assignment. The job that needs to be done in all systems quality control is wider than the scope of this discussion and includes analysis and design review, module and system testing, maintenance, and modification review. We are concerned here only with the review and control of programming.

Whoever is responsible for introducing modular COBOL concepts should first develop local guidelines from the information in this book.

Obviously, for the systems staff to understand how to produce clean and modular program code, some instruction may have to be provided. Some of this instruction is really "selling" the concept, showing systems staffs why flexibility is beneficial. Similar to many concepts, there is room for interpretation and there are latitudes in implementation. If the project leaders do not understand what the concept is they will not be able to evaluate their project staffs as to how well the concept is being implemented. If designers do not understand it, their designs may be mismatched to modular concepts, forcing programmers either to redesign or compromise the modularity of the system. Obviously, programmers have to understand it.

One of the very best ways to begin teaching these concepts is to plan educational involvement around an actual project. There is nothing more informative than real examples and no better way to reinforce the concepts than to apply them in practice immediately.

Clearly, the person who is to head up the implementation, the quality control project manager, needs to be a qualified consultant, and a believer. The role is that of technical evangelist, with active participation in selected projects with informal lectures, actual design effort, coding, and documentation at critical points.

RESPONSIBILITIES: APPLICATIONS PROJECT LEADERS

In many organizations it is the project leader who evaluates the code being produced and who functions as advisor and auditor. Initially, in larger organizations there may be a staff consultant available for advice, but eventually the primary quality control role must pass to the leaders of the various applications projects. The lead programmer may also take on this responsibility, especially on large projects.

It is the responsibility of an applications project leader (as regards modular matters) to evaluate his project staff. The most desirable environment is naturally one in which the programmers are themselves enthusiastic about modular concepts. This will only result if they have the understanding (through initial education and the availability of guidance during projects) and are being evaluated. Evaluation implies the obvious; if programmers will not use clean, simple, modular code, perhaps they should seek another profession. Systems groups cannot become dependent on the personal quirks and partialities of individuals. If someone hatches brilliant ideas, these concepts may make even better use of that brilliance. If an individual will not use these concepts, any number of less brilliant individuals who will use them can do a better job of programming.

There may indeed be examples (there have been in the past) in which an individual resists these concepts. Pride can be a significant factor. Some individuals may feel a personal attachment to their own constructs. They have often created them with great difficulty, without examples on which to model their efforts, and with horribly uninformative manuals.

However, if what they are doing creates the kind of problems I have mentioned, something has to be done. Key people who have otherwise strong skills may have to be very carefully handled. Consider giving them jobs that do not involve programming.

On the benefit side, project leaders may expect that the use of modular methods will permit them to refine their estimates of job cost and duration, and the level of effort required. This happens in two ways. First, project leaders are usually accustomed to estimating in relation to the anticipated complexity of a program. The more complex the program, the more one finds a deviation from the expected. The use of simple modular code greatly improves the situation. In the preliminary design phase, one identifies the modules required for a system. These modules should be specified in sufficient detail such that each of them represents a single simple program module. Interfaces between modules should also be considered modules. If all the modules have been identified as being as small and simple as they should be, then the estimate will be closer to the time required to develop a single module multiplied by the number of modules in the system.

As modules are developed that represent generalized or repeat capability, they are put "on the shelf" for future use. The more of these generalized routines that can be employed on a project, the more accurate the estimate will become. More of the development phase will represent a "known" factor.

The development of on-the-shelf capability does not necessarily imply that total systems costs can be reduced. The programming and testing phase should demonstrate significant savings. This permits resources to be shifted to the areas of problem analysis, documentation, installation, and user training and assistance where performance is deficient in many organizations.

Efficiency and Systems Tuning

Almost always, early in discussions about modularity and clean code the question of efficiency arises. Since this is an issue project leaders can expect to encounter, an overview is in order. The usual concern of programmers is with what may be termed "microefficiency." A typical example is the comparable execution time of two COBOL statements or constructs such as PERFORM and GO TO. Another example is the cost, in machine time, of subroutine linkage as opposed to in-line coding. Much training in programming has stressed "bit" or microefficiency. The probable reason is that in early computing, with subminiature storage and tortoise cycle times, this was a critical concern. Such microefficiency is also an easy concept to grasp; arranging a program to shave some time from its execution, or to reduce the number of statements, became a convenient model of elegance.

Today the situation in computing is different. Completing a computing job technically is no longer miraculous; our problems involve responsiveness, solving the right problems. To gain responsiveness we must have a flexible structure. This does not contradict concerns of efficiency; in fact, flexibility is a prerequisite to real efficiency. Distinction must be made between efficiency in the macro- and microsense. The most dramatic reductions in resource requirements (time and core) in computer systems come from the ability either to make large readjustments in the structure or to pinpoint for modification those modules that contribute most to the execution time.

An example of a macroimprovement (they are often feasible only if they can be easily implemented) is the reduction in the number of times a data base needs to be referenced. "Stacking" functions such as update and file selection for reporting are examples. Consider a specific instance in which there are three input streams in a system, each of which contains information with which a sequential data base is to be updated. By gathering and merging the input streams before passing what may be a large data file, significant time savings may be obtained. While it can be said that such a decision should have been made in the original design phase, frequently, in the real systems world, it is only after some coding effort that such opportunities become apparent. If the structure is modular, the change may be trivial; if the structure is "spaghetti," the programmer may be left holding a cold meatball. There can scarcely be too much emphasis on this point. The number of times such a decision point is encountered in systems development efforts is very great. The tuning of systems should most naturally come in the "soft" phase of implementation. "Soft" indicates a period in which the system is being run in a trial mode. The users are receiving reports and otherwise trying out their interfaces, but the business operation the system will support is not yet dependent on it. Too few systems actually have such a phase, which is a source of a great deal of trauma. Again, it is only in such an exercise, or, lacking a soft cut-over, when a system is up and running, that many of the opportunities for macroefficiency emerge.

It must be said about microefficiency that whenever it contradicts modularity or clarity it should be discounted. First, most arguments for microefficiency are rather weak. PERFORM versus GO TO is an example. Taken on a one-to-one basis, PERFORM (in the usual implementation—IBM/370 rather than Honeywell 600) requires six more machine instructions than GO TO. What is often overlooked is the additional coding (IF statements and setting flags) it may take to implement more than one logical path passing through an in-line coded segment. PERFORM, as will be stressed, is one of the more powerful tools for modularity in COBOL and to avoid using it to gain microefficiency is being extremely short-sighted. The use of CALL is another example. CALL is significantly more time-consuming than PERFORM, but the benefits it offers in generality and flexibility more than offset its cost.

Microefficiency may be turned into macroefficiency, but only if the structure of the system permits. This is where the odds shift overwhelmingly in favor of modularity. Only when a system is in an advanced stage may all its critical points become clear. A great deal of effort may be expended on making code in a program or system microefficient, and much of this effort may be wasted; there is negative gain from tuning code that is seldom exercised in a program. If the code is modular, one can very easily (through testing and timing, or by using "snooper" hardware/software aids) isolate and identify the critical code.[2]

If in extreme cases assembly-level code is clearly called for, substitute it for COBOL only in the most critical modules. For system conversion or transfer, always maintain the equivalent COBOL module. In this way moving or altering that part of the system will involve only a loss of efficiency (temporary until the assembly code can be rewritten), not of capability.

Testing

Another area of responsibility for the project leader is the testing of programs and systems. This is a topic that deserves a great deal of research, analysis, and comment; too much, indeed, for the scope of this monograph. The reader is invited to consult other sources dealing with this subject.[3] The important point is that testing is a hierarchic process and implies modularity. One should begin with small modules which are testable by virtue of their limited function. As these are determined to be reliable, the next level may be tested. Interface should be thought of as a separate function for testing purposes, too. If at all possible, do not test both the logic of a module and its interface with other models at the same time. Only by means of a well-defined modular structure can one approach the desirable end of testing in a "software test bench" environment.[4] Only by facilitating the testing of single modules can these modules be developed independently and (in PERT terms) removed from the critical path.

RESPONSIBILITIES: THE SYSTEMS DESIGNER

The systems designer also needs to understand modular concepts. The software and language facilities used to implement a solution greatly influence how the problem should be expressed. Conversely, the way a design has been formulated greatly influences the resultant solution. The systems designer's decisions frequently have the greatest effect on both the developmental and operational costs of a system. If there is a mismatch between the design and implementation tools, further definition will be required. Frequently, this is what happens when systems designers have a different (often incomplete) understanding of the programmer's tools. A case in point is the use of decision tables. If a problem is expressed in decision tables by a systems designer and given to a programmer who has no tools for direct implementation, he will reformulate before programming. If the programmer has a decision table processor (such as DETAB/65)[5] but the designer has no understanding of decision table use, the programmer will again have to reformulate before using his tools.

The same is true of many of the flexible techniques described in this monograph. If the output of a design effort does not specify table-driven constructs, or overintegrates segmentable functions, additional design effort will be required. Usually, the resources for this additional design add to the cost of the programming phase. The reuse of capability requires that designers think in terms of developing and using building blocks.

RESPONSIBILITIES: THE PROGRAMMER

The programmer is the one who ultimately will sink or save the whole issue of modularity. He is the one who commits code to core. His responsibilities are to perform the effort to be described in the remainder of this monograph.

Rather than preview here what is to come, let us discuss briefly what appears to be a change in the programmer's role, both perceived and actual.

It has been reported that one of the fathers of computers and computer programming, the mathematician John von Neumann, was horrified to find how many programming errors he and his staff had committed (on the ENIAC computer in 1946). He expected each program to run successfully the first time. (Now of course things are different; we expect a program to run only after the first successful compilation.) Programming early gained a reputation as a complex business; after all, if it was difficult for von Neumann, it is difficult for you and me. In fact, the idea of difficulty was carried so far that soon programming really was not programming unless it was complex. This particular model of programming was especially prevalent in university circles, but spilled over into the commercial world as well. A phenomenon called superprogrammer began to emerge in the computer environment.

A superprogrammer was a person who had a reputation for being able, single-handedly, to write the longest and/or most complex and/or most perversely tricky program and make it run. What a superprogrammer did was to demonstrate the ability to scale a mountain or to survive a kayak trip through the rapids of a river. The problem is that, first, the path to most finished systems did not have to pass through either mountains or rapids. Second, for subsequent trips (for maintenance or alteration) over the mountains or rapids, the superprogrammer may not have been available and the hapless replacement may not have survived. Maintenance programmers who inherited superprograms tended to develop quite a different view of the ingredients of a good program. For some programmers somewhere, going through someone else's spaghetti may be a challenge and a joy, but for most programmers that kind of work is very depressing. There are innumerable examples of programmers who have fled their jobs rather than maintain some tangle of a system. I know of one system that is responsible for the departure of several individuals.

Large systems are created by teams of individuals, not by a single person. Programmers who have worked in a team environment have begun to appreciate that simple programs are elegant programs. There is a growing awareness that successful programming requires a structured approach. It is easy to create complexity in a program, indeed, a level of complexity that exceeds that of most other mental activities; the solution to a simple problem can be made a difficult task. To solve a truly complex problem requires that all the components be kept as simple as possible.

The Creative Environment

What the remainder of this book does is to define a fairly rigid COBOL programming style. When this material is introduced to programmers in organizations, there will be a predictable number who will be concerned that their creativity is being threatened. My contention is that only by highly structuring the tools of programming can programmers become really creative. Many programmers do not have the time to solve truly interesting problems or to develop new capabilities and ideas because they are tied up debugging excessively complex programs and redoing variations of capability that should have been on the shelf. Much of the time this is not the programmer's fault, but that of measurement which emphasizes immediate results at the expense of future need. At least there is a growing awareness on the part of managers of systems development efforts that a near-sighted attitude is very costly in the longer run.

To create a healthy work environment, a balance must be obtained between creativity and structure. Organizations need to maintain an environment where individuals are able to contribute and implement new ideas. However, certain goal orientations must be heeded. Programming tricks and techniques that inhibit the goals of flexibility must be disallowed.

Job Definition

Another difficulty has been in the definition of the scope of the programmer's job. Historically, in systems efforts there has been a deficit in the capability for information analysis and problem definition. To fill this gap systems designers have functioned (frequently unsatisfactorily) as analysts. Similarly, since this left certain aspects of the design function unfulfilled, programmers have taken over these portions of the design responsibility.

The result is that there are almost no "coders," nor in the pure sense, programmers. Most programmers beyond the entry level function as programmer/designers (often called programmer/analysts). When (more typically in large organizations than small) there is not a clear understanding of the roles of the various members of a systems team, tension may arise as to the territorial prerogatives of the respective members.

The sharper definition of design and programming tasks brought about by the implementation of flexible, and so on, concepts may heighten this tension. The trend toward better role definition in systems projects should take the direction of providing more analyst and interface responsibilities for the systems designer and more overt design responsibilities for the programmer. It should be made clear that the programmer's first job is to not to begin to code, but to begin planning and detailed designing. Programmers and their supervisors are too frequently in a hurry to see program code. A redefinition of their jobs should help to prevent the design of systems in "real-time." The programmer's job should include developing better programming tools and capability for the organization. Wider recognition should be given to the ability of experienced programmers to save time and money for an organization.

SUMMARY

To create an environment where clean modular code is written requires a commitment from systems management to initiate the program, insure that the measurement environment is supportive, and assign definite responsibility for the quality control function.[6] Applications project leaders should understand the importance of better project definition and the relationship of modularity to cost estimation, efficiency, and testing. Systems designers should understand the tools of modularity. Programmers should understand their roles and job definitions as being more responsible than in the past. Programmers need to recognize their position as members of a team and as developers of capability.

REFERENCES

1. Weinberg, Gerald M., *The Psychology of Computer Programming,* Van-Nostrand Reinhold, New York, 1972. Contains a section on the desirability of reading programs. In general, this excellent book offers many suggestions for improving the systems work environment.
2. For further discussion on this point see: Constantine, Larry, "A Modular Approach to Program Optimization," *Computers and Automation,* March 1967, pp. 35–37.
3. Refer to Jackson, Michael, and Swanwick, Anthony B., "Segmented Level Programming," *Computers and Automation,* February 1969; also Gruenberger, Fred, "Program Testing and Validating," *Datamation,* July 1968, pp. 39–45; and Cohen, Alan, "Modular Programs: Defining the Module," *Datamation,* January 1972, pp. 34–37.
4. The best discussion extant on testing a test-bed environment of which I am aware is in the material on Hoskyns Systems Research's "Testmaster" proprietary test package.
5. Pollack, Solomon L., Hicks, Harry T., and Harrison, William J., *Decision Tables: Theory and Practice,* John Wiley, New York, 1971.
6. A very informative article describing the approach of a group using PL/I is in: Baker, F. T., "Chief Programmer Team Management of Production Programming," *IBM Systems Journal,* No. 1, 1972.

CHAPTER **3**

Transferability and Portability

There are two different, although frequently intermixed, factors involved in the mobility of systems. One is the ability to move a system from one brand or model of computer to another. A term for this attribute is transferability, also referred to in computing literature as transportability.

A second attribute which may be applied to systems is portability, the ability to move a system from one location to another in a business sense. Thus a budget control and responsibility accounting system may be used by more than one division or by a subsidiary.

As far as computing literature goes, portability has been almost totally neglected. The problem of moving a system in the business sense is not only the larger problem but also the most ill-structured. While the incompatibility of computer equipment creates difficulties, they are difficulties that can be handled. Portability, however, is greatly dependent on the behavior of individuals. It is obtaining agreement among diverse users or predicting the future behavior of unknown users that makes portability interesting.

The reason for discussing the problems of transferability and portability in this book is that their solutions are very closely related to modularity and the standardization of constructs. Reviewing these problems provides a better background for the material to come, as well as more reasons for using it.

This chapter is not intended to be either a thorough analysis of the problems involved in transferability among the many COBOL compilers available, or a complete guide to the variability of business practices that impact systems. Such analysis could go on and on. The aim is rather to illuminate the problems and recommend general means for approaching their solutions. Let us discuss the easier one, transferability, first.

TRANSFERABILITY

An organization must address the concerns of transferability under the following circumstances.

1. When it is desirable to move a system from one part (division, group, etc.) of the organization to another and there are equipment differences.
2. When an organization is considering the acquisition of a computer different from the one they are currently using, that is, conversion.
3. When an organization intends to market, trade, give away, or otherwise produce code which they plan to export from the organization.

When faced with the problem or prospect of transferring systems, an organization should carefully define the range of the problem for their systems staffs, especially the programmers. A document should be prepared [it would be reasonable to obtain aid from the computer vendor(s) involved] which defines the scope of the transferability or conversion requirements.

This document should list the differences in character representation, core size, file access and storage, COBOL source statements, and operating system and control language, as well as other pertinent differences, between the two (or more) computers involved. The following discussions highlight some of the specific COBOL concerns that should be covered in a transferability document, followed by some additional recommendations on its other contents.

ANS COBOL

The problem in COBOL is that, while there exists a standard COBOL, ANS (American National Standard) COBOL, no computer manufacturer offers a COBOL compiler that is both full and pure ANS. The situation is roughly as follows:

1. Small machine compilers are often subsets of ANS. Frequently, the choice of subset facilities is strange indeed. In one manufacturer's small machine compiler, ALTER has been included, and GO TO . . . DEPENDING ON has not. Manufacturers offer subsets to reduce compile time and storage (both at compile time to reduce the number of passes required and at run time to reduce the run-time subroutine support required for COBOL object programs).
2. Many manufacturers wish their COBOL compilers to reflect certain hardware features of their machines. These features frequently offer certain microefficiencies in compile and execution speed but just as often are included because of compatibility with some prior generation COBOL compiler or to provide some feature otherwise available only to the assembly language programmer. One manufacturer's COBOL represents a quite dramatic philosophical departure in that it is treated as a subset of ALGOL. In this case one can point to some very interesting benefits, but they are of nostalgic interest, and nostalgia does not help us in a production environment.
3. Combining the above two tendencies, especially in the larger machine's COBOL compilers, one may obtain either a subset of ANS COBOL with extensions or a full set, but still with extensions.

ANS incompatabilities create problems in system transferability which range from simple to ghastly.

Data Representation

The internal representation of character sets differs rather widely among the various vendors' machines. With only minor exceptions this creates no problem in the compiling of programs. The incompatability of punched card inputs is a problem frequently handled in systems installations. However, real problems may be created in the use of these internal codes when the collating sequence is involved.

Collating sequence is the order in which internal bit configurations are assigned to incoming patterns of bits from an input medium. Thus, in the IBM 360/370 world, a card punch of 12-6-8 is interpreted as the special character "+" and assigned an internal value of 4E (hexadecimal; 78 is the decimal equivalent). In the Honeywell 600 the same punched card code 12-6-8 is interpreted as a "<" (less than) and assigned an internal value of 36 (octal, which is 30 decimal). Further difficulties may occur in sorting data files. In the collating sequence of the IBM 370, numerics 0 through 9 are treated as the highest-valued legitimate characters (decimal 240 through 249). In the standard Honeywell 600 sequence, numerics have the lowest value (decimal 0 through 9).

In an attempt to sort an input field into ascending order in the above situation, the field "123A" would be sorted preceding "A123" on the Honeywell machine, while the reverse would be true on the IBM machine. The situation is improved somewhat by the fact that many non-IBM compilers have the option to declare the collating sequence COMMERCIAL, which then causes code to be generated which at least treats the relationship between alphabetics and numerics the same as in the IBM 370 usage (EBCDIC).

Table 1 shows the relationship between the Honeywell 600 Commercial and IBM collating sequences. Note that there are still discrepancies in the way special characters are treated in just these two machines. What this means is that particular care needs to be taken not only in sorting but also in testing any inequality (GREATER THAN or LESS THAN).

By coding elements in the data base using either strictly alphabetic or strictly numeric codes in the sorting fields, one may elude the consequences of the problem. If the construction of such codes is not feasible, then there are other ways to handle the problem. One would be to specify that a data base from one machine undergo translation when used on a machine in which the respective collating protocols cause problems. This might be done en masse, or as an additional preliminary job step in the execution of a system.

Another option would be to provide sort routines that observe the desired collating sequence from the families of machines with which an organization deals.

In general, the safest way to treat the inequality problem in program code is not to use inequalities, if at all possible. Rather, use IF . . . EQUAL . . . or IF . . . NOT EQUAL . . . . A systems organization may facilitate the exclusive use of equalities by structuring their data base accordingly.

Table 1

IBM System/370 and Honeywell 600 Commercial Collating Sequences

Sequence Number	IBM System/ 370	Honeywell 600 Commercial	Sequence Number	IBM System/ 370	Honeywell 600 Commercial
1	Blank	Blank	29	N	P
2	.	.	30	O	Q
3	<	)	31	P	R
4	(	"	32	Q	S
5	+	$	33	R	T
6	$	*	34	S	U
7	*	–	35	T	V
8	)	/	36	U	W
9	;	,	37	V	X
10	–	=	38	W	Y
11	/	(	39	X	Z
12	,	>	40	Y	0
13	>	+	41	Z	1
14	=	A	42	0	2
15	"	B	43	1	3
16	A	C	44	2	4
17	B	D	45	3	5
18	C	E	46	4	6
19	D	F	47	5	7
20	E	G	48	6	8
21	F	H	49	7	9
22	G	I	50	8	<
23	H	J	51	9	;
24	I	K			
25	J	L			
26	K	M			
27	L	N			
28	M	O			

COBOL Source Statement Differences

When one begins to examine differences in the source statement requirements for the various COBOL compilers, the scope of the transferability problem begins to look very messy indeed. There are many detailed differences which can and do cause problems. Some manufacturers provide translators to convert from one COBOL set to another. A typical translator handles the easy, straightforward, and "linear" cases and merely flags the difficult cases for a programmer to handle. By taking care of the small problems, these translators render a useful function, but they are not the whole solution.

The ANS COBOL standards have improved the format and layout of vendors' COBOL manuals (although much more could be done in this regard). The inclusion of "meta-language" notation for source statement facilities is a great improvement which permits more rapid feature comparison. An example is[1]:

Format 1

EXAMINE identifier TALLYING

UNTIL FIRST
ALL literal-1
LEADING

(REPLACING BY literal-2)

Format 2

EXAMINE identifier REPLACING

ALL
LEADING
FIRST literal-1 BY literal-2
UNTIL FIRST

For the transferability document the meta-language notation is a useful first level method of syntax comparison for source statement differences. Figure 2 shows the comparative meta language for the WRITE verb for the IBM 360 DOS[2] and Honeywell 200 Series Mod 1 (MSR)[3] COBOL compilers. For the previous example, the EXAMINE verb, the two compilers are the same; the WRITE statement was chosen especially for the richness of variability (and difficulty presented to transferability) implied by the differences. This is especially true when one considers the interaction of WRITE with SPECIAL-NAMES, the INPUT-OUTPUT SECTION of the ENVIRONMENT DIVISION, the FILE SECTION of the DATA DIVISION, and USE. All of these are equally rich in variability among different compilers.

Indeed, the largest problem involves the COBOL necessary to carry on input and output processing. So much is different in the way interaction is specified for printers, disk access methods, and tape and disk label handling that one may safely say there is no standard.

IBM System/360 Disk Operating System
American National Standards COBOL

Format 1

```
WRITE record-name [FROM identifier-1]
  [ { BEFORE } ADVANCING  { identifier-2 LINES } ]
  [ { AFTER  }            { integer LINES      } ]
  [                       { mnemonic-name      } ]

[AT { END-OF-PAGE } imperative-statement]
    { EOP         }
```

Format 2

```
WRITE record-name [FROM identifier-1]
AFTER POSITIONING { identifier-2 } LINES
                  { integer      }
[AT { END-OF-PAGE } imperative-statement]
    { EOP         }
```

Format 3

```
WRITE record-name [FROM identifier-1]
INVALID KEY imperative-statement
```

Honeywell Series 200
MOD 1 (MSR) COBOL Computer

Option 1

```
WRITE record-name [FROM identifier-1]
  [ { BEFORE } ADVANCING  { identifier-2 LINES } ]
  [ { AFTER  }            { integer LINES      } ]
  [                       { mnemonic-name      } ]
```

Option 2

```
WRITE record-name [FROM identifier-1] { AT END      }
                                      { INVALID KEY }
  any imperative statement
```

Figure 2.

The procedural verbs for internal manipulation are much less volatile. There may be alterations such as:

1. Absence of a standard verb or format, such as GO TO . . . DEPENDING ON or COMPUTE.
2. Addition of a nonstandard verb or clause, such as TRANSFORM, CALL (a serious omission from the ANS standard), or MOVE . . . TO . . . THRU . . . or REWRITE.
3. A difference in the notation, such as disallowing the abbreviation CORR for CORRESPONDING, or permitting "FROM" or "EQUALS" instead of "=" in the COMPUTE verb.
4. The addition or absence of some clause in a verb, such as not providing for obtaining the REMAINDER in the DIVIDE verb or REVERSED in the OPEN verb, or permitting TO TOP OF PAGE with the ADVANCING clause.

One could go on providing examples of nuisances and variations in the COBOL compilers of various vendors. However, the important question is how a system's organization addresses the transferability problem.

Identify and Isolate

Two words, identify and isolate, may sum up the strategy of preparing transferable programs. Identification must be made of the scope of the problem. This is the aim of the transferability document mentioned earlier. The document should provide comparative information on the computers involved in the problem. If multidivision/multicomputers is the problem, more than two computers will be included. If conversion is the problem, perhaps the document will describe only two machine environments. (However, early in a conversion study a transferability document covering the leading candidate machines is a valuable planning aid). The table of contents of this document should include the following.

1. Data representation and collating sequences
2. COBOL reserved words
3. Meta-language comparison of syntax of COBOL facilities
4. Notes on usage and interaction (semantics) of COBOL facilities
5. File environment
6. Operating system environment
7. Specification of transferability strategy
8. Definition of COBOL language subset
9. Recommendations and/or specifications for constructs

We have already discussed the first three topics. Item 4, notes on usage and interaction, is required to support the meta-language comparisons. Check your local COBOL manual and see how much explanation and qualification is included with the facility descriptions (especially, again, input and output). Topic 5, the file environment, should include access methods, declarations requirements, and the operational implications for COBOL statements (INVALID key handling, seeking or otherwise positioning, the use of physical and logical addresses, etc.)

The operating system environment (topic 6) should provide a comparative view of job control requirements. This comparison should not only be on a one-to-one basis but should delineate models for commonly used job streams.

Specification of the transferability strategy (topic 7) involves a global discussion of how the whole problem is to be addressed. This part of the document should specify the conditions for the choice of alternate transfer strategies. An organization can attempt to develop systems in parallel for more than one machine and in doing so can make the conversion process more efficient than if it develops a system for first one machine and then modifies it for other machines (unless unnecessary thrashing of design ensues). A conversion may merely transfer systems, or some redevelopment might take place. (Usually the first is planned but the latter becomes reality.)

Topic 8, definition of the subset of COBOL statements, should be an attempt to isolate a workable set of programming facilities out of the COBOL compilers for the two or more machines involved. The aim is to identify, among the respective machines, as many items as possible that can be transferred without change. The probability of achieving this naturally declines as the number of target computers increase to more than two. The strategy then shifts to the isolation of anomalies.

The last topic, the specification of constructs, carries the subset definition one step further. In addition to identifying single facilities, constructs that are frequently used may also be delineated. Examples are the standardized modules for READ and WRITE, including the ENVIRONMENT and DATA DIVISION requirements. Specifications for standard printer formatting and form handling constructs might be the next level of definition. Models for file update and general extraction and reporting might be another level of specification.

Once identification has been made of differences in the respective COBOL compilers and a strategy for accounting for these differences has been formulated, work can begin. Habit is the worst enemy of the programmer in this regard, and some live education on the COBOL differences will benefit a staff. Compile errors have visibility as an attribute, and the differences that cause them will be quickly absorbed by the programming staff. More care must be taken with those differences in object code implementation and effect. Examples are truncation and alignment of data fields, data type handling (will the machine blithely add alphameric data together?), class edit conventions (how is an alphabetic character in the rightmost position in a numeric field regarded?), and internal defaults and checks (what happens if the index is less than one or greater than the number of paragraphs in the list in a GO TO . . . DEPENDING ON?).

One additional functional consideration may then be added to the definition of a flexible system, that it be transferable. In actual practice, since we define modularity at the microlevel, the situation may most often take care of itself. Put another way, as long as the unique coding appears in a very few already discreet micromodules, all that remains is to identify it as unique in the documentation.

Taking a specific example, say there is an opportunity to obtain greater throughput in a program if the TRANSFORM verb is used, but that there is a requirement to use the same program on a machine with a COBOL compiler that does not support TRANSFORM. This is a case in which isolation is clearly indicated. By preparing an alternatively coded module which produces the same results, capability is not lost and potential efficiency can be retained. The decision to code in parallel (to obtain local efficiency) rather than to construct the capability from simple subset ANS COBOL can be made intelligently only when the machine code (and its timing) generated by the COBOL compiler is understood. It well may be that the timing of an "exotic" higher-level language facility and its standard equivalent coding are not sufficiently different to justify the extra effort of dual coding and isolation.

In any case the two methods of isolation are modular separation and documentation, such as the placement of a special comment in the NOTE associated with a paragraph.

Moving to a Different-Sized Machine

Overlaid on the rest of the transferability problem are the considerations of moving from a larger to a smaller machine, or conversely. The smaller-to-larger problem is usually simple, the consideration being taking advantage of the size and speed of the larger machine.

This is not a problem of regaining capability but of increasing efficiency.

One of the immediate areas in which the greater memory size of larger machines may be used is expansion of the buffer size, the number of buffers, and/or the blocking factor of the peripheral records. This allows more processing to take place before an input/output interrupt occurs, which must request and perhaps wait for a peripheral-to-core transfer.

Many operating systems make it easy to provide additional buffering. If for some reason this is not true of a machine, the user may provide a subroutine which implements the equivalent. Instead of issuing a READ or WRITE, the user can CALL a subroutine, the function of which is to MOVE a record to or from a table, and READ or WRITE only when the table of records is full or needs to be replenished. Moving among different-sized machines is merely a matter of adjusting the table size.

A second obvious advantage of a larger machine is that more code can be contained in core. Systems developed on smaller machines which require an overlay structure (of which more is said in Chapter 7) may be recomposed into a single core (or partition) load. Care must be taken, when making such a move, to preserve the cleanliness of structure. The driver routine that formerly controlled the overlay protocol should be altered (if necessary for the operating system environment involved) to maintain the same protocol by simple CALLs.

Moving from a larger to a smaller computer may not be as simple. This is particularly true if the possibility of this being required was not planned for in the original design.

As would be the converse of the small-to-large problem, in going from large to small, the number of buffers and their size, and the size of the record blocking factor, may have to be reduced.

The big problem may be in the decomposition of a single large core or partition load into a smaller memory size. This may be done either through the use of overlay or by increasing the number of job steps. Generally, to avoid carrying a lot of intermediate results and control information on files, an overlay structure will prove more attractive. This is where micromodular programming again proves its worth. A clearly hierarchic structure in the program provides a guideline for the formation of an overlay structure.

Transferability involves a great many small details. Fortunately, many of them, such as format and syntax, can be provided for by automatic translation programs. The details left, those of usage and implementation, still may seem formidable. Pessimistically, one may be led to say that transferability does not exist. However, the situation may be greatly improved by understanding, planning, and care in the preparation of programs.

PORTABILITY

Moving systems in the business sense is much less predictable than transferring systems among computers. There is no clean rule book that can be written to map from one situation to another in a business. Situations are too fluid. Organizations change; people move in and out of positions; priorities shift; plans turn into unanticipated realities. The game of designing systems to move from one business function to another is a highly probabilistic one. However, as in most gambling situations there are some good bets.

If, included in the design phase, consideration is given to the portability problem, then certain strategies may be adopted. The problem is predicting the future of a system and its interactions with not only the business environment but also frequently with the larger social environment as well. If this sounds formidably "prognostalgic," the actual problems usually involve (simply) the exercise of common sense.

For an examination of the problem and suggestions for its solution, let us take a greatly overworked example from the business world: the payroll system. Business systems literature suffers from a surfeit of payroll system examples, as if no other system ever existed. However, if the reader will bear with us, we can illustrate that even this most universal and mundane example suffers from the portability problem in many organizations. There are numerous companies in which payroll programs are frequently reprogrammed, in which there are as many different-from-scratch payrolls systems as computer installations, or in which payroll is running under simulation or emulation because it was not transferable.

Payroll can suffer from the following volatility:

1. Differences in IRS rulings on amount, withholding schedules, surcharges, and general accounting and reporting procedures.
2. Differences in state and local taxes which may be required.
3. Differences in union rules for the calculation, and so on, of pay.
4. Nontax deductions (credit unions, pension or health insurance contributions, FICA).

5. Nonpayroll use of payroll files (as mailing lists for company publications, locator files, etc.).

Two strategies are immediately suggested for the above differences: modular separation of function and the use of table driven code. There exists at least one commercial version (written by a software consultant firm to sell to other companies) of a payroll program which has a separate module for each state.

Thus, in the payroll system, the logic to handle federal tax, state tax, local tax, FICA, other deductions, union reports, check formatting, check writing, interface with general ledger accounting, and so on, should be separated, each into its own module or module hierarchy.

Such commonly volatile items as the upper limit for FICA collection or the withholding rate are obvious candidates for table entries. For the FICA limit, it being a single number (under current rulings), placement in the DATA DIVISION or embedding in the code may seem to be a matter of indifference, but it is not. It is much easier to document and identify items if they are in the DATA DIVISION, as is explained in Chapter 4. As we emphasize repeatedly, cumulative attention to small advantages adds up to a much greater flexibility of systems.

Other examples, in other systems, could also be cited: charts of accounts, vendor codes, location codes, responsibility codes, inventory item codes, and project numbers. One of the best reasons for exposing modular concepts to individuals performing the information analysis function is to make them aware of the need to identify those items that are most prone to change in the environment in which the system will operate.

In gathering a majority opinion from multiple future users as to the requirements of a system, an information analyst should also develop an ear for the minority opinion. Many of the items that may be overruled out of expediency or to obtain a working definition may well crop up later as firm desires. A good understanding of the probable future of the system reinforces the desirability for flexible design and development.

Most of the references I have made are to systems of the operational type, those systems that perform an organization's daily business. It should be noted that all the recommendations made in this monograph apply equally to other types of systems as well. The issue of volatility is particularly appropriate when considering planning systems involving business models. The potentially most fragile logic in a business model is that which contains its assumptions about the nature of reality. Clear identification of these assumptions is mandatory if a system is to model the perceived reality of managerial users in a credible fashion. These models must be adaptable to change, hopefully improvements, in that perceived reality.

SUMMARY

The problem of transferring a program from one computer system to another may be reduced by careful preplanning, including development of a transferability document citing important differences. Preparation for the possibility of transfer is a matter of identifying and isolating or avoiding differences.

Moving an applications system to an alternative business location can be a complex problem. The best strategy for portability in a systems organization is to develop flexible systems. Modularity and table-driven data-independent code are the most useful tactics.

REFERENCES

1. American National Standards Institute, *ANS Standard COBOL,* ANSI X3.23-1968, Washington, D.C., 1969.
2. International Business Machines, *IBM System/360 Disk Operating System American National Standard COBOL,* S360-24 GC28-6394-2, New York, 1968, 1969.
3. Honeywell Information Systems Inc., *MOD 1 (MSR) COBOL Compiler,* 123.1205.141H.0*D-17,* Newton Highlands, Massachusetts, 1970, 1971.

CHAPTER 4

Documentation

Before continuing with details on how to write clean and modular COBOL code, it is appropriate to discuss documentation. There are two good reasons for this. Documentation begins in the analysis and design phases of systems development and, as this chapter demonstrates, a great deal of the documentation of a program should be completed before any significant coding begins. The second reason for including documentation here is that in the examples of COBOL coding that appear in Chapter 5, I have for consistency's sake, used certain naming and layout conventions. Programmers will be much more comfortable with these examples if they first find out what these conventions are and why I have used them. Analysts, designers, and especially project leaders also should continue reading.

DOCUMENTATION IS COMMUNICATION

The spirit of documentation is communication. Such communication meets several needs:

1. Documentation can function as an ongoing mechanism for checking program logic

during the development process. The programmer communicates with his own logic.

2. Documentation is required for making changes in a system or for readapting it to an alternate environment.

3. Documentation permits systems management or their planners to "window-shop" among systems and to select candidates for reuse or modification.

The focus of this monograph is on the flexibility of programs in a system. For this reason we do not cover the whole topic of documentation but consider only documentation within a program itself or closely associated with it. As the reader will see, this is a fairly significant amount.

DOCUMENTATION AND THE SYSTEMS ENVIRONMENT

There are two extreme approaches to documentation: to ignore it (as frequently happens in small organizations); or to make of it a gross superstructure of bureaucratic paper production (as is the case in many large organizations). Of course, neither of these approaches is appropriate. Documentation is a vital part of a system. In fact, the stipulation should be made that a computerized system is a *system* only if documentation and user education materials are part of it. If a system is to be properly developed, tested, and maintained, documentation is necessary.

Consultants and top systems management offer the following advice for systems developers:

"Begin documentation early."
"Document before, during, and after a project."
"When in doubt, document."

Systems project management, designers, and programmers say:

"I'll do it later; I'm in a hurry now."
"The schedule has slipped. . . ."
"The budget slipped. . . ."

While the advice in favor of documentation is appropriate, the difficulties of systems groups are real. Code rather than documentation produces the reports that management requires.

Documentation must become a habit with systems designers and programmers, and developing the self-discipline to acquire this habit often is not easy. Systems management has a responsibility to understand the importance of scheduling and budgeting for documentation. Just as for programming quality control, documentation must be evaluated as part of an individual's job. Too often programmers are brought to a project and put to work, coding, before they are given the problem. This is because the general notion is that a programmer is working only if code is being written. When the problem becomes identified later in the project, what might have originally been fairly clean programming is subjected to patchwork alteration.

Part of the programmer's job should be planning how to program; some of this planning, if written down, will become a portion of the useful documentation of a system.

In some documentation the problem is that too much expensive effort is put into it too early. An example is flow diagramming. Often there is emphasis on the production of neatly inked flow charts coming out of the design phase, only to be made obsolete by the programming phase and the almost inevitable changes in program logic and structure. Conversely, documentation done too late—as an afterthought to the process of system building—may also waste resources. A frequent example is a program narrative written after the program has been completed and which merely parrots the action of the language code in the program listing.

The targets to aim at in managing documentation are: (1) to reduce documentation to the useful and required amount, eliminating paperwork for its own sake, and (2) to make the documentation as much as possible part of the development process. The latter requires that documentation be done at the appropriate time in the process but also increases its utility to the process.

In most organizations the most reliable, up-to-date, and useful source of detailed information about a program is the source code listing. There are good reasons for this. In most organizations it is difficult to control documentation. When emergency maintenance procedures or quick-reaction modifications are performed on a program, the code is altered but the documentation may not be updated to reflect these changes. Maintenance programmers quickly learn that they must turn to the source listing to find out what is really going on. To counteract this situation an organization must have clearly defined follow-up procedures to insure that the documentation is updated. If an organization has not planned and budgeted for program and documentation maintenance, there will be more pressure to slight these procedures when they become necessary. The discussion in this chapter recommends one method of helping to tie documentation to program code, and that is to include as much documentary information as possible in the source listing.

PROGRAM DOCUMENTATION

The desirable minimum items of program documentation are:

1. Program abstract
2. Problem narrative
3. Run-to-run flow diagram
4. Section directory
5. Data dictionary
6. Hierarchic flow diagram
7. File format
8. Report format
9. Notes—section narratives
10. Source code listing

Each of these is discussed in turn, including its purpose and at what point in the development process it should be completed. Examples of the less familiar items may be found in a sample program in the Appendix.

Program Abstract

A program abstract is a brief description of the tasks a program performs, the files used, and miscellaneous other information a particular installation may require.

The program abstract is a more detailed backup to a general system description and is therefore useful not only to programmers and designers but planners or analysts window-shopping for potentially useful programs. The abstract should be part of the original design activity in a system's development. As soon as the problem has been separated into system modules, the abstract should be available as the first item of programming documentation. The way to incorporate it into the source COBOL listing is to have the designer who describes the task each program should perform write it down on a coding sheet rather than on the back of an envelope, a shirt sleeve, or the equivalent. It makes sense to have designers begin to develop the source listing documentation for each program with an abstract on cards, on tape, or in a system library file. Figure 3 outlines a suggested format for the program abstract. It is placed in the REMARKS SECTION of the IDENTIFICATION DIVISION.

System:	Name of the system or subsystem to which this module belongs.
Program:	PROGRAM-ID name or any ENTRY names used.
Process:	A "one-liner" describing the program's function.
Input:	Files: name, medium (tape, disk, etc.), and contents. (For a subprogram, the USING variables).
Working files:	Name, medium, and contents of any scratch space needed.
Output:	Files: name, medium, and contents.
Subprograms used:	Name of any subprograms called by this program.
Comments:	Miscellaneous data a given installation might need to include, for example, frequency (how often a program is executed), library references, assumptions, restrictions, and so on.

Figure 3. **Contents of program abstract.**

Problem Narrative

The problem narrative is, first, a description of the applications problem to be solved by the program in which it appears. It is not a description of the COBOL code but is an outgrowth of the analysis phase of systems development. Second, the narrative may be extended or revised during the design phase to add to or modify the problem according to those constraints imposed by the requirements of a computer solution. The problem narrative is used to develop NOTEs to describe the function of each section of the program. The code is then written using the NOTEs descriptions as a guideline.

Run-to-Run Flow Diagram

This is a graphic depiction of the sequence of programs, the files used, and the reports produced for a subsystem or series of programs. The run-to-run diagram is a familiar piece of systems documentation.[1]

The run-to-run diagram is developed early in the design phase, close in time to the design additions to the program narrative. Since it is graphic, it unfortunately cannot be included with the code. Because it is subject to revision at later stages in the development cycle, it should not be elaborate or expensive. Figure 4 is an example of the segment of a run-to-run diagram that illustrates the precedence relations, files, and reports for a single program. It may also include an indication of options, alternatives, and the conditions of choice for the execution or bypass of given programs in a subsystem. A run-to-run flow diagram is also useful for obtaining an overview of a sub-

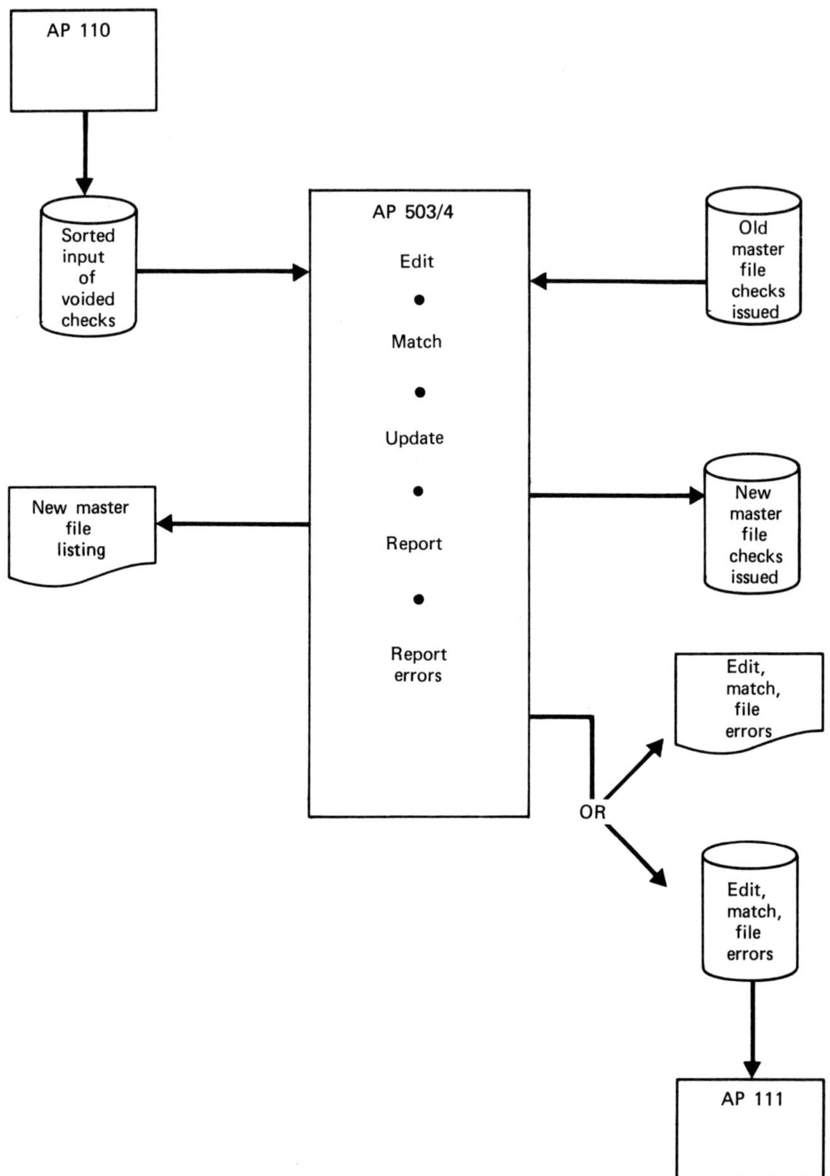

Figure 4 **Run-to-run flow of AP 503/4.**

system for systems management, systems planners, business planners, and analysts shopping for a system.

Section Directory

As the program is being designed, one of the tasks is to develop, from the implications of the problem narrative, descriptions of several program sections, each performing some part of the problem. The first step in this process is to provide a descriptive name and a brief phrase describing each section's function. If these descriptions are alphabetically combined, they serve as a handy guide to where in the program a given function is performed. The section directory is also placed in the IDENTIFICATION DIVISION. The "by-product" nature of the section directory becomes more clear in the description of program development in Chapter 6.

Data Dictionary

It is beyond the scope of this volume to discuss the development of a data dictionary in the larger framework of data base management. Indeed, it might be that to describe what I am about to discuss as a data dictionary is an exaggeration, but, at least at the program level, it is a beginning. Whatever one wants to call it, and however one arranges it, an essential part of documentation is a listing of the meaning of each data name used. Datum represents either some real-world entity (a voucher number or a customer account number), or some data-processing entity (an index to a table or a logical flag to signal that the last record of a file has been read). A programmer needs a guide to the meaning of data names either to maintain a program written by someone else or, in the case of the originator of a program, to become reacquainted with it. This is the most slighted, yet probably the most important, part of all documentation.

The layout of a data dictionary (it should also appear with the code in the IDENTIFICATION DIVISION) may be either straight alphabetical, for all the data names, or subdivided into sections according to type. Later in this chapter I discuss layout and alphabetization and show how both of these may be combined.

As useful categorization of data items by function is the following:

```
FILE SECTION
   Input
   Output
   Working
```

WORKING STORAGE SECTION
  Working structures
  Constants
  Tables
  Indexes
  Flags

The FILE SECTION entries are self-explanatory, but input items are of particular interest. Since they come into a program from the "outside world," there are a few things one needs to know about them.

In the following discussion of how to present the pertinent documentation for various data types, I use a tabular "model" similar to the meta-language notation used to describe COBOL language options in most COBOL manuals. The reader should not be put off by the apparent formality of this notation; the actual examples are simple and straightforward.

For input file entries, the following information is desirable.

```
(Data-entry-name)    (Usage description);
                     RANGE (of values it can have);
                     (Edit status) IF (condition-description)
```

An example is:

```
B-CHECK-NUMBER       SEQUENTIAL CHECK NUMBER;
                     RANGE 1 TO 99999999;
                     FATAL IF NEGATIVE OR NOT NUMERIC;
                     FATAL TO JOB IF NO MATCH WITH INPUT MASTER
                       FILE
```

This means that this check number may have any eight positive digits and, if not, the current transaction is to be terminated. Further, if the number cannot be matched to the master file, the run is to be aborted. Possible entries relating to the edit status are:

```
IGNORED FOR EDIT
WARNING MESSAGE ONLY
FATAL (TO TRANSACTION)
FATAL TO JOB
```

The remaining two FILE SECTION entries, output and working (input/output), may be documented more simply with only the name, usage description, and output format required.

In the WORKING-STORAGE SECTION the working structures may usually be documented with a simple description. Frequently, these structures receive data from input areas for comparison or other manipulation and may be cross-referenced to their corresponding description in input. See M-MASTER-WORK in the data dictionary of the sample program in the Appendix for an example of this.

Constants also require only brief descriptions. See Q-CATEGORY-CODES in the sample program.

Tables, indices, and flags require more information. For tables:

```
(Table-name)          (Function);
                      SIZE (characters);
                      OCCURS (number of times);
                      INDEXED BY (data name);
                      FOR (usage description)
```

An entry might be:

```
K-ERROR-TABLE         ACCOMMODATES ERROR MESSAGES AND THE
                        FAULTY INPUT RECORD IMAGES;
                      SIZE 132;
                      OCCURS 100;
                      INDEXED BY WI-INDEX-ERROR FOR EACH ERROR
                        OR BLANK LINE
```

Here the OCCURS is redundant with the DATA DIVISION entry, as INDEXED might be when using the SEARCH verb. However, it is a minor redundancy and readers are left to decide for themselves.

For an index to a table, there is some particular information that is valuable. When one encounters a table-name indexed by a variable, to determine its possible value implies the following questions:

What is its initial value and where is it set?

By what value is it incremented and where?

To what and where is its value limited (what is the upper bound)?

If it is reset to an initial value, to what, where, and under what condition?

The meta-language construct for these questions is:

```
(Table-index-name)    INITIAL VALUE (literal)
                        in W-S or WORKING-STORAGE or paragraph-
                        name);
                        (Function);
                      INCREMENTED BY (literal or identifier)
                      IN (paragraph-name);
                      VALUE LIMITED BY (identifier or literal)
                      IN (paragraph-name);
                      RESET TO (value) IN (paragraph-name) ON (con-
                        dition-description);
```

An example of how the documentation would appear is:

```
WI-INDEX-ERR      INITIAL VALUE 1 IN W-S;
                  POINTS TO NEXT AVAILABLE SPACE IN ERROR
                    TABLE;
                  INCREMENTED BY 1 IN TN-TABLE-LOOP;
                  VALUE LIMITED BY WI-ERRTAB-LIMIT IN TN-
                    TABLE-LOOP;
                  RESET TO 1 IN TN-TABLE-LOOP ON TABLE FILLING
                    AND BEING DUMPTED TO DISK.
```

For an index used in PERFORM . . . VARYING, the format can be much the same as for indices of tables except that instead of repeatedly listing the paragraph names the fact that all the functions are controlled by the VARYING may be indicated. If the loop is of the usual FROM 1 BY 1 variety, skip the increment portion also, for example:

```
W-HEADING-LOOP    NO INITIAL VALUE;
                  SET BY LOOP IN TP-END-PAGE TO FIND
                  BOTTOM OF PAGE;
                  LIMITED BY W-PAGE-END IN WRITE STATEMENT
```

A flag may be defined as a variable used to control the program logic. It may have some initial value; often ZERO or "N," is set under some program condition (end-of-file, error in input) and then may be reset to an alternate value under some other program condition. Here again, when one encounters a program statement that tests the value of a flag, the "what" and "where" of setting and resetting are what one wishes to know.

The meta-language construct for flags is:

```
FLAG-NAME         INITIAL VALUE (literal) IN (W-S or WORKING
                    STORAGE or paragraph-name);
                  SET TO (value) IN (paragraph-name) ON (condition-
                    description);
                  RESET TO (value) IN (paragraph-name) ON (con-
                    dition-description)
```

An example is:

```
W-MATCH-FLAG      NO INITIAL VALUE;
                  SET TO "Y" IN MA-MATCH-CHECKS;
                  RESET TO "N" IN DD-DETAIL-MATCH IF A GOOD
                    MATCH HAS NOT BEEN FOUND BETWEEN MAS-
                    TER AND INPUT RECORD
```

I realize that the foregoing is probably the most distasteful, seemingly pedantic recommendation in this monograph. The data dictionary items are going to be the most easy to let slip, especially the index and flag entries, because there are several of these to document in a program. However, because of the difficulty that indices and flags may cause (they are the primary decision element in program control), of all the items in the data dictionary they are the most valuable. The two most persuasive arguments against data dictionary documentation are: (1) it involves a lot of writing and (2) programmers are used to looking in the DATA DIVISION and the code to find this information.

For the first argument, it is true that a lot of writing may be involved; however, it is writing that should be done sometime during a project. If it is done on coding forms, it can be placed with the code, handy for the programmer. Coding forms with the key words required for data dictionary entries preprinted (so that the programmer merely fills in the blanks) can be a great aid. Also useful is an abbreviational COBOL preprocessor (see Chapter 9).

For the second argument, one of the main purposes of documentation is to reduce the time it takes for a programmer to find out what a program is designed to do. Frequently, a programmer is asked to look at a program to see if it can be quickly adapted for use in a system, or whether a new program will have to be written. Good documentation can greatly accelerate the time required to answer to this question. The rest of this book is devoted to increasing the number of times the answer will be, "Yes, this program can be easily adapted."

Another point is that filling in data dictionary entries is a valuable form of desk checking. The activity of creating and using these entries helps a programmer to achieve the desired level of intimate understanding of a program. By having documented how a flag is used, a programmer is much less likely to leave out one of its functions.

The data dictionary should be developed gradually throughout the analysis and design phases and be nearly complete by the time programming begins. The *organization* of data files does not have to be frozen to be able to identify the data contained in the files, so this activity does not contradict the general desirability of organizing files late in the development cycle. More is said about the use of flags and indices in Chapter 8.

Flow Diagrams

Flow charts, the familiar type depicting program logic, should be produced in pencil, probably without use of a template (which takes too much time) by a designer or programmer as a planning or design tool *preparatory* to coding a program. Shy away from attacking not a

A logical flow either proceeds from left to right, as in the case of successive process blocks:

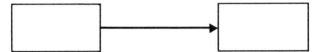

or, in the case of a decision block, the .TRUE. case proceeds to the right and the .FALSE. case downward to a pointer to a page name—line number on the same or another page of the flow diagram.

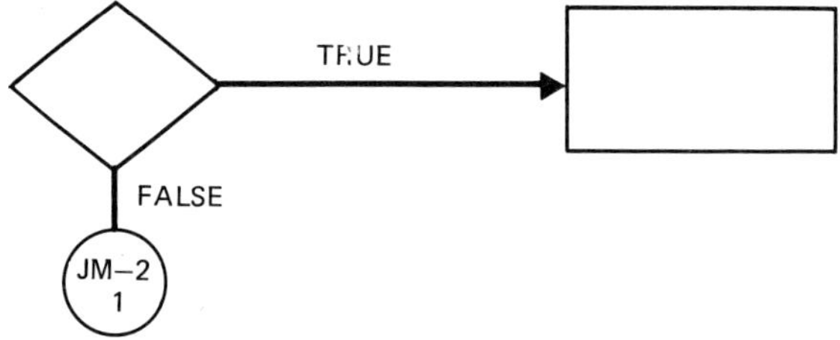

Label the branches YES, NO, TRUE, FALSE, and so on, for clarity.

At the end (right side of the page) of a line, a page name—line number connector is used.

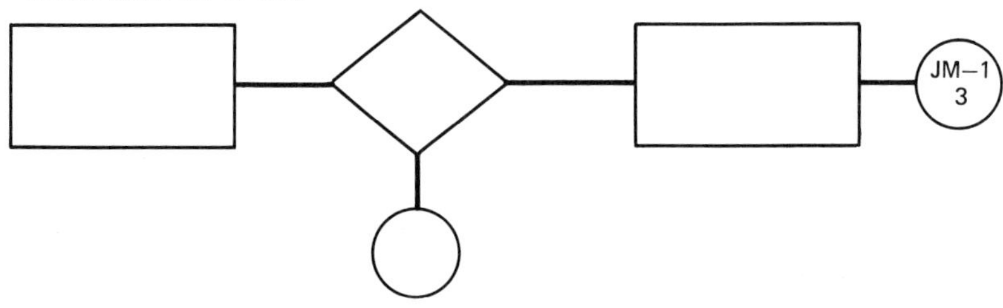

PERFORM may be graphed as follows.

PERFORM
Page name—line
number FOR con–
dition description

Where the loop logic is a separate control entity frequently on a separate page.

GO TO. . . DEPENDING ON may be graphed as follows.

GO TO DEPENDING ON variable name value	PL_1	PL_2	PL_3	PL_N
	1	2	3	N

or

GO TO DEPENDING ON variable name value	PL_1	PL_2	PL_3	PL_4
	1, 4, 10	5, 6	7–9, 11–13	14–16

Where PL is page name–line number.

The second example above shows the case in which more than one value of the variable name results in a branch to a given paragraph label in the program.

The beginning and end points may use a terminal symbol, such as

→ (RETURN)

Otherwise, only the rectangle and diamond should be used (even for input/output, since the run–to–run flow diagram describes the file interfaces.)

Figure 5 **Flow-charting conventions.**

systems but a graphic arts problem by laying out an exotic chart with long connecting lines. A simple left-to-right convention is better. The most useful flow chart conventions are outlined in Figure 5, and an example of one portion of a flow chart is shown in Figure 6.[2]

Final flow charts, if they are determined useful to some function (and it is not ever clear that they are), should be prepared, as needed, by running the source deck through one of the automatic flow charting programs available.

Another type of flow diagram which is very useful, both for program design and permanent documentation, is what I call a hierarchic module diagram. Such a diagram depicts the "parent-child" relationships among modules that CALL or PERFORM and other modules in a system or program. The general structure of such a diagram is the same as the familiar organizational chart.

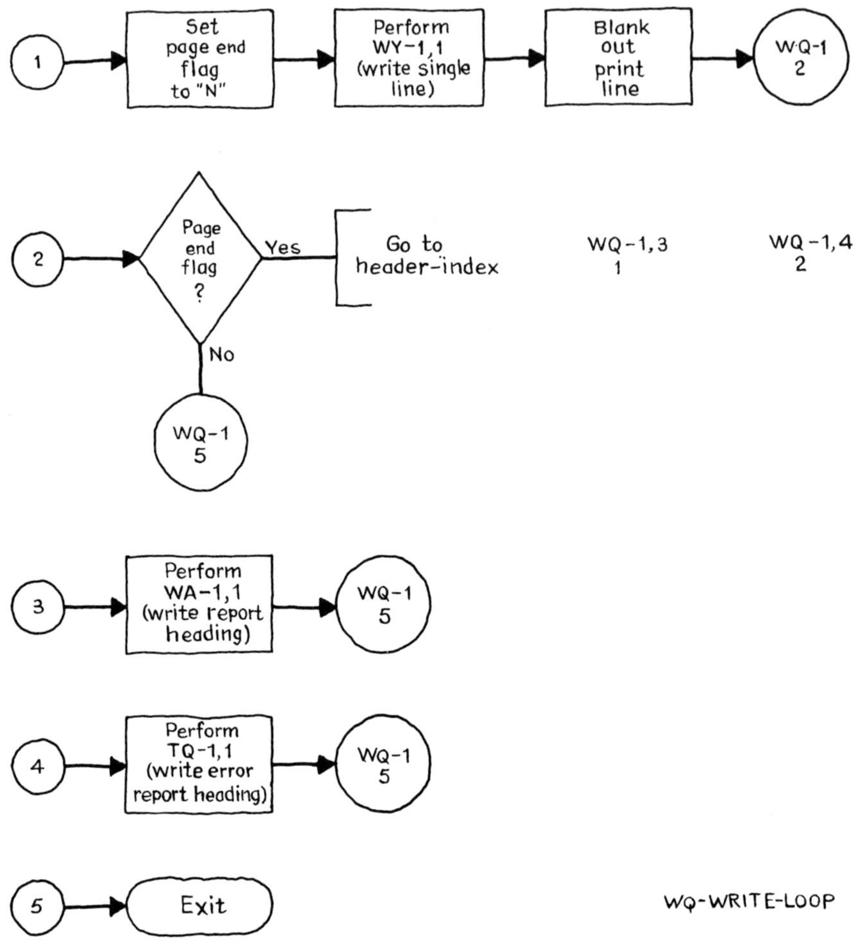

Figure 6 **Sample flow diagram.**

A hierarchic diagram may be useful on several levels in a system, and is very important when a system is highly modular. No example is given here, since a detailed discussion of a program-level hierarchic module diagram is included in Chapter 6 (in discussing the sample program).

File and Report Formats

These are familiar to data processing, and little more needs to be said of them. Examples for the sample program would be so rudimentary that they have been excluded.

Notes

The use of the NOTE feature in COBOL permits blocks or single lines of comments to be inserted into the code. NOTEs should be developed at the time of program design. Just as the program abstract is developed when a subsystem is modularized into programs, so section NOTEs should be developed when the program is substructured into sections. NOTEs are a guideline to what will be done, from the programming standpoint, in each section and, because of this, should be written in a kind of codelike subset of English. The code should parrot the NOTEs, but if any "tricky" code develops in the programming of a section, the NOTE should be updated to explain it. Any assumptions that have been made which are not transparent in the code, once it has been completed, should be added. Refer to the sample program in the Appendix for examples. Generally, the sample NOTEs have not been altered; they appear as they did when the paragraphs were being designed, before the code was written, and have been updated only if the code deviated from the expected. This is to emphasize that the writing of NOTEs need not be a literary art as long as they communicate.

Alphabetic Location Coding

We finally come to the code itself. There are several naming and layout conventions that increase the readability and intelligibility of the program. These are small details which taken as a whole can make it easier and faster to scan a program and which are easily incorporated into the program-writing process.

The coded examples in this monograph all use alphabetic prefixes for paragraph names. AA-BEGIN, HA-HOUSE-KEEP, XA-FINAL-PROCESS, TC-CHECK-VALUE are all names that might appear in a program; a two-character prefix has been placed in front of an otherwise descriptive paragraph name. If the paragraphs are placed in alphabetic sequence in the program, any paragraph can be quickly located in the listing. Try to find any of the paragraphs in the sample program listing in the Appendix, and you will find it an easy matter to skip through the PERFORM and GO TO structure of any branch of logic in the program.

Naturally, the alphabetic sequencing should follow some rational scheme of program organization. The mainline portion of a program should be prefixed in the As, so that it appears at the start of the code. Some programmers prefer to prefix the paragraphs so that, as one goes deeper "down" into a hierarchic structure of sections, the prefixes move from A toward Z. Others prefer to use prefixes to indicate certain types of processing. W profixes sections that *W*rite files, T prefixes *T*able handling code, and so on.[3] In actual practice one will find that the selection of designations is not critical. The important point of the alpha sequencing is that one can find paragraphs or sections quickly.

I have found the following prefixing convention most useful: PERFORM TA-TABLE-LOAD THRU TAX-TABLE-LOAD-X. The "X" suffix is a good convention for identifying the EXIT paragraph, and by using this convention one always knows the EXIT paragraph name for the THRU part of the PERFORM. Intervening paragraphs within this section can be named TAB-TYPE-CHECK, TAF-COMPLETE, and so on. Gaps may be left for the insertion of modifications (such as TAC, TAD, or TAE between TAB and TAF). If a paragraph name is NA-EDIT-COUNT, the NOTE preceding this code may be named NA-NOTE.

Data Division Names

Just as paragraph names are more easily located if an alphabetic prefix is used, the same is true of data names. File descriptions and their data records may be prefixed starting with A, B, C, and so on. All the subelements in a structure should use the same prefix.

```
01  L-CARD-WORK.
    05  L-CARD-REC.
        03  L-CHECK-NUMBER          PICTURE X(8).
        03  FILLER                  PICTURE X.
        03  L-VENDOR-IDENT          PICTURE X(6).
```

The prefixes A through H might be reserved for FILE SECTION names; I through P for working structures; Q, R, S, for constants; T, U, and V for tables; W, Y, and Z for flags; and X for indices.

If the working areas for files are consistently prefixed in parallel, A is moved to I, B to J, C to K, and so on, simply another consistency has been added to the process.

When using the REDEFINES option, an informative convention is to maintain its relationship to the data name it references. This may be done by appending an R after the original alpha prefix:

```
AR-VENDOR-RECORD REDEFINES A-VENDOR-RECORD
```

Where it is desirable to use the CORRESPONDING option, the substructure of the redefined structures may use the same unprefixed names. As long as no reference other than in CORRESPONDING is made to the unprefixed names, the quick locatability of data names will not be compromised.

Additional motivation for data naming becomes clear in Chapter 7 on the subject of interface design.

Meaningful Data Names

Frequent reference is made in discussions of programming practice of the usefulness of meaningful data names. It is true that a name such as C-PART-NUMBER is much more descriptive than FLD-10. The object is to establish as much real-world relationship to the data name as possible; if the programmer is reminded of the function of a datum he is less likely to misuse it. Another recommendation is to differentiate one data name from another as much as possible. Thus using a sequence such as C-PART-NUMBER-A, C-PART-NUMBER-C, and so on, violating both the ultimate meaningfulness and differentiation. It would be better to use C-MAJOR-ASSBY-NUMBER, C-MINOR-ASSBY-NUMBER or C-GEAR-BOX-NUMBER, C-SPINDLE-NUMBER, or whatever fits the purpose. A rather bad example of naming from an actual COBOL program are the data names: PRYDEPB, CYRDEPB, PRYDEPT, CYRDEPTX. These are acronyms, PRYDEPB being prior year depreciation base, but they lend themselves to spelling errors and other misuse.

When referring to a data name to be used as a flag, or index, use these terms in the name. Thus W-BAD-DATA-FLAG or P-PARTS-TABLE-INDEX fairly reeks with meaning. Other names suggest themselves: W-BATCH-BALANCE-TOTAL, W-NUMBER-OF-LINES. One caution is in order. What is a meaningful name to one person may not be to another, or may have a different meaning. Be sure. Meaningful names are an adjunct to, not a substitute for, documentation.

Program Layout

It is also desirable to make the program more responsive to change by increasing the speed at which it can be physically scanned.

First, only one statement should occupy any one line. This makes the code easier to follow and makes modifications much easier. Even consider placing each part of a compound conditional on a separate line.

```
IF A-VENDOR CODE=W-TEST-CODE
AND B-CARD-SEQUENCE-NUM=1
OR W-BYPASS-SWITCH=Y
   MOVE "Y" TO W-OUTPUT-SWITCH
   MOVE-A-VENDOR-WORK-AREA TO L-OUTPUT-AREA
   PERFORM SA-WRITE-OUTPUT THRU SAX-WRITE-OUTPUT-X
   GO TO DA-VENDOR-TEXT-X.
MOVE "Y" TO W-OUTPUT-SWITCH.
```

Branches are easier to read if the yes or "TRUE" condition branch of statements coming from the IF statement is indented. The margin should return to normal for the default or "FALSE" branch. Refer to the above example. Note that for desk checking a quick scan will tell if an extra "." has been inadvertently placed at any of the indented sentences other than the final one.

The separation of modules will be more visually apparent if open space surrounds them in the listing. Most compilers support an asterisk in card column 7 which may be used for this purpose. Some compilers permit the use of blank cards (which pass them without indicating an error), otherwise a dummy NOTE statement achieves the same result.

```
K3-EXIT.
   EXIT.
KZ-SPACE-NOTE.
NOTE X
     X
     X
     X
     X.
L-SEQ-ERROR-SECTION.
```

Essential Minimum Documentation

The foregoing has been a discussion of what I consider "desirable minimum" program documentation. I would like now to amend this list to the "essential minimum":

1. Combined program abstract and data dictionary
2. Run-to-run flow diagram
3. Hierarchic flow diagram
4. File formats
5. Report formats
6. Notes
7. Source code listing

For situations in which systems management does not wish to control the working habits of its systems staff, the essential minimum is at a level more acceptable to the average working programmer. Interestingly enough of course the items on the "desirable" list that are missing here are those items that would be generated as part of the analysis and design phase. The after-the-fact generation of these items is more difficult and distasteful.

The format of the combined program abstract and data dictionary follows; the sample subprogram "PRINTER" in the Appendix contains an example.

System:	Name of system or subsystem to which this module belongs.
Program:	PROGRAM-ID or any ENTRY names used.
Process:	A description of the action of the program, to provide an overview of its function and operational options.
Interfaces:	
Input argument list:	If a subprogram, include the data dictionary entries for data structure in the ENTRY . . . USING that provide input to the module.
Input files:	The name, medium, and contents of input files.
Working data structures:	The data dictionary entries for data structures referenced only within the bounds of the module.
Working files:	Files used as both input-output, for temporary storage, and referenced only within the bounds of the module.
Output argument list:	If a subprogram, include the data dictionary entries for data structures in the ENTRY . . . USING that provide output from the module. If a structure has also been listed in the input interface entry, repeat it here.
Output files:	The name, medium, and content of output files.
Logical interface:	This entry includes the subprograms to be called by this module, the size of the working storage required, and the file codes required for the operating system job control input.
Other comments:	Special techniques used, references, and other miscellany as required may be placed in this category.

SUMMARY

Documentation can be an aid in developing, maintaining, and reusing programs. The keys to successful documentation are scheduling and budgeting for it, doing it at the proper time in a project, selecting the most useful minimum, and making it a by-product of the development process. The most important and easily slighted documentation is the description of the meaning and usage of data items.

REFERENCES

1. Sometimes this is called a data flow diagram, see Benjamin Robert, *Control of the Information System Development Cycle,* John Wiley, New York, 1971.
2. My first general introduction to this flow charting method was at a seminar on Segmented Level Programming sponsored by Hoskyns Systems Research in New York in 1968.
3. Some recommendations on naming conventions may be found in: Wigg, J. D., "COBOL Coding Standards," *Computer Bulletin,* July 1971, pp. 254–257.

CHAPTER 5

Modularity

It is widely accepted that modular programming is desirable. Nearly every programmer or exprogrammer will say that his or her programs are or were modular, yet in most cases the benefits we expect to achieve from modularity are not forthcoming. The reasons for this are as follows.

1. Modularity exists on several levels in the production of systems and must be considered at each level. Usually, the problem is in not applying modularity at a sufficiently detailed level.
2. Modularity and how to obtain it in detail have not been sufficiently well defined in the literature.
3. Obtaining modularity is just part of the solution. In order to gain maximum benefits from modularity, programs must also be documented and written in a simple, trouble-free manner.

This chapter discusses the first point, the various levels of modularity and their definition and interaction. Chapter 6 addresses the second point; point 3, documentation, was covered in Chapter 4, and Chapter 8 discusses simple and trouble-free code.

Systems modularity begins with the gross

structure of the information needs of an organization. Since the systems analyst and systems designer may play a large role in the specification of this structure, modularity begins with them. This chapter, while providing a background for the technical COBOL programming details to come in later chapters, should also be read by analysts and designers to clarify their views of modularity.

LEVELS OF MODULARITY

If one takes the structure of an organization and begins to delineate the organization's various information needs, one way to categorize initially these needs is into three groups: long-range planning, annual planning, and operational control. Each one of these groups may be divided into more detailed subsystems. Let us look more closely at operational control, for it is in the mechanization of routine daily operations that computer systems have had their largest and most successful application.[1] The components of an operational control information system may be delineated as follows.

Logistics:
1. Raw materials
2. Production
3. Salable product

Physical assets:
1. Property and equipment
2. Capital projects

Financial:
1. Accounting
2. Treasury

Manpower.
1. Payroll
2. Benefits
3. Personnel administration

We might describe these components as applicational modules at the systems level; they represent the information processing environment which is the on-going concern of the systems staff. What this permits us to do is to describe more precisely the limits of any one of the modules; the first implication of modularity is the process of subdividing a whole into some simpler constituent parts.

We may proceed to define application modules on an even more detailed level. A useful way to display this process has been devised by Robert Benjamin in *Control of the Information System Develop-*

ment Cycle.[2] In Figure 7 I have applied his terminology and structure for the various levels in an information system specifically to accounting control.

At the top of Figure 7 are the familiar subsystem components of an accounting system: accounts payable, accounts receivable, and so on. Each of these components describes a set of on-going activities. Selecting one of these, accounts payable, one may proceed to the cycle level, that is, to those activities that occur on an iterative, time-controlled schedule. While accounts payable is always "going on" in a sense, updating the open invoice file occurs only every so often,

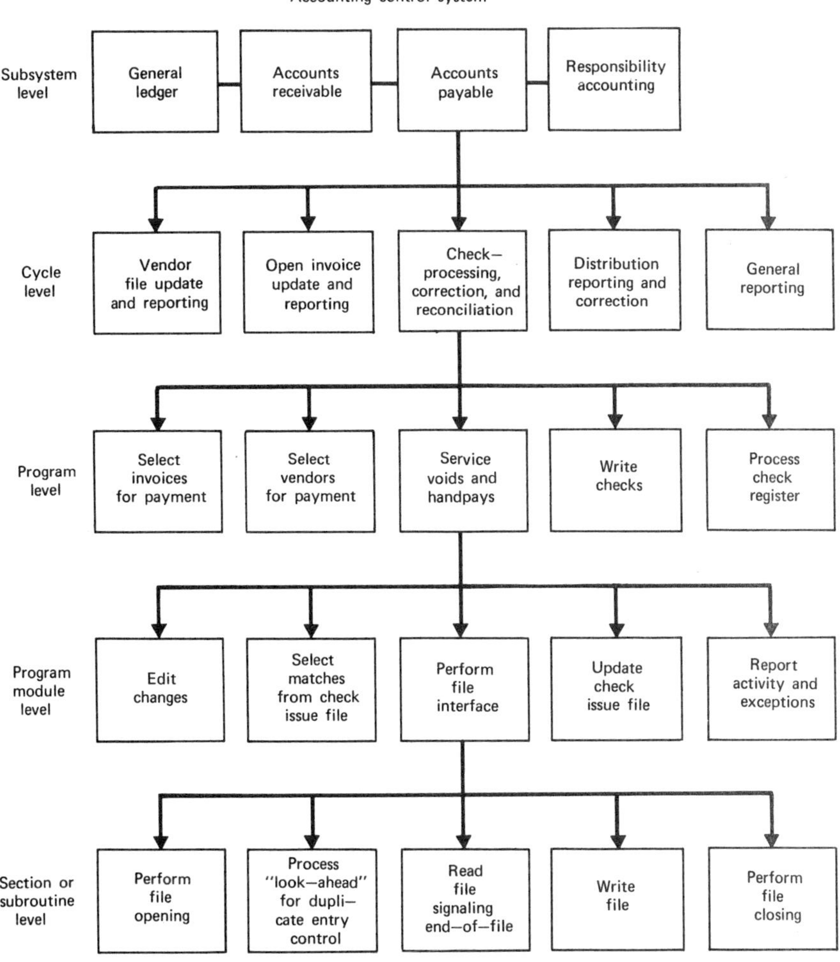

Figure 7 **Levels of modularity.**

perhaps biweekly. If one of the cycle-level aggregations, check processing, is followed to the next lower level of modulation, one may describe it in terms of a group of programs. Program is used here in the sense of a multiple set of job steps, any of which may further contain a subprogram structure. Programs are also cyclic.

The next lower level is termed the module level, module in the sense of a single mainline program and any subprograms it may use. Figure 7 depicts the module contents of the program that services (updates) the checks-issued file for voided and hand-paid checks. It is at this level that the familiar activities of edit, select, update, and report are found. Finally, taking the subfunctions of a module, one may identify section- or subprogram-level activities. The section-level elements of file interface are shown in Figure 7.

Figure 7 illustrates a path that has been followed from one of the major application areas in a business, accounts payable, down through a hierarchy of increasingly detailed definition.

The implications of this are as follows.

1. The basic reason why one seeks to modularize a system is to subdivide a complex problem into separate, smaller, more simple problems.

2. Each modular element should be discrete and visible. An analyst or programmer looking for one of these elements should be able to find it easily, regardless of the level of detail.

3. Each modular element should be self-contained and easily rearranged at the next higher logical level. It should be possible to modify any one of these modules without affecting any other module, as long as there is no major redefinition of function that affects the relative contents of two or more of the modules. To alter the order in which any of the parts is processed should be a simple change.

All that has been discussed here so far involves subdividing an application into modules and modularizing the task (or problem) but not the implementation (or solution). In this book the process of defining the problem into modules is called applicational modularity.

APPLICATIONAL MODULARITY

The definition of applicational modularity begins with procedure and work simplification analysis in the business and is further defined by the efforts of business and computer systems analysts. The process is not one of arbitrarily drawing lines between functions but of identifying or constructing self-contained entities. To use an analogy to an automobile, it does not seem reasonable to have to remove or readjust the fuel pump in order to change a fan belt, yet in computer systems something of this nature happens too frequently.

The ability to define modularity successfully at a given level is dependent on how well the definition has been carried out at the next higher level. Modularity means that a system is built as several self-contained elements. These elements or modules require a definition of how they are to be arranged and how information is to flow among them. This process is interface design and is very important in achieving the benefits of modularity. Interface design is simplified if the modules have been specified so that each one performs a well-defined task and is logically complete.

The definition of what constitutes a module is variable. What one group or individual may decide are appropriate functions to be combined into a module may differ from what another group considers appropriate. What is proper for a given group depends on their model of the requirements and their perception of how change may affect the system.

Analysts, then, can significantly abet the cause of modular systems design, and the efforts of systems designers can in turn greatly aid in the production of modular programming. Since the techniques for defining modularity above the program level are beyond the scope of this book, analysts are referred to the previously cited Blumenthal[1] reference. Systems designers should refer within this book to Chapter 6, on module interface methods, and will find that many of the guidelines for module design to be found in subsequent chapters apply to the design of multimodule programs and multiprogram systems.

Modularity in Computer Systems

So far a module has been defined as:

1. Part of a larger entity
2. Discrete
3. Logically self-contained

In applying the above to a module in a computer system, a more precise definition is necessary.

1. The functions of input and output are well defined.
2. The module has a single entry point and a single exit point.

3. It exits to a standard return point in the module from which it was executed.

Separating a problem into systems, programs, or modules merely refers to a particular level of modularization. The degree of modularization this book advocates extends down to the section level in COBOL. In order to distinguish this more detailed level of modularity from the usual program or subroutine level, we may refer to it as "micromodularity." This level of detailed modularity is required if one wishes to maximize the benefits of modularity. At the program level the usual structure is the "antimodular" one shown on the left in Figure 8. A program with this type of structure may be broken up into pieces. By our definition, however, these pieces are not modules,

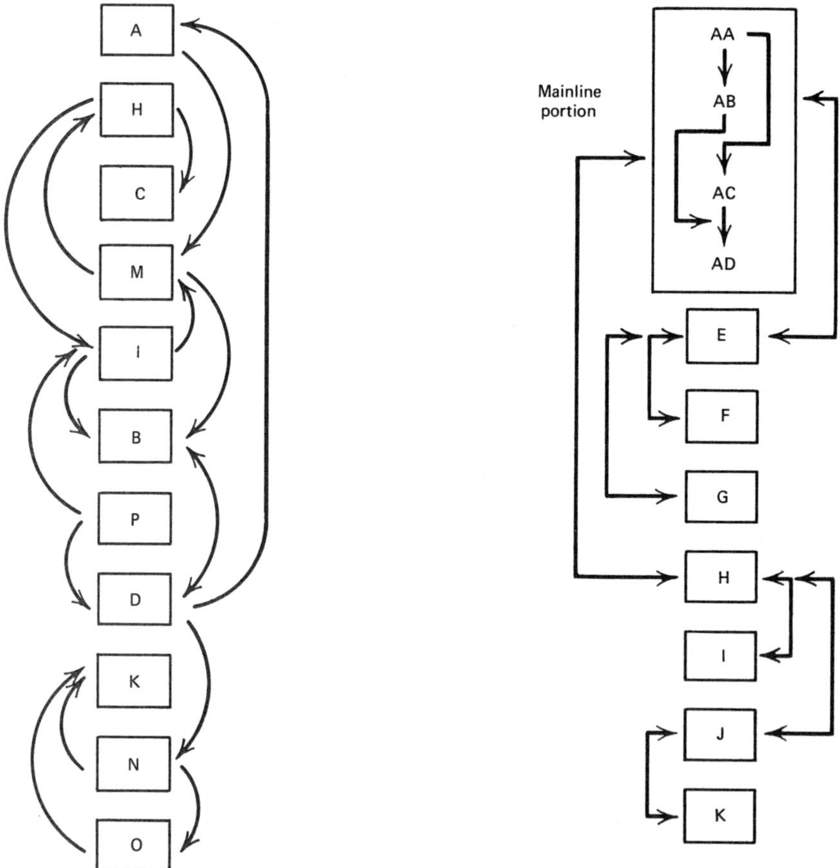

Figure 8 **Antimodular and modular.**

since they are clearly neither independent nor easily rearrangeable. The tangle on the left is intended to depict what happens when an unstructured approach is taken in controlling the logical branches in a program. Such a program causes great suffering when a change has to be made, since it is difficult to evaluate how each of many logical paths that cross through a section may be affected by the change. On the right in Figure 8 is shown the clarity that results from modularity. The right-hand part of the figure shows a short mainline section followed by a hierarchic structure of closed subroutines. A closed subroutine should have a single entry point and a single exit point and should return to the statement following that which causes its execution (as a PERFORM or CALL in COBOL). The lines in Figure 8 with an arrow at each end symbolize the PERFORM relationship. In the antimodular example it is difficult to identify the mainline, let alone any other structure.

Such a structure is hierarchic in nature. It can also be depicted as

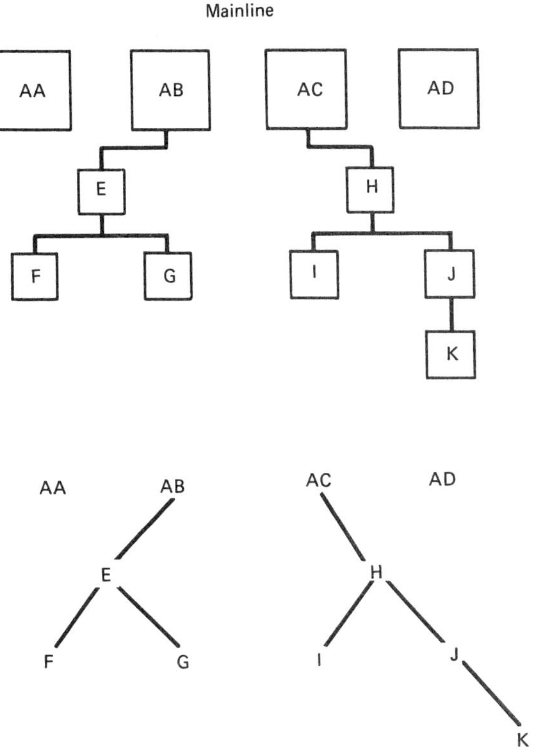

Figure 9 **Alternative representations of modular structures.**

in Figure 9, either in the form of an organizational chart or as a tree structure.

PROCEDURAL MODULARITY

In addition to the applicational modularity resulting from decomposition of the problem, there is another dimension of modularity which becomes significant at the program level. The rigid procedural requirements the use of a computer imposes upon a solution make further categorization necessary (for more complete success).

The basic procedural functions found in a program module are:

1. Logical interface
2. Process
3. Housekeeping
4. File interface
5. Exception

Logical interface is the control function, choosing what process (problem-solving) code is to be executed. Housekeeping is concerned with preparing and tidying up the computer environment (clearing storage, opening files, etc.). File interface is simply input and output, involving any references to peripheral devices. Exception is the handling of errors, given special emphasis here because it is frequently slighted. These functions are developed in detail in Chapter 6 which includes an example showing how a table of the intersections between applicational and procedural functions at the program module level can aid in designing reasonable modules.

Linear and Hierarchic Structures

Most commercial programmers have learned to think in linear terms. Systems are viewed as a set of sequential programs (or indeed as simply core or partition loads). As an illustration, Figure 10 shows a set of programs which make up an accounts payable subsystem. Usually, such a subsystem can be divided into streams; the six separate lines in Figure 10 arbitrarily represent six streams. Although conceptually the entire group, AP101 thru AP603, could be executed in the order shown here, usually the various streams are executed according to a cyclic schedule. A linear structure seems appropriate for processing a requirement of this type. There is, however, an opportunity to acquire some bad habits when using such a structure,

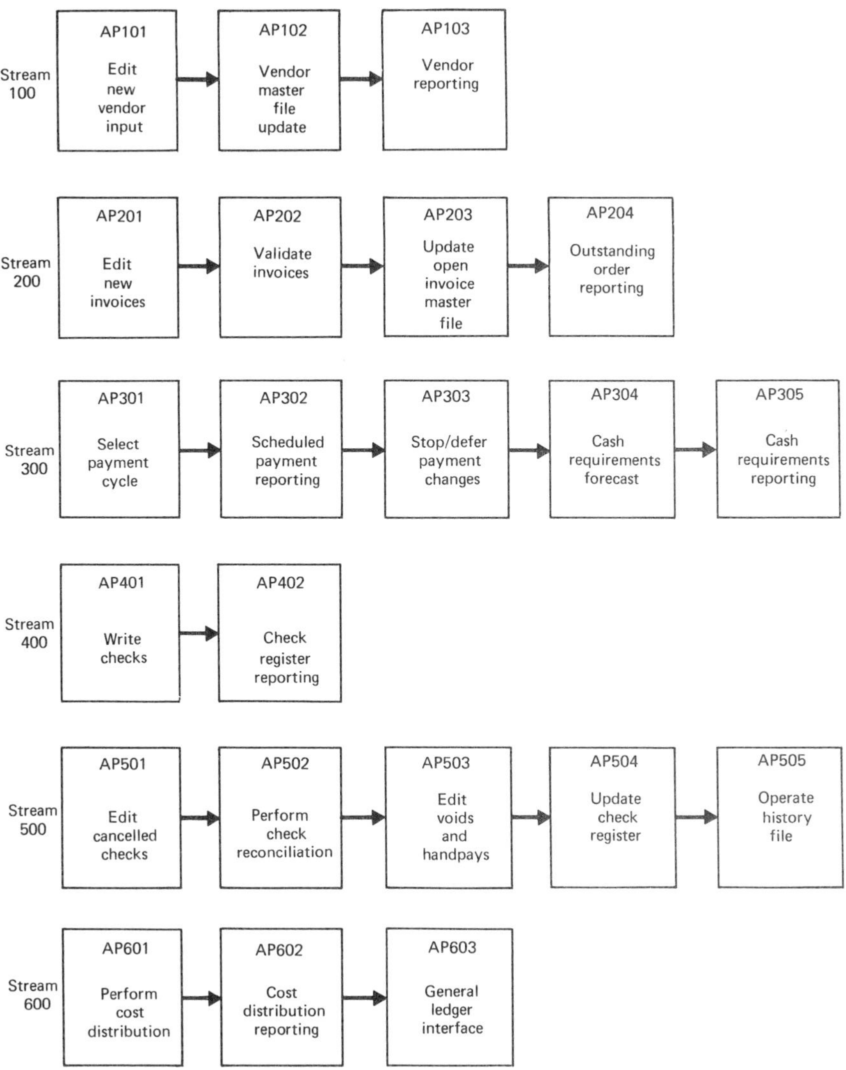

Figure 10 **Accounts payable system.**

one of which is the tendency among programmers (and designers) to ignore the frequent repetition of subfunction in a linear structure.

If one takes note of the functions being performed in the linear subsystem flow in Figure 10, there is a strong likelihood that separate programs will contain quite similar functions. For example, some editing occurs in AP101, AP201, AP501, AP503. Some file interaction likely occurs in all programs, but file update specifically occurs in AP102, AP203, AP504, AP505. Formatted reporting occurs in six of the programs. In most systems of this type, the probability is high that there is a variety of code for these similar functions.

At the program level a linear attitude may also result in needless repetition. The programmer, often working within a poorly formed design model, proceeds to code as the problem occurs to him. Thus multiple READ and WRITE statements are issued against the same file, when one of each could well suffice, or values in the input data stream are needlessly evaluated or tested in more than one location. We have seen that it is possible at the subsystem level to maintain a reasonable separation of functions. This is achieved in a linear structure, however, at the expense of redundancy of subfunction. The same is true within a program. There is a tendency to dissolve procedural modularity by spreading a logically cohesive subfunction throughout a program. Thus the housekeeping function, or file formatting, or the regulation of end-of-file processing may be woven all through the program. Just as in a subsystem, if one must search out the pieces of a given functional element in order to modify that function, extra time, effort, and a higher probability of error are incurred.

A hierarchic structure, such as the example in Figure 9, has been most often associated with scientific or software programming. Training and the complexity of the problems may direct individuals in these areas toward the use of hierarchic models. (Parenthetically, one may find antimodular examples in both scientific and software programming.) As we have seen, however, modularity is inherently hierarchic.

Figure 11 rearranges the functions of the accounts payable subsystem in Figure 10 in a hierarchic structure. Note how the procedural functions of logical interface, housekeeping, file interface, and process are separated. All input is shown passing through the same filter with the input control program first triggering the edit, and then passing the accepted input to the remainder of the system via work files or structures. The edit portion of this system could use tables for each type of system input to control the process through generalized edit functions. Viewed in this manner, most of the processing—selection, matching, and calculation—would be reduced to very simple modules. File handling, too, would be performed through a single interface to a subhierarchy of modules whose function it would be to service the subsystem on a get-and-put basis, irrespective of file structure processing. It is not within the scope of this monograph to deal in formalities, but one is led to suspect that any but the most simple of linear structures can also be depicted as a hierarchic struc-

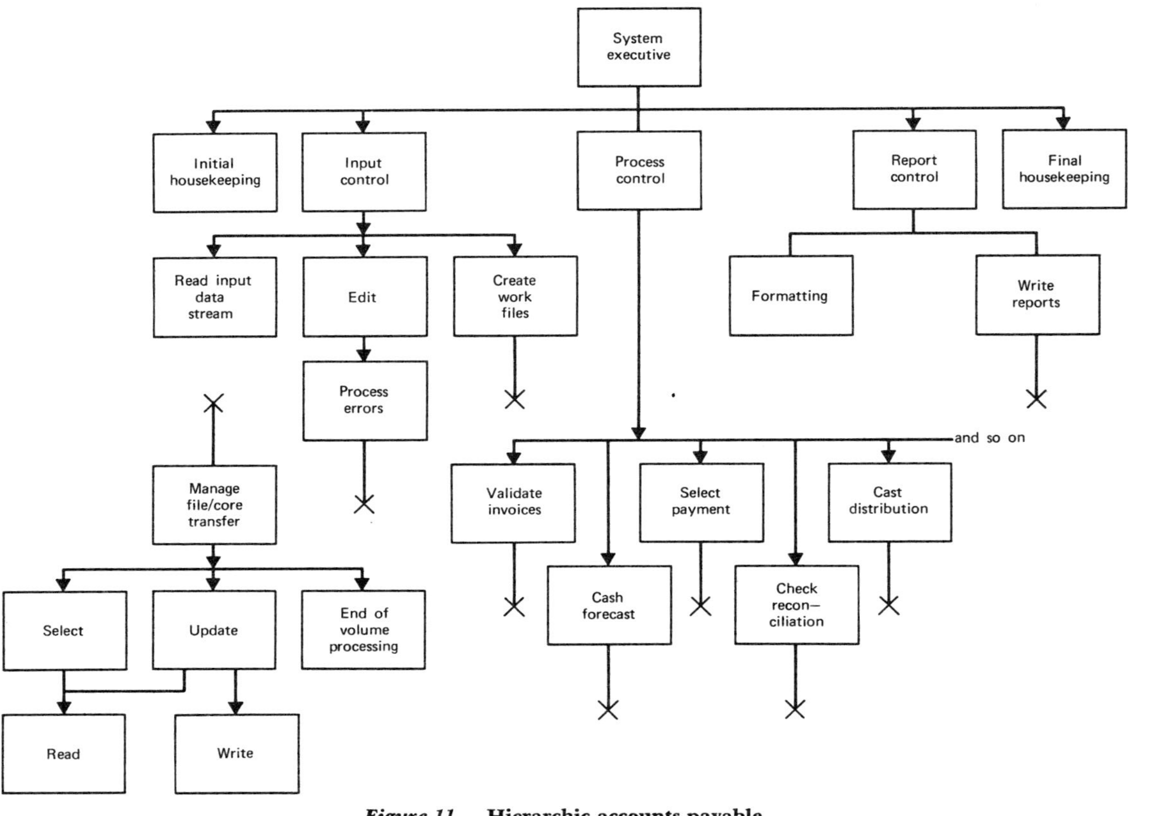

Figure 11 **Hierarchic accounts payable.**

ture, and in the case of applications systems it is profitable to regard them as such. The hierarchic implementation of Figure 11 would most likely involve an overlay structure and some generalized, table-driven processing modules. We deal with those possibilities in later chapters. For now, the observation should be that, even if one maintains the essentially linear structure of Figure 10, one can take advantage of the repetition of basic functions. This may be done by providing, if not generalized, standardized ways of approaching those procedural functions that are recurrent. By this means an installation could reduce much of the busy work that currently surrounds applications programming and lend considerable clarity to the process.

STRUCTURAL MODULARITY

Before proceeding to specific examples of how to achieve flexibility in COBOL, one additional concept should be covered.

A given module may be conceived of as consisting of three basic parts: data, code (or process), and control (see Figure 12). Data enter the module as input, are operated upon by the code, and leave as output. Control is the function that chooses which code and data are brought together for processing. Data and code are passive; control is the active element. This model of a module works equally well for nearly any process. Consider a drill press (along with the human

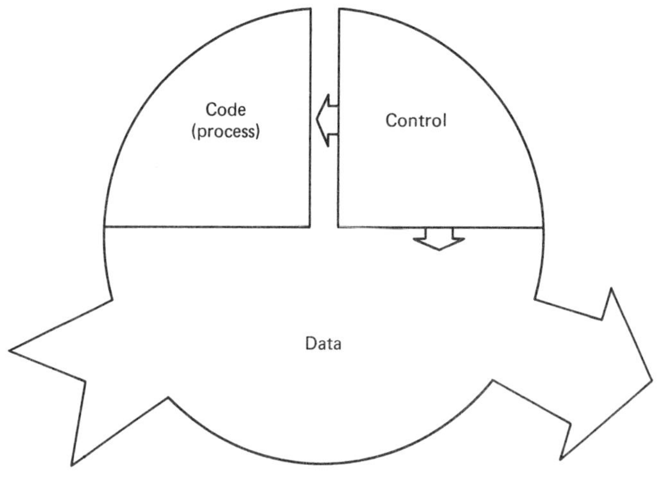

Figure 12 **Structural components of a module.**

operator) the *code* (that which operates on the data); the *data* are pieces of stock in which we wish to drill holes; and *control* is exercised through the choice of bit, positioning of a stop on the bit, choosing a rate of descent, and so on. Control involves sampling and decision making. In computer programs control is performed through testing and branching. We define this level of modular separation as "structural."

COBOL, with the DATA DIVISION separate from the PROCEDURE DIVISION, helps to separate data from both code and control. It is still possible to effect some mixing of data in the code (by using literals in procedural statements), and this is dealt with in more detail in Chapter 7. Code and control are not easily separated from each other, however, and Chapter 8 deals with how to obtain effective separation by maximizing the visibility of the control structure.

SUMMARY

We have identified, then, three types of modularity:

1. Applicational—involved with the business at hand, for example, cash requirements forecasting.
2. Procedural—concerning the basic computing tasks, for example, housekeeping, process, and so on.
3. Structural—the separation of data, code, and control.

Procedural modularity tends to be logically nested within applicational modularity, while structural modularity is all-pervasive. Having this view of modularity provides a solid framework with which to approach the achievements of modularity. Indeed, it can hardly be overemphasized that this view of modularity is not academic but provides a working model. With this model one can isolate language facilities and develop appropriate language constructs (groupings of language statements), whatever the computer language choice, to achieve modularity and simplicity in the solution of a problem.

REFERENCES

1. Blumenthal, Sherman, *Management Information Systems,* Prentice Hall, Englewood Cliffs, N.J., 1969.
2. Benjamin, Robert, *Control of the Information System Development Cycle,* John Wiley, 1971.

CHAPTER 6

Module Design

The most easily discussed (and acquired) aspects of programming are the methods for using single statements and constructs. What is not so easy in programming is the resolution of semantic problems, how to combine constructs into a working program, and how to modularize functions in a useful and meaningful fashion.

The ability to separate functions into modules tends to be considered an "art." This is because there is a lack of structured understanding of modularity. The aim of this chapter is to provide some examples; the desired result is to move the modularization process away from "witchcraft" and toward engineering (highly systematized witchcraft). The focus here is on the resolution of modularity within a single COBOL program—micromodularity.

THE PERFORM VERB

The PERFORM verb and paragraph structure in COBOL naturally lend themselves to closed subroutine structures. Taking the diagrammatic example of modular structure from Figure 8 in the previous chapter, its exact

COBOL implementation may be outlined. Figure 13 shows the PERFORMs, paragraph entries, and paragraph exits that define a clean, hierarchic structure of strictly closed subprograms. However, COBOL is not strict in its definition of PERFORM and one may easily violate its natural utility in implementing closed subroutines. Since PERFORM can be easily mishandled, and the micromodularity of a program (or subprogram) is dependent on its proper use, it needs to be given special attention.

The PERFORM verb should be used only as follows.

```
PERFORM paragraph-name THRU paragraph-exit-name.

                        Procedure division
AA.
        IF conditional-statement
           GO TO AB.
        GO TO AC.
AB.
        PERFORM E THRU EX-X.
        GO TO AD.
AC.
        PERFORM H THRU HX-X.
AD.
        STOP RUN.
*
*
*
*
E.
        IF conditional-statement
           PERFORM F THRU FX-X.
        PERFORM G THRU GX-X.
EX-X.
        EXIT.
*
*
*
F.
        processing-code
FX-X.
        EXIT.
*
*
*
G.
        processing-code
GX-X.
```

```
         EXIT.
*
*
*
H.
         IF conditional-statement
            GO TO HX-X.
         PERFORM I THRU IX-X.
         PERFORM J THRU JX-X.
HX-X.
         EXIT.
*
*
*
I.
         processing-code
IX-X.
         EXIT.
*
*
*
J.
         IF conditional-statement
            GO TO JX-X.
         PERFORM K THRU KX-X.
JX-X.
         EXIT.
*
*
*
K.
         processing-code
KX-X.
         EXIT.
```

Figure 13. **Skeletal code of COBOL module.**

Paragraph-exit-name should be an EXIT paragraph. By using the THRU option, the scope of the code referenced by the PERFORM is clearly indicated; there is no doubt where the code begins and ends. I refer to this construct as a paragraph-group. This is preferred to PERFORMing a SECTION, since programmers tend to forget more easily to define the scope of a SECTION (by another SECTION statement). SECTION may be used to group together one or more paragraph-THRU-exit constructs for documentation, or to specify their priority in paging or virtual memory environments, but should not be referred to by a PERFORM.

An example of correct usage is.

```
PERFORM WD-DOGGEREL THRU WDX-DOGGEREL-X.
.
.
.
.
WD-DOGGEREL.
    IF M-MOON NOT EQUAL W-BLUE
        GO TO WDC-JUNE.
    MOVE J-SPRING TO C-SEASON.
    GO TO WDX-DOGGEREL-X.
WDC-JUNE.
    MOVE J-SUMMER TO C-SEASON.
WDX-DOGGEREL-X.
    EXIT.
    .
    .
    .
```

The above satisfies the structural requirements for the purpose use of PERFORM, even if poetic license has been taken with the apparent function of the code.

The scope of these PERFORM . . . THRU (exit) constructs should never overlap. In the above example one should not PERFORM WDC-JUNE THRU WDX-DOGGEREL-X. This violates the clear single entry point–single exit rule governing a closed subroutine. This example is a trivial one, and the reader can probably see little harm in PERFORMing the inner paragraph WDC-JUNE. However, it can safely be said that if this rule is violated it will at some time cause systems difficulties.

CONTROL OF GO TO

This brings us to a second topic in program structure, the use of GO TO. One of the primary contributors to complexity in computer programs is the branches. Unless the scope of the branches in a program is limited, severe difficulties may arise in following the logic. It takes only a very few interwoven branches in a program to exceed a reasonably efficient level of complexity. GO TO, if misused, may also ruin the cleanliness of the closed subprogram structure. In current computing literature there are several articles which provide evidence that GO TO is both troublesome and unnecessary and so advocate its elimination from future programming languages. While

COBOL programs can be written in a GO TO-less manner, it is impractical to attempt to revolutionize a few generations of COBOL users. Besides, such programs would likely be less readable than programs in which GO TO is used sparingly and intelligently.[1]

Using PERFORM as the primary structural element in a program will in itself reduce the number of GO TOs in a program, but there are three rules (each more limiting than the previous) that should be adhered to as closely as possible.

1. GO TO should refer only to a name within its own paragraph-group. This means that a programmer neither has to look very far nor perform much analysis to understand the scope and impact of a program branch. This rule also prohibits branching out of the middle of one paragraph-group to some other paragraph-group, something which not only creates confusion in the control structure but destroys the independence (hence modularity) of the paragraph-groups involved.

2. GO TO should branch only forward in the program (downward on the page), and (by rule 1) only to an intermediate paragraph or to the EXIT paragraph within the paragraph-group. To branch backward implies a loop, and the appropriate loop construct in COBOL, PERFORM . . . VARYING . . . UNTIL is more visible. Chapter 8 discusses loops and program structure in more detail.

3. GO TO should branch forward only to the EXIT paragraph in its paragraph-group.

The most desirable degree of GO TO control is achieved by adhering as closely as possible to rule 3. This is not always feasible, but because of habit rather than for technical reasons. GO TO has always provided an easy way out of structural difficulties, so much so that programmers have been able to avoid designing their programs. As an individual gains experience in developing modularity and consciously seeks to reduce the untamed use of GO TO, this style of programming will become more natural; it takes practice to use new tools. The reward will be modules that are more readable, easier to document, and eventually faster and easier to program and verify (a term I prefer to the pesticidal "debug").

The two main tools for achieving COBOL program modularity thus are: (1) separation of the code into PERFORMed paragraphs, and (2) preservation of their separateness by restriction of the use of GO TO.

THE HIERARCHIC MODULE DIAGRAM

One of the useful adjuncts to a micromodular program module is an organization chart of its modules (paragraph-groups). The term I use for such a chart is hierarchic module diagram. This diagram depicts, in a global manner, the PERFORM relationships of the paragraph-groups in a module.

Figure 14 is the hierarchic module diagram of a program designed to edit card images and update a check-issued file in an accounts payable system. For general information this program roughly conforms to the combined AP503 and AP504 in Figure 10. Parts of this program are used in several examples, and a complete listing appears in the Appendix.

The PERFORM relationship of one paragraph to another is depicted by a connecting line with an arrow at each end. No GO TO relations need be shown, since they have been severely limited in scope and should be easy to understand from the code itself. The alphabetic prefixes of the names of paragraph-groups are all that is required to identify them. Note that if a module has been structured properly, creation of this diagram is easy, and if it is not easy, something must be wrong with the structure.

A paragraph PERFORMed by more than one other paragraph may be repeated in the structure. It is useful to show repetitive occurrences of a paragraph-group by circling its second, third, and so on, appearances. If a paragraph implies a substructure of paragraphs and is referred to more than once, the one case in which it is not circled depicts the lower-level structure. In Figure 14 the printer module (WP) is used in several places. It is expanded down the AA-AF-SD-WP branch of the diagram and is seen to include the WQ (WY, WA, TQ) structure. Modules that perform no other modules (leaves on our tree) are found uncircled and at the structural end of a branch of the tree. EA is such an example and may be found at the end of the AA-AF-EN-EA branch. As might be expected, TA-ERR-TAB is used by more than one module, since its job is to service the exception modules SA, SD, and SF. If a module appears again, lower in a branch in which it already appears, there may be a danger of attempted recursive processing.

A hierarchic module diagram provides a useful overview of the relationship of paragraph-groups in a program module and can also serve as a development aid. If a diagram does not fit handily on a single page, it may be separated at obvious break points (final housekeeping, printer module, etc.). Constructs that are reused may also appear on separate pages; documentation may also be modular.

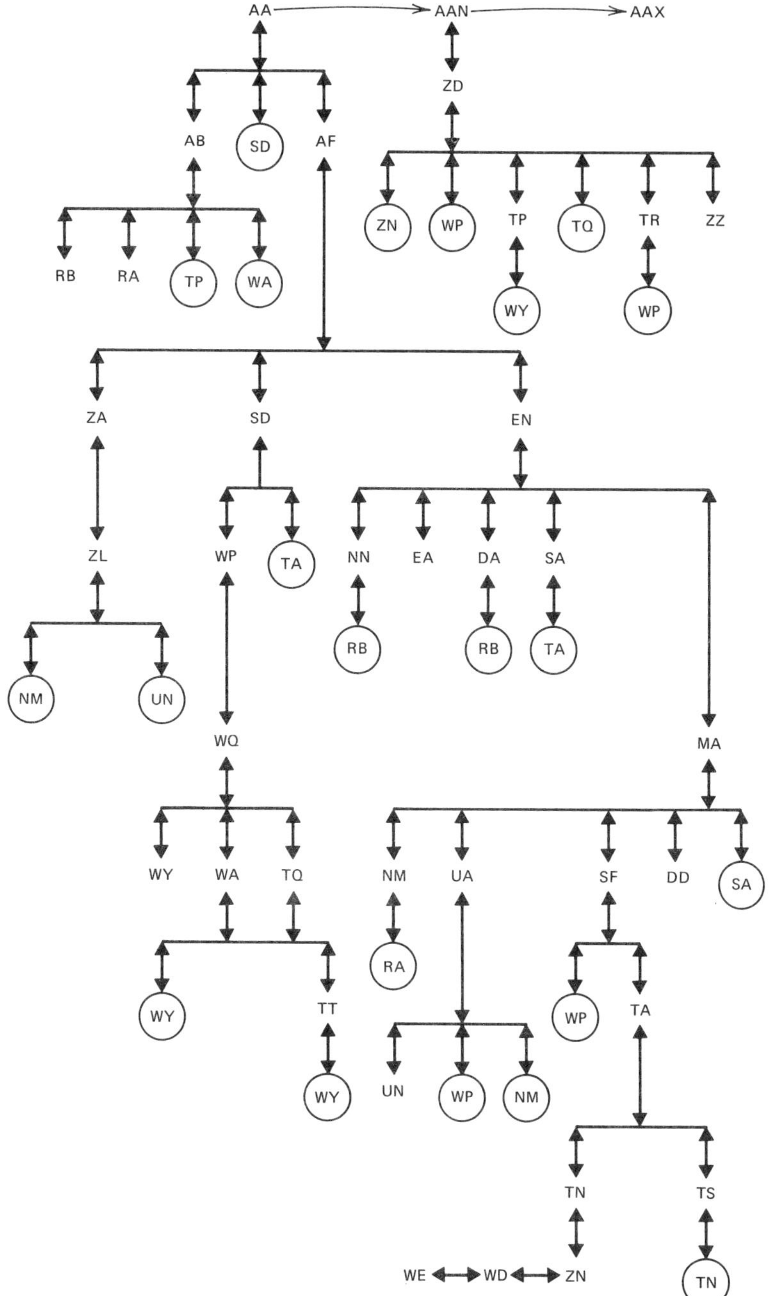

Figure 14 **AP 503/4 hierarchic tree diagram.**

PROCEDURAL STRUCTURE

In Chapter 5 we discussed applicational, structural, and procedural modularity. It is worthwhile to define the contents of the procedural functions more precisely. The five functions are logical interface, process, exception, housekeeping, and file interface.

In a hierarchic structure of program modules, the top of the hierarchy is occupied by the mainline. While it is perhaps implied, it is worth making explicit that the function of the mainline is that of the primary logical interface. Logical interface is the control function, the coding that tests and chooses (IF), which results in the selection of lower-level modules (PERFORM or GO TO . . . DEPENDING ON in our well-structured COBOL environment). Similarly, in all but the most simple programs, the mainline selects modules which also have the function of logical interface. These middle-level modules with the task of logical interface may be called "driver" modules. (Which is a better term than "submainlines," for example.) In a complex structure a driver may drive another driver on a lower level.

Distinguished from interface modules are what may be called process modules. These have the function of manipulation (MOVE) and calculation (COMPUTE) and may test and choose among functional alternatives local to the section (IF . . . GO TO). Only for exceptions does a process module make choices at the section level (IF . . . PERFORM . . . THRU . . .). A much clearer structure will result if a general rule is followed that only process modules make any changes in the data in the data stream (input, work, output) of a program.

In logically low-level IF evaluation (low-level in that branching is ordinarily within the scope of the paragraph-group), a process module may encounter an exception condition. Exception processing may then legitimately be PERFORMed by the process module. Typically, exception processing involves issuing a message (either to a user file or for "immediate" display on a printer) and setting one or more flags which will cause (in an interface module) the current transaction or the program to be aborted.

Housekeeping is a familiar functional entity. Housekeeping is analogous to setting up a machine to prepare to mill stock. The obvious system tasks involved in housekeeping are opening of files, zeroing or blanking data fields, and initializing a data table from a file. Other housekeeping functions may be: obtaining the date or time from the operating system, or processing file labels. In short, anything that deals more with preparing to run a computer program than accomplishing the business at hand may be termed housekeeping. Most housekeeping is performed once, such as file opening; some is performed cyclically, such as zeroing or blanking fields after the completion of each transaction in a series. One-time functions should be kept separate in a modular sense from functions to be performed more than once.

The last basic procedural module type is file interface. The READs and WRITEs and their special problems make this an obviously segmentable function.

To summarize:

Logical interface

Tests and chooses among module alternatives, using:

```
IF . . . PERFORM . . . THRU . .
IF. . . CALL
   or
GO TO . . .
   DEPENDING ON . . .
constructs.
```

With the exception of setting a flag value, it does not use MOVE or COMPUTE, nor does it contain input or output statements.

Process

Manipulates and calculates, tests, and chooses among local paragraph choices, using:

```
MOVE
COMPUTE (ADD, SUBTRACT, MULTIPLY, DIVIDE)
EXAMINE
SEARCH
SORT
IF . . . GO TO . . .
```

Exception

A special case of process for anticipated but undesired logical paths. Uses:

```
MOVE
PERFORM . . . THRU . . .
```

Housekeeping

Input/output—services files, using:

```
OPEN
CLOSE
```

Sets values, using:

```
MOVE
```

May PERFORM modules which have nothing to do with the main logical flow of the program module (e.g., obtain current DATE from operating system).

File interface

Performs input/outputs processing, using:

READ
WRITE
DISPLAY
ACCEPT

CASE STUDY: PROGRAM DESIGN

As an example, a single program out of a simple, medium-sized accounts payable system is analyzed to demonstrate how applicational (business) modules and system (procedural) modules may interact. To simplify the example, a few applicational niceties have been ignored. A complete listing of this program appears in the Appendix. The problem statement and rough design statement follow.

The program accepts, edits, and updates a sorted input stream of corrections to a master file containing records of checks which have been printed.

While there should be only one input card per check number, there may be several records on the master file to be updated, since a single check may apply toward payment of several invoices. The master file has been edited previously so there are: (1) no gaps in the check numbers; all check numbers are sequential and have been accounted for; (2) all records for different invoices for the same check number agree in detail.

There are two categories of corrections, "hand-voided" which is noted on the master record by an "H," and "stop-payment" which is noted by an "S." The input format is as follows.

Field Name	# Characters	Range	Remarks
1. CHECK-NUMBER	8	1-99999999	FATAL
2. VENDOR-IDENT	6	NUMERIC	FATAL
3. ISSUE-DATE	6	NUMERIC	FATAL
4. AMOUNT-PAID	6	0V01-9999V99	FATAL
5. VOID-CATEGORY	1	"S" or "H"	FATAL

The card arrangement for the above five fields is as follows; "B" represents a blank.

11111111B222222B333333BB444444BB5

The input to this program has been sorted by check-number. Vendor-identification (a numerical code), issue-date, and the amount-paid on the check may be compared as a safety measure to insure that the proper deletion has been made. The master file input is also in sorted order by check-number (major) and invoice-number (minor). Its format is:

	Field Name	# Characters	Remarks
1.	VENDOR-IDENT	6	NUMERIC CODE
2.	VENDOR-NAME	30	ALPHA
3.	CHECK-NUMBER	8	NUMERIC
4.	ISSUE-DATE	6	DATE OF CHECK
5.	INVOICE-NUMBER	10	NUMERIC
6.	AMOUNT-PAID	6	AMOUNT FOR THIS INVOICE
7.	VOID-FLAG	1	"S" or "H"

The file is packed with no blanks intervening between fields.

Processing of this file is to proceed as follows.

Read the input file and edit it for nonnegative numeric data. Read the old master file until a match is found between the check numbers on the two files. Read the next input record to insure that there is no duplication of check numbers. If a duplicate is discovered, do not process any input records with that check number. Report errors. Continue to read until a new number is encountered. Repeat the match and duplicate checking procedure.

Records on the old file for which there is no match condition are written to the new master file as they are encountered. Prepare a listing of the new master file. When a valid match occurs, further compare the vendor codes and the issue dates. If there is a no-match condition, write out an error report and repeat the process. On a match of the above fields, update the flag field in the old master record and write the record to the new master file. The master file will be cycled, updating, until a new check is encountered.

If the old master file goes to end of file before the update input file, this will invalidate the new master file and the program will have to be rerun. At the normal end of the program, cycle any of the old master file remaining unread to the new master file.

The program will be run in a small-shop environment. When an error is encountered, place an image of the input along with an error message in an in-core table. Print the error table at the end of the program so as not to conflict with the listing of the new master file. If there are more errors than the table will hold, dump the error table into a file, both on the full condition and at the end of the job, for subsequent dumping onto the printer. Issue a message that this has been done.

A functional matrix may be constructed by making the significant phrases from the above problem statement column headings and using the procedural system functions as row entries (refer to Figure 15). Intersections between the applicational and procedural tasks in this matrix provide a rough-cut solution to modularizing the problem. This is not a precise process; some of the process leaves identified at this point may turn out to be drivers, and other functions initially thought of as discrete may later be combined.

As a module is identified, it should be described on a coding sheet

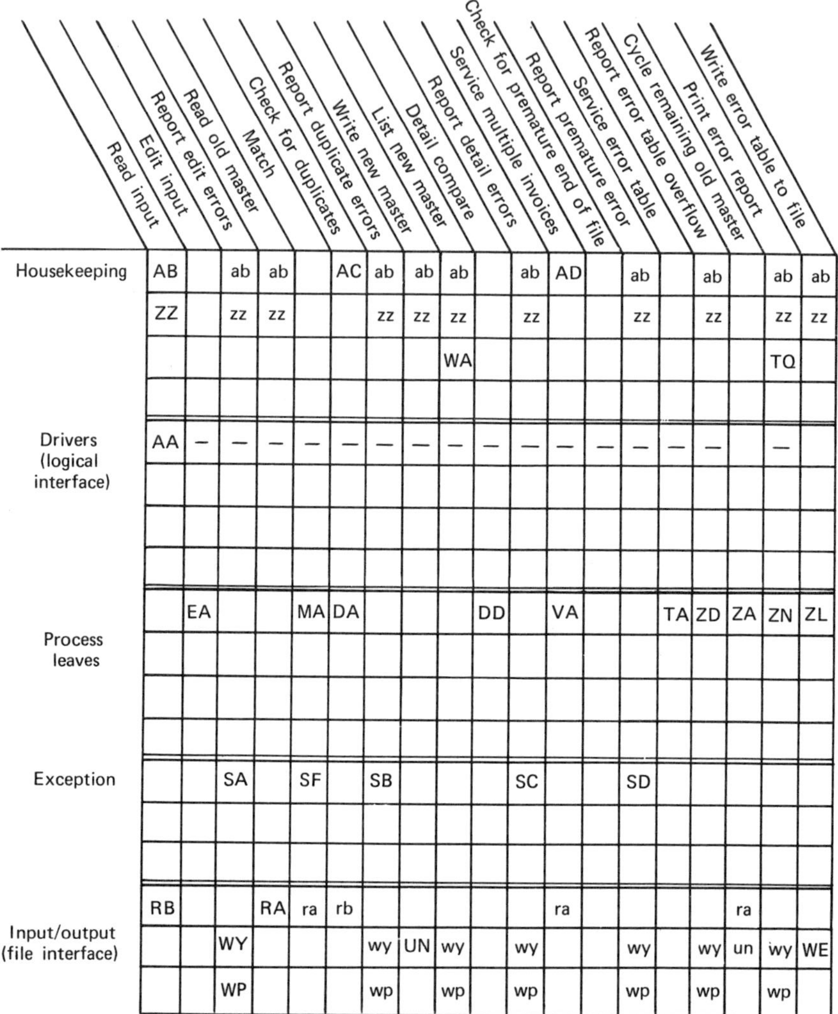

	Read input	Edit input	Report edit errors	Read old master	Match	Check for duplicates	Report duplicate errors	Write new master	List new master	Detail compare	Report detail errors	Service multiple invoices	Check for premature end of file	Report premature error	Service error table	Report error table overflow	Cycle remaining old master	Print error report	Write error table to file
Housekeeping	AB		ab	ab		AC	ab	ab	ab		ab	AD		ab		ab		ab	ab
	ZZ		zz	zz			zz	zz	zz		zz			zz		zz		zz	zz
									WA									TQ	
Drivers (logical interface)	AA	–	–	–	–	–	–	–	–	–	–	–	–	–	–	–		–	
Process leaves		EA			MA	DA				DD		VA			TA	ZD	ZA	ZN	ZL
Exception			SA		SF		SB				SC			SD					
Input/output (file interface)	RB			RA	ra	rb						ra					ra		
			WY				wy	UN	wy		wy			wy		wy	un	wy	WE
			WP				wp		wp		wp			wp		wp		wp	

Figure 15 **Applicational/procedural matrix.**

as an entry in the program section directory. It might not survive actual design and programming but, if it does not, nothing is lost and, if it does, a piece of the desirable documentation is finished. For discussion purposes let me describe some of the thinking that resulted in the example matrix (refer to Figure 15). The entries in the matrix are prefixes that will be assigned to a paragraph-group name. An uppercase entry refers to the first occurrence of a module; lowercase means it has appeared before but is also required for an additional applicational function. The first definition is that of the housekeeping.

AB-INITIALIZE	Some housekeeping will be required. Specifically, a file will have to be OPENed for every entry that has "read," "report", "write", "print," or "list" as the action verb.
AC-INPUT-AHEAD	In order to check for duplications in the input, two records will have to be in core. In order not to clutter the processing with a repeated test for first record, the first READ may be treated as housekeeping.
AD-MASTER-AHEAD	The same case in AC is true for the master file, since it is also necessary to look ahead for duplicate check numbers with different invoice numbers for update.
ZZ-CLOSE	For all files that are OPENed, a CLOSE is required.
WA-PAGE-HEADING	Since the newly updated master is listed on the printer, a page heading needs to be printed. Housekeeping is a good place to perform the first one of these.
TQ-ERROR-HEADS	The same case as in WA applies to the heading for the error report. This will not be performed as initial housekeeping, but only if the report is written in this job step.

The run-to-run flow diagram (refer to Chapter 4) indicates that there will be five files. All error reporting and listing, including the conditional listing of the error table, will be done through a single printer output file. At this point the primitive input/output routines (those that contain the READ or WRITE statement for a given file) may be identified.

RB-READ-INPUT	Read input file.
WY-WRITE	Write printer file.
RA-READ-MASTER	Read old master file.
UN-UPDATE-WRITE	Write new master file.
WE-WRITE-E	Write, conditionally, the error table to disk.
WP-PRINT	A printer line heading and page control module will have to be built around (or taken off the shelf for) WY-WRITE.

Next the process modules may be identified, since probably not enough to known at this point of the structure of the program to specify the driver modules.

EA-EDIT-INPUT	Edit input record.
MA-MATCH-CHECKS	Cycle old master file until a match is made with an input check number.

DA-DUP-CHECK	Test for and service duplicate check number on successive input.
DD-DETAIL-MATCH	Perform detailed comparison of input to master record.
UM-CYCLE-LOOP	Check for repeat of check number, if repeat cycle writing output file.
TA-ERR-TAB	Service table of error messages.
ZD-END-JOB	Print message if error table is dumped to disk.
ZA-FLUSH-LOOP	A loop will have to be used to print out the error table line by line.
ZL-FLUSH-LOOP	Same as ZN; true for error table cycle to disk.

The exception routines may be identified next. They will each conform to the general model of an exception routine: set an exception flag and (for the table in this program) move an error message to the table.

SA-EDIT-EXCEPT	Service edit errors.
SB-DUP-ERRORS	Service duplicate errors.
SC-DETAIL-ERRORS	Report detail match errors.
SD-PREMATURE-EOF	Report unexpected end of master file.
SF-BAD-FILE	Report bad sort sequence errors.

Drivers are a problem. At this point the only one we can be sure of is that there will be a mainline.

AA-MAIN-LINE	Mainline.

There are several ways in which one can proceed, and to a large extent it may depend on how an individual thinks about program structure and what process level capability already exists on the shelf. Some individuals prefer to think from the top of the structure down; others proceed from the bottom up. Perhaps a combination is best. One could begin to write the narrative for the procedural leaves identified thus far and perhaps gain more insight into the remaining structure. Alternatively, one might begin to sketch a hierarchic diagram of the proposed structure.

The control structure probably represents the greatest difficulty. What needs to be known is where to place the tests for end of file, cancellation of the transaction due to edit errors, printing of page headings, and so on. In most programs the uppermost level of control comes from the input files. If there is only one input file, the problem is usually simplified. When the input file is exhausted, the end-of-job processing is executed. In a multiple input file, one must consider what to do when one or the other or all (or other combinations) of the input files are exhausted. Many nonhierarchic, nonmodular programs present difficulty at end-of-file time. The AT END option of the READ statement is a strong invitation to make a great leap across the program structure to the termination code. The problem comes when there is more to do than simply DISPLAY "END OF JOB," CLOSE the files, and go home. In the sample program with the "look-ahead" read on both input files, there is still transaction processing to be done AT END. In order not to introduce clutter into the structure in a hierarchic modular program, the AT END should be used to set a flag. This flag is then tested in the control structure to determine what to process toward job end. Thus instead of jumping to AT END processing, the hierarchical method is to cascade upward to the driver which also has "command" over end-of-job processing. In this way processing may be terminated in an orderly and graceful fashion. Also, this reduces the temptation to jump through the program and tie up terminal loose ends. The cascading is achieved using

```
AT END
MOVE "Y" TO W-INPUT-FLAG.
```

in the READ statement, and

```
IF-W-INPUT-FLAG="Y"
```

statements in process and interface modules. The "true" action of these IF statements should frequently be to EXIT the module. See the program sample for examples.

Returning to the applicational/procedural matrix (Figure 15), one should first insure that the input READ primitives appear in all the columns in which they may reasonably be needed. For example, RB, the input file READ module, will also be needed when reading ahead to check for duplicate input check numbers, so that it appears in the "check for dupes" column.

Since DA is in the same column, W-INPUT-FLAG, signaling end-of-file processing in RB, will most likely have to be tested in DA and perhaps also in the as yet unidentified driver(s) which will PERFORM DA, and in AA, the mainline. (The mainline is in an all-pervasive position.)

Similarly, RA, the master file READ, will be PERFORMed to search for a match in the master file, to search for multiple invoices, and to complete reading of the master file at job end. One may expect then to test W-MASTER-EOF (the end-of-file flag name to be assigned) in AA, MA, UM, and ZA. As the hierarchy is built, anytime either RA or RB is a leaf on the current branch, an evaluation must be made as to whether an end-of-file flag needs to be tested. The flag

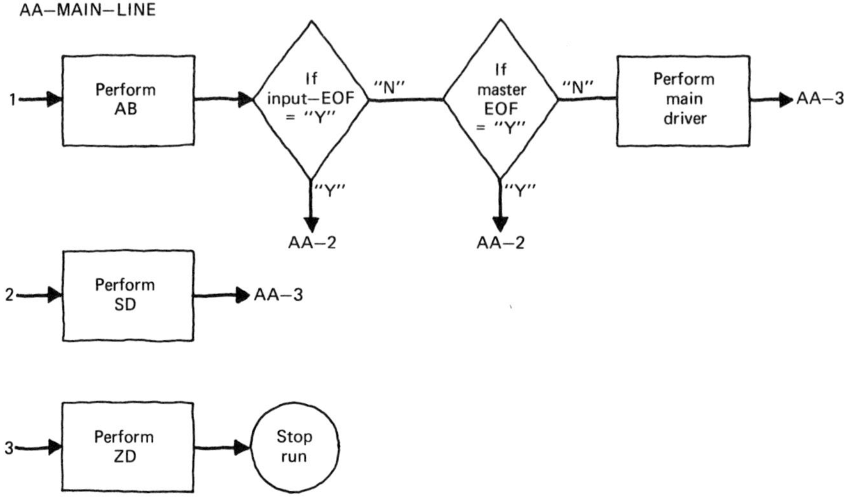

Figure 16 **Mainline and control AP 503/4.**

will not necessarily have to be tested in every module in the branch, as demonstrated in the sample program. The clearer the problem is understood, the cleaner the structure may become and fewer tests are likely to be required. If this technique is new to a programmer, it may result in what seems to be a lot of flag testing. As this approach becomes more familiar, the situation should improve.

This approach to the definition of the control structure has been more or less from the bottom up. More frequently, control design is attacked with a top-down approach, and this is appropriate, as discussed in other program design literature.[2] The utility of the bottom-up method is in providing a preview of the problem to facilitate the top-down "pass."

A top-down evaluation naturally begins with the mainline. The mainline should PERFORM three functions: initial housekeeping, the main driver, and end-of-job processing. Since the section descriptions indicate that AB-INITIALIZE executes READs for both input files, both flags should be tested. The flow diagram for AA-MAINLINE is Figure 16.

The job of the main driver is to handle the primary control. A graphic flow of the narrative of the driver, AF, is shown in Figure 17, and the flow diagram in Figure 18. This is the main program loop; each time it is entered a check will be made for the conditions specified in Figure 17, and the appropriate action will be taken.

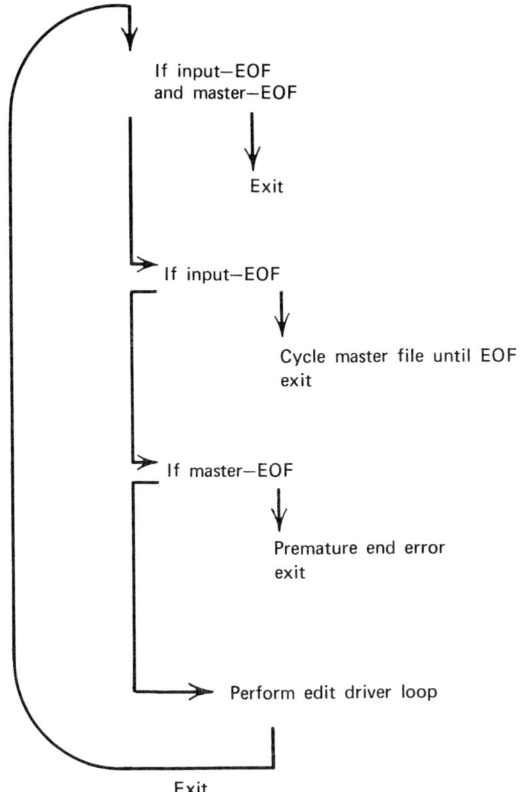

Figure 17 **Main driver loop (AF) control requirements.**

In the listing of the sample program, note that EN-DRIVER (which is the edit subdriver) does not have to test either W-INPUT-EOF or W-MASTER-EOF. While the former may be set downstream from DA-DUP-CHECK and the latter downstream in MA-MATCH-CHECKS, they do not interact in EN. The input flag will be set in DA only if an exception occurs, in which case the EXIT will be taken in EN as a result of W-NO-DUP-FLAG being set to "N." In DA the result of testing and finding W-INPUT-EOF="Y" causes DA to EXIT. In a more complex system, it might be necessary to test such a flag in every module in the branch in which it influences control. If the sample program were given as a problem for modification, a predictable source of error would be the failure to account for the downstream setting of the input flags if additional PERFORMs needed to be placed in EN or if a restructuring of EN were called for. This is

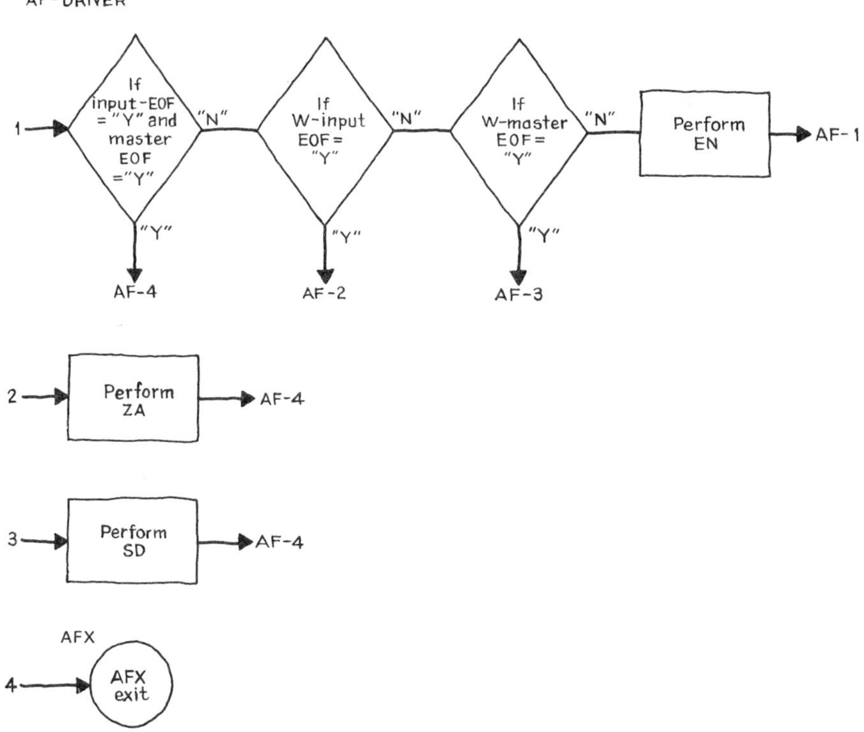

Figure 18 **Main driver and control AP 503/4.**

an example of why it is important to illuminate the use of flags and indices in the documentation.

A few additional points about the sample program are worth mentioning. Refer to Figure 15, the applicational/procedural matrix, and compare it to the program listing, or better to the hierarchic tree diagram to see how the actual program structure conforms to the original matrix. Housekeeping was fairly predictable, although AC and AD were condensed into paragraphs within AB rather than PERFORMed separately. Two new housekeeping modules were added, TS, to permit blank lines to be easily inserted in the error table, and TP, a "find the end of the page" routine for the printer (the latter was written to avoid discussing the differences in how various COBOL compilers implement printer control tape handling) and TT for blank lines when needed for the printer module.

As the drivers AF and EN were identified, they were added. MA became a driver rather than a leaf, and the same can be said for TA and WP since they perform simple control functions at the top of a hierarchy of process paragraphs.

The "fetch-a-record" modules NN and NM were added. It should not be overlooked that these routines, which move an input record to a work area and then replace the input record with a READ, helped simplify the structure. The end-of-file condition may then be tested after processing a transaction, since one transaction is left in the work area when the replacement READ encounters the AT END.

The substructure under WP has added WQ, and TA has TN, TR, and WD as new additions. The latter were added simply as a result of using a PERFORM . . . VARYING and needing a paragraph-name to reference. UN came under the control of UA, which also incorporated what was to have been UM. In the exception category it was found that SA was sufficient for indicating the errors that SA, SB and SC were planned to handle.

What I have done is present a brief anatomy lesson illustrating how one might profitably use some of the seemingly abstract concepts (applicational, procedural) to help design the modules for a program. The program here was short and noncomplex, but that should cause little loss of generality; all programs should be as short and noncomplex as possible. If this method does not seem to apply to a problem because of size, resegment the problem.

IMPROVING THE STRUCTURE OF AN EXISTING PROGRAM—A SAMPLE

Frequently, the problem in programming is to improve the quality of a structure to lend more clarity to it. Some programs have so little structure that it is not worth the effort; these programs often end up being rewritten. The subject of improving programs in maintenance is one that needs some serious research beyond the scope of this monograph. As a systems group introduces modularity, there will be many cases in which the structure is fairly good but not as clean as might be desirable. The sample program segment that follows was written under such conditions. The intent is neither an exhaustive analysis nor an exposition of any principles, just presentation of a sample of how one program was improved.

This is an example of how subtle complexity might be easily and inadvertedly introduced into the branching structure of a program. The example was taken from an actual coded program; only the data names have been changed to protect the innocent.

```
 AA-BEGIN.
     PERFORM BA-HOUSEKEEP THRU BZ-HOUSEKEEP.
     PERFORM XA-GET-INPUT THRU XZ-GET-INPUT.
*
 AB-OUTER-LOOP.
     IF MASTER-SWITCH = '0'
          PERFORM WA-GET-MASTER THRU WZ-GET-MASTER.
     MOVE '1' TO MASTER-SWITCH.
*
 AC-CHOOSE-RECORD.
     IF INPUT-CONTROL LESS THAN MASTER-CONTROL
          GO TO AD-NEW-MASTER.
     IF INPUT-CONTROL = MASTER-CONTROL
          AND INPUT-CONTROL = HIGH-VALUES
          GO TO ZA-END-OF-JOB.
     MOVE AM-INPUT TO AM-OUTPUT.
     MOVE '0' TO MASTER-SWITCH.
     MOVE '0' TO NEW-MASTER-SWITCH.
     GO TO AF-COMPARE.
*
 AD-NEW-MASTER.
     IF T-SEQ-NUM = '1' AND T-RECORD-CODE = 'A'
          GO TO AE-NEW-M-SET-UP.
     MOVE '90' TO T-ERROR.
     PERFORM DA-DELETE-TRAN THRU DZ-DELETE-TRAN.
     GO TO AB-OUTER-LOOP.
*
 AE-NEW-M-SET-UP.
     IF T-SOURCE NOT = HOLD-SOURCE-CHECK
          MOVE HOLD-CONTROL TO HOLD-CHECK.
     IF T-COMP-NUMBER = '00' AND HOLD-COMP-CHECK NOT '00'
          MOVE '92' TO T-ERROR
          PERFORM DA-DELETE-TRAN THRU DZ-DELETE-TRAN
          GO TO AB-OUTER-LOOP.
     IF T-COMP-NUMBER NOT = '00' AND HOLD-COMP-CHECK = '00'
          MOVE '93' TO T-ERROR
          PERFORM DA-DELETE-TRAN THRU DZ-DELETE-TRAN
          GO TO AB-OUTER-LOOP.
     MOVE SPACES TO AM-OUTPUT.
     MOVE HOLD-CONTROL TO AM-CONTROL.
     MOVE SPACES TO NEW-MASTER-SWITCH.
     MOVE AM-SOURCE TO SEARCH-SOURCE.
     PERFORM YA-SEARCH THRU YZ-SEARCH.
     ADD 1 TO TOTAL.
*
 AF-COMPARE.
     IF HOLD-CONTROL NOT = AM-CONTROL
          GO TO AH-MASTER-DONE.
     IF T-SEQ-NUM = '1'
          AND T-TRAN-CODE = 'A'
          AND NEW-MASTER-SWITCH = '0'
          MOVE '91' TO T-ERROR
          PERFORM DA-DELETE-TRAN THRU DZ-DELETE-TRAN
          GO TO AF-COMPARE.
     IF T-SEQ-NUM = '1'
          AND T-TRAN-CODE = 'D'
          MOVE AM-SOURCE TO SEARCH-SOURCE
          PERFORM YA-SEARCH THRU YZ-SEARCH
```

```
        ADD 1 TO TOTAL
        PERFORM NA-PRINT-SET THRU NZ-PRINT-SET
        GO TO AB-OUTER-LOOP.
    PERFORM NA-PRINT-SET THRU NZ-PRINT-SET.
    PERFORM HA-UPDATE THRU HZ-UPDATE.
AG-NEXT.
    PERFORM XA-GET-INPUT THRU XZ-GET-INPUT.
    GO TO AF-COMPARE.
*
AH-MASTER-DONE.
    PERFORM TA-PUT-OUTPUT THRU TZ-PUT-OUTPUT.
    GO TO AB-OUTER-LOOP.
```

Figure 19

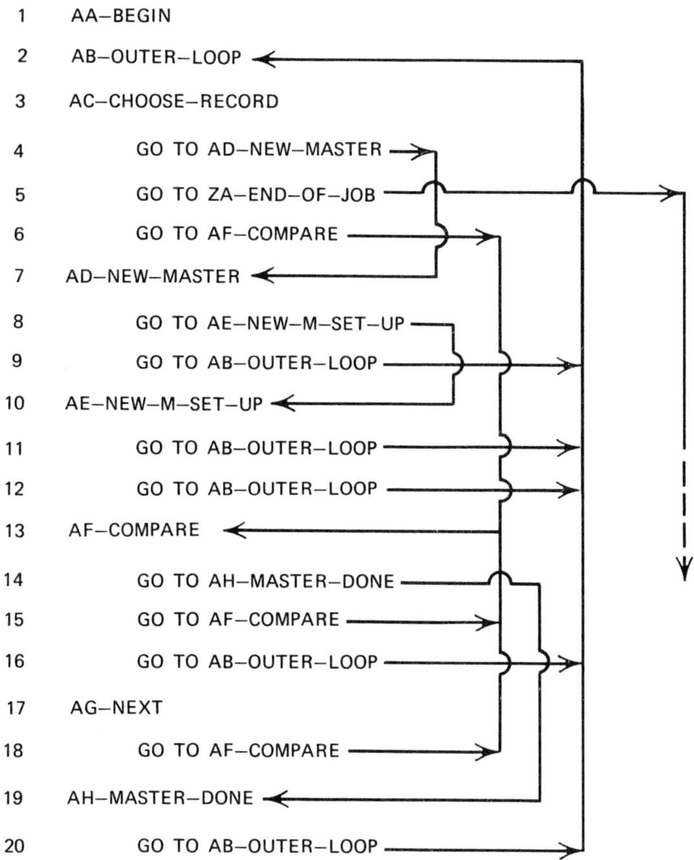

Figure 20 **Branching structure.**

The function of the program from which this example was taken is the update of a master file from a sorted and edited transaction file. Notes have been omitted from the program listing in order to focus on the structure, not the functions being performed. While this program was written with much better than average attention to the beneficial use of PERFORM, the mainline portion (shown in Figure 19) is more complex than need be. If the GO TO branches in this segment are diagrammed as in Figure 20, some interesting facts about its structure become apparent.

For one, the branch in line 5 is to a too distant location for quick reference. Two loops are implied: an outer loop spanning AB and AH, and an inner, smaller one, spanning AF and AG. There is a potential problem of scope brought about by the branch at line 16; it jumps out of the middle of the implied inner loop and may cause difficulty during a future modification. The branches at lines 9, 11, 12, 16, and 20 imply a PERFORM . . . THRU construct, including substitution of a branch to an EXIT for each GO TO AB-OUTER-LOOP. The branches at lines 4, 8, and 14 are short (of local scope), forward-moving branches and are clean and acceptable. The inner loop may be made explicit by changing the branches at lines 15 and 18 to branches to the EXIT of AF. AF will then be PERFORMed THRU its EXIT.

These revision in the coding appear in Figure 21. Note how short and clear the mainline segment has become with AC and AF now being PERFORMed. A flag, END-SWITCH, has been added to clarify the end-of-job logic. It is reset in AC. A revised structure at ACA-INNER-LOOP permits the choice between executing AH or reexecuting AF to be made clearly outside of the loop. Use of a flag, INNER-LOOP-CONTROL, also makes the choices to continue recycling the PERFORM or EXIT. The new structure makes an EXIT to ACX the equivalent of the former branch to AB. Figure 22 diagrams the revised branching structure. All branches to the EXITS, AC and AFX, have been eliminated since this is also a well-formed construct and the PERFORM relationship of AC and AF is shown by the separating dots. Figure 22 shows definite improvement, but there is still a bit of spaghetti caused by the backward branches to ACA.

If ACA is also PERFORMed, the branching structure may be cleaned up neatly. AH may also be eliminated as a separate entity by moving its code to under the first IF in ACA. The final revised coding of the inner loops is seen in Figure 23.

Figure 24 diagrams the final revised structure. Note how straight forward it has become.

```
AA-BEGIN.
    PERFORM BA-HOUSEKEEP THRU BZ-HOUSEKEEP.
    PERFORM XA-GET-INPUT THRU XZ-GET-INPUT.
*
AB-MAIN.
    IF MASTER-SWITCH = '0'
        PERFORM WA-GET-MASTER THRU WZ-GET-MASTER.
    MOVE '1' TO MASTER-SWITCH.
    PERFORM AC-RECORD-PROC THRU ACX-RECORD-EXIT.
    IF END-SWITCH = 'Y'
        GO TO ABX-END-OF-JOB.
    GO TO AB-MAIN.
*
ABX-END-OF-JOB.
    PERFORM ZA-WRAPUP THRU ZZ-WRAPUP-X.
    STOP RUN.
*
AC-RECORD-PROC.
    IF INPUT-CONTROL LESS THAN MASTER-CONTROL
        GO TO AD-NEW-MASTER.
    IF INPUT-CONTROL = MASTER-CONTROL
        AND INPUT-CONTROL = HIGH-VALUES
        MOVE 'Y' TO END-SWITCH
        GO TO ACX-RECORD-EXIT.
    MOVE AM-INPUT TO AM-OUTPUT.
    MOVE '0' TO MASTER-SWITCH.
    MOVE '0' TO NEW-MASTER-SWITCH.
*
ACA-INNER-LOOP.
    IF HOLD-CONTROL NOT = AM-CONTROL
        GO TO AH-MASTER-DONE.
    MOVE 'N' TO INNER-LOOP-CONTROL.
    PERFORM AF-COMPARE THRU AFX-COMPARE-EXIT.
    IF INNER-LOOP-CONTROL = 'N'
        GO TO ACA-INNER-LOOP.
    GO TO ACX-RECORD-EXIT.
*
AD-NEW-MASTER.
    IF T-SEQ-NUM = '1' AND T-RECORD-CODE = 'A'
        GO TO AE-NEW-M-SET-UP.
    MOVE '90' TO T-ERROR.
    PERFORM DA-DELETE-TRAN THRU DZ-DELETE-TRAN.
    GO TO ACX-RECORD-EXIT.
*
AE-NEW-M-SET-UP.
    IF T-SOURCE NOT = HOLD-SOURCE-CHECK
        MOVE HOLD-CONTROL TO HOLD-CHECK.
    IF T-COMP-NUMBER = '00' AND HOLD-COMP-CHECK NOT '00'
        MOVE '92' TO T-ERROR
        PERFORM DA-DELETE-TRAN THRU DZ-DELETE-TRAN
        GO TO ACX-RECORD-EXIT.
    IF T-COMP-NUMBER NOT = '00' AND HOLD-COMP-CHECK = '00'
        MOVE '93' TO T-ERROR
        PERFORM DA-DELETE-TRAN THRU DZ-DELETE-TRAN
        GO TO ACX-RECORD-EXIT.
    MOVE SPACES TO AM-OUTPUT.
    MOVE HOLD-CONTROL TO AM-CONTROL.
    MOVE SPACES TO NEW-MASTER-SWITCH.
```

```
     MOVE AM-SOURCE TO SEARCH-SOURCE.
     PERFORM YA-SEARCH THRU YZ-SEARCH.
     ADD 1 TO TOTAL.
     GO TO ACA-INNER-LOOP.
*
 AH-MASTER-DONE.
     PERFORM TA-PUT-OUTPUT THRU TZ-PUT-OUTPUT.
*
 ACX-RECORD-EXIT.
     EXIT.
*
 AF-COMPARE.
     IF T-SEQ-NUM = '1'
         AND T-TRAN-CODE = 'A'
         AND NEW-MASTER-SWITCH = '0'
         MOVE '91' TO T-ERROR
         PERFORM DA-DELETE-TRAN THRU DZ-DELETE-TRAN
         GO TO AFX-COMPARE-EXIT.
     IF T-SEQ-NUM = '1'
         AND T-TRAN-CODE = 'D'
         MOVE AM-SOURCE TO SEARCH-SOURCE
         PERFORM YA-SEARCH THRU YZ-SEARCH
         ADD 1 TO TOTAL
         PERFORM NA-PRINT-SET THRU NZ-PRINT-SET
         MOVE 'Y' TO INNER-LOOP-CONTROL
         GO TO AFX-COMPARE-EXIT.
     PERFORM NA-PRINT-SET THRU NZ-PRINT-SET.
     PERFORM HA-UPDATE THRU HZ-UPDATE.
     PERFORM XA-GET-INPUT THRU XZ-GET-INPUT.
*
 AFX-COMPARE-EXIT.
     EXIT.
```

Figure 21

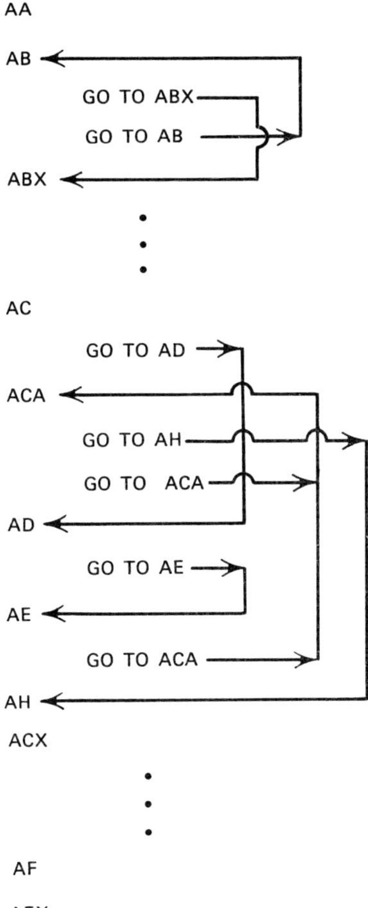

Figure 22 **First revision of structure.**

```
 AA-BEGIN.
     PERFORM BA-HOUSEKEEP THRU BZ-HOUSEKEEP.
     PERFORM XA-GET-INPUT THRU XZ-GET-INPUT.
*
 AB-MAIN.
     IF MASTER-SWITCH = '0'
          PERFORM WA-GET-MASTER THRU WZ-GET-MASTER.
     MOVE '1' TO MASTER-SWITCH.
     PERFORM AC-RECORD-PROC THRU ACX-RECORD-EXIT.
     IF END-SWITCH = 'Y'
          GO TO ABX-END-OF-JOB.
     GO TO AB-MAIN.
*
 ABX-END-OF-JOB.
     PERFORM ZA-WRAPUP THRU ZZ-WRAPUP-X.
     STOP RUN.
*
 AC-RECORD-PROC.
     IF INPUT-CONTROL LESS THAN MASTER-CONTROL
          GO TO AD-NEW-MASTER.
     IF INPUT-CONTROL = MASTER-CONTROL
          AND INPUT-CONTROL = HIGH-VALUES
          MOVE 'Y' TO END-SWITCH
          GO TO ACX-RECORD-EXIT.
     MOVE AM-INPUT TO AM-OUTPUT.
     MOVE '0' TO MASTER-SWITCH.
     MOVE '0' TO NEW-MASTER-SWITCH.
     PERFORM AF-INNER-LOOP THRU AFX-INNER-EXIT.
     GO TO ACX-RECORD-EXIT.
*
 AD-NEW-MASTER.
     IF T-SEQ-NUM = '1' AND T-RECORD-CODE = 'A'
          GO TO AE-NEW-M-SET-UP.
     MOVE '90' TO T-ERROR.
     PERFORM DA-DELETE-TRAN THRU DZ-DELETE-TRAN.
     GO TO ACX-RECORD-EXIT.
*
 AE-NEW-M-SET-UP.
     IF T-SOURCE NOT = HOLD-SOURCE-CHECK
          MOVE HOLD-CONTROL TO HOLD-CHECK.
     IF T-COMP-NUMBER = '00' AND HOLD-COMP-CHECK NOT '00'
          MOVE '92' TO T-ERROR
          PERFORM DA-DELETE-TRAN THRU DZ-DELETE-TRAN
          GO TO ACX-RECORD-EXIT.
     IF T-COMP-NUMBER NOT = '00' AND HOLD-COMP-CHECK = '00'
          MOVE '93' TO T-ERROR
          PERFORM DA-DELETE-TRAN THRU DZ-DELETE-TRAN
          GO TO ACX-RECORD-EXIT.
     MOVE SPACES TO AM-OUTPUT.
     MOVE HOLD-CONTROL TO AM-CONTROL.
     MOVE SPACES TO NEW-MASTER-SWITCH.
     MOVE AM-SOURCE TO SEARCH-SOURCE.
     PERFORM YA-SEARCH THRU YZ-SEARCH.
     ADD 1 TO TOTAL.
     PERFORM AF-INNER-LOOP THRU AFX-INNER-EXIT.
 ACX-RECORD-EXIT.
     EXIT.
*
```

```
AF-INNER-LOOP.
    IF HOLD-CONTROL NOT = AM-CONTROL
        PERFORM TA-PUT-OUTPUT THRU TZ-PUT-OUTPUT.
    GO TO AFX-INNER-EXIT.
    MOVE 'N' TO INNER-LOOP-CONTROL.
    PERFORM AG-COMPARE THRY AGX-COMPARE-EXIT.
    IF INNER-LOOP-CONTROL = 'N'
        GO TO AF-INNER-LOOP.
AFX-INNER-EXIT.
    EXIT.
*
AG-COMPARE.
    IF T-SEQ-NUM = '1'
        AND T-TRAN-CODE = 'A'
        AND NEW-MASTER-SWITCH = '0'
        MOVE '91' TO T-ERROR
        PERFORM DA-DELETE-TRAN THRU DZ-DELETE-TRAN
        GO TO AGX-COMPARE-EXIT.
    IF T-SEQ-NUM = '1'
        AND T-TRAN-CODE = 'D'
        MOVE AM-SOURCE TO SEARCH-SOURCE
        PERFORM YA-SEARCH THRU YZ-SEARCH
        ADD 1 TO TOTAL
        PERFORM NA-PRINT-SET THRU NZ-PRINT-SET
        MOVE 'Y' TO INNER-LOOP-CONTROL
        GO TO AGX-COMPARE-EXIT.
    PERFORM NA-PRINT-SET THRU NZ-PRINT-SET.
    PERFORM HA-UPDATE THRU HZ-UPDATE.
    PERFORM XA-GET-INPUT THRU XZ-GET-INPUT.
AGX-COMPARE-EXIT.
    EXIT.
```

Figure 23

SUMMARY

Modular design in COBOL is primarily related to using the PERFORM verb exclusively as a closed subroutine construct and exercising strict control over the scope of any GO TO. It is useful to identify five procedural functions for any program module: logical interface, process, exception, housekeeping, and file interface. The process of defining modules in a program may be thought of as identifying the interaction between the applicational and the procedural. A good approach to the design of program control, often a difficult area, is a combination of top-down and bottom-up techniques.

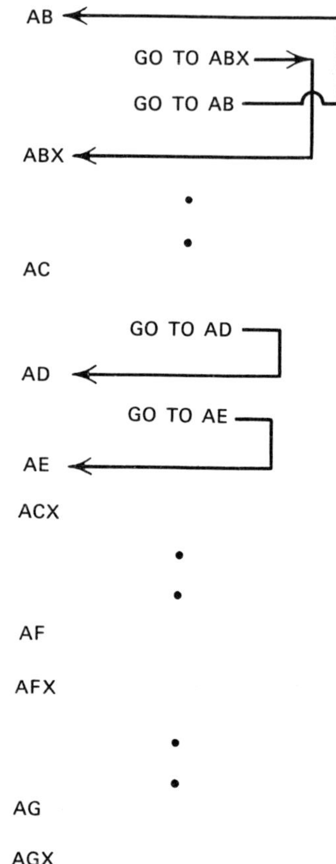

Figure 24 **Second revision of structure.**

REFERENCES

1. Dijkstra, E. W., "GO TO Statement Considered Harmful" letter, *Communications of the ACM,* March, 1968. "For a number of years I have been familiar with the observation that the quality of programmers is a decreasing function of the density of GO TO statements in the programs they produce."

   For a good presentation of the whole GO TO issue refer to the three papers in the section:

   "Control Structures in Programming Languages: the GO TO Controversy," *25th Proceedings of the ACM*, 1972.
2. Baker, F. T., "Chief Programmer Team Management of Production Programming," *IBM Systems Journal,* No. 1, 1972.

CHAPTER 7

Interface: Linkage and Subprograms

Designing programs with the desirable degree of modularity (i.e., *very* modular) can create problems if the interface between modules is not well defined. Or perhaps it would be more appropriate to say that the problems caused by poor interface design become more visible and critical in a very modular program or system. This chapter attacks interface design at both the intramodule and the intermodule levels.

INTERFACE AND DATA

Interface between modules is effected through data at every level of modularity. Interface between program modules is effected either through files or, in the case of subprograms, by the data passed in the USING portion of the CALL[1] verb. Within a module the interface between paragraph-groups is also achieved through data, as will be illustrated shortly.

Since data represent the key element of an interface, it is appropriate to describe the process and attributes of data binding. Binding is a term applied to the computer systems process of linking a logical data element with a physical storage address. In COBOL, when A-VENDOR-ITEM is assigned storage position X (displaced +318 bytes from the contents of register 9, for example), it has been logically bound. At execution time the contents of the register establish the base address for the storage of which A-VENDOR-ITEM is a part. The actual physical address is not bound at the time the COBOL program is compiled, so that the operating system may relocate the program. However, the relative position of A-VENDOR-ITEM to the program has been fixed, so that its logical binding is complete and irrevocable.

Time is one of the attributes of binding, so that we may speak of compile time binding (static) as in COBOL, or execution time binding (dynamic) as in ALGOL or PL/I. CALL raises yet another attribute of binding, mode, the two options being name binding or positional binding. If a data storage position is defined as L-ISSUE-DATE in the DATA DIVISION, and a statement says MOVE SPACE TO L-ISSUE-DATE, the compiler binds the reference to storage by name; L-ISSUE-DATE is taken to mean the same storage location in both references. However, the CALL . . . USING statement may appear:

```
CALL "DISTABLE" USING L-VENDOR-REC, K-CONTROL-BLOCK.
```

and the corresponding ENTRY . . . USING in the subprogram:

```
ENTRY "DISTABLE" USING H-CUSTOMER-INFO, I-PARAMETERS.
```

While there is name binding of the CALL and ENTRY names, the binding of the data names in the USING is on a positional basis. Thus the names themselves do not have to correspond, only some understood equivalence in the data descriptions of the names occupying respective positions in the two USINGs.

INTRAMODULE INTERFACE

Within a COBOL program module, all the data in the data division are accessible to any code in the program; all data are global to the module. This is not necessarily the case in languages with a block structure, such as ALGOL or PL/I, in which a variable may be local, that is, may be referenced only by the code in a given block (which is one of the potential trouble spots in those languages).

Although all data are globally accessible within a program module, certain structures are naturally associated with a given section of code. A typical example may be found in the sample program (in the Appendix) in the paragraph-group, SA-EDIT-EXCPT.

```
SA-EDIT-EXCPT.
    MOVE "ERRORS" TO L-ERROR-MSG.
    MOVE I-INPUT-EDIT-MSG TO J-PRINT-LINE.
    PERFORM TA-ERR-TAB THRU TAX-ERR-TAB-X.
    MOVE L-CARD-WORK TO J-PRINT-LINE.
    MOVE 1 TO W-BLANK-LINES.
    PERFORM TA-ERR-TAB-THRU TAX-ERR-TAB-X.
SAX-EDIT-EXCPT-X.
    EXIT.
```

SA-EDIT-EXCPT is performed when an error has been detected in one of the process modules, at which time it MOVEs an error message to J-PRINT-LINE, PERFORMs TA-ERR-TAB, MOVEs the input line itself to J-PRINT-LINE, sets W-BLANK-LINES to 1, and PERFORMs TA-ERR-TAB again. TA-ERR-TAB takes the contents of J-PRINT-LINE, whatever they are, and places them in a table of error messages, followed by however many blank line table entries have been specified.

The function of these MOVEs is to "stage" the data to the TA group, the data names that hold the data defining, in part, the TA group's data interface.

For any given module data interfaces may be subdivided into the following categories:

1. Process interface
2. Control interface
3. Working interface
    a. Stable
    b. Perishable

The first, the process interface, contains the data on which the module will operate; for the TA paragraph group this is J-PRINT-LINE (see Figure 25). The control interface variable is W-BLANK-LINES, which is set to the number of blank table entries to follow the contents of J-PRINT-LINE. The working interface may be thought of as being separated into two categories: stable and perishable. Stable working data represent storage used internally to a module, which must retain its integrity throughout the entire execution. In other words, a stable working structure cannot be REDEFINEd and used for an alternate purpose by another module, nor should it be altered by an outside module. Table KI-ERROR-REC, its index WI-INDEX-ERR, and the limiting value in WI-ERRTAB-LIMIT may be thought of as stable working data, since they must remain bound for TA's use. W-ANY-ERROR is a flag used to signal that at least one error has occurred and, although it is available to

```
TA-ERR-TAB.
    MOVE "Y" TO W-ANY-ERROR.
    MOVE J-PRINT-LINE TO K1-ERROR-REC (WI-INDEX-ERR).
    PERFORM TN-TABLE-LOOP THRU TNX-TABLE-LOOP-X.
    IF W-BLANK-LINES NOT=ZERO
        PERFORM TS-BLANK-LOOP THRU TSX-BLANK-LOOP-X
            VARYING W-LOOP-INDEX FROM 1 BY 1 UNTIL
            W-BLOOP-INDEX GREATER THAN W-BLANK-LINES
        MOVE 0 TO W-BLANK-LINES.
TAX-ERR-TAB-X.
    EXIT.

TN-TABLE-LOOP.
    ADD 1 TO WI-INDEX-ERR.
    IF WI-INDEX-ERR GREATER THAN WI-ERRTAB-LIMIT
        MOVE "Y" TO WZ-TABLE-FLUSH
        PERFORM ZN-FLUSH-LOOP THRU ZNX-FLUSH-LOOP-X
        MOVE 1 TO WI-INDEX-ERR.
TNX-TABLE-LOOP-X.
    EXIT.

TS-BLANK-LOOP.
    MOVE SPACES TO K1-ERROR-REC (WI-INDEX-ERR).
    PERFORM TN-TABLE-LOOP THRU TNX-TABLE-LOOP-X.
TSX-BLANK-LOOP-X.
    EXIT.
```

Figure 25. **TA Paragraph-group.**

external modules for testing, it should be considered as "read-only" stable working data; the same is true of WZ-TABLE-FLUSH, which is a flag indicating table overflow has occurred.

Perishable working data are data used for temporary storage, usually of intermediate results, and do not have to retain their value from one PERFORM to the next. If TA were a subprogram, its perishable working data would be the loop index W-LOOP-INDEX, since it is reinitialized for each execution of the TA group. Interfacing within a module, perishable working data frequently have less meaning than when interfacing with a subprogram, all the data within a module being global. One should avoid, if at all possible, gratuitous use of a single storage location or structure for multiple purposes (through REDEFINEs or otherwise). If such reuse is necessary to conserve storage, defining what is and is not perishable is absolutely critical.

In cases in which there is a fair amount of change, especially if it is asymmetric, one should maximize the visibility of a module's data interface. While documentation is a partial solution, placing the data in a structure that mirrors the structure of the interface also enhances visibility.

For TA-ERR-TAB an appropriate structure is:

```
01  TA-INTERFACE.
    05  TA-PROCESS-DATA.
        10  TA-PRINT-LINE          PICTURE X(132).
    05  TA-CONTROL-DATA.
        10  TA-BLANK-LINES         PICTURE 9(4) VALUE 0 COMP.
    05  TA-STABLE-WORK-DATA.
        10  TA-ANY-ERROR           PICTURE X  VALUE "N".
        10  TA-ERROR-INDEX         PICTURE 9(4) VALUE 1 COMP.
        10  TA-ERRTAB-LIMIT        PICTURE 9(4) VALUE 100 COMP.
        10  TA-TABLE-FLUSH         PICTURE X  VALUE "N".
        10  TA-ERROR-TABLE
               OCCURS 100
               TIMES.
            15  TA-ERR-REC         PICTURE X(132).
```

This structure defines TA's (and its subsidiary modules') relationship to the hierarchically superior remainder of the program modules. A module PERFORMing TA need not be involved in TA's inner workings, nor it with theirs. This is the essence of interface, that it effects clean communication between independent modules.

INTERMODULE INTERFACE: SUBPROGRAMS

COBOL programmers use too few CALLed subprograms (largely because of their training and experience), in spite of the fact that the positional binding of subprogram interfaces greatly enhances the reusability of modules. Most frequently, systems organizations do not exercise the data-naming discipline or library protocol that might facilitate the reuse of code that already exists, so that, although a programmer may know that useful code can be found in another program, it cannot be used directly because data names do not match what has already been defined. (See a further discussion on this point in Chapter 9.) Thus to be reusable code does not only have to be modular, but it has to be easily unfastened and reattached. CALL . . . USING solves this naming problem, and the subprogram provides a handy container for a reusable module of code. It is true that CALL . . . USING incurs some overhead, but with the benefit that large chunks of code become quickly reusable.

In a multisubprogram system it is essential that all the interfaces be well defined. Not only is it useful to distinguish between the interface categories already discussed (process, control, stable working, and perishable working), but also within those categories what is input and output to the subprogram. Before looking at the data interface in detail, it is worthwhile to note that there is also a logical interface between program modules. Ideally, a paragraph-group in the calling module is devoted to interfacing with the subprogram. Its structure may be schematized as follows.

```
Interface-paragraph.
   Gather interface data.
   CALL . . . USING interface data.
   Distribute interface data.
Interface-paragraph-exit.
   EXIT.
```

The job of the logical interface module (referred to in Chapter 6 as drivers) is to MOVE the data elements into the interface data sets (if necessary), CALL the subprogram, and redistribute the results into the WORKING STORAGE or output buffers of the calling program. Many times in actual practice these models of the logical and data interface are too strict to be useful. There may be no need for one or another of the functions of gathering or distributing, no working data, or no control. However, strict models provide a convenient frame of reference for when there is sufficient complexity to warrant either their strict implementation or an equivalent substitute.

A useful example in studying interface may be constructed by taking the printer logic (WP and its subsidiary modules) from the sample program and converting it to a subprogram. The purpose of this subprogram, called "PRINTER," is to fill the need for simple reports on a standard form.

The problem narrative is:

> PRINTER will accept a 132-character line of code and write it to the printer, followed by some number of blank lines specified by an input variable. PRINTER will control page overflow, printing one to five lines of heading information, as specified by an input table and control variable. Given an initialized value for page count, PRINTER will increment it by one on each page overflow. The status of the page overflow flag should be available to the calling module.

The data interfaces for PRINTER may be structured as follows, as they would appear in its LINKAGE SECTION.[2]

The process data consist of the print line and the table of heading lines.

```
01  P-W-DATA-INTERFACE.
    02  P-PROCESS-DATA.
        05  P-PRINT-LINE                      PICTURE X(132).
        05  P-HEADING OCCURS 5 TIMES.
            10  P-HEAD-RECS                   PICTURE X(132).
```

Control is the two input variables that regulate the number of blank lines to follow the printed line and specify the number of heading lines. Also, since PRINTER is now in a subprogram, a code should be provided to allow the calling module to OPEN the printer file, print, or CLOSE the file.

```
02  C-CONTROL-DATA.
    05  C-OP-CODE                             PICTURE 9(4) COMP.
    05  C-NUMBER-LINES                        PICTURE 9(4) COMP.
    05  C-HEAD-LINES                          PICTURE 9(4) COMP.
```

The stable work data are the two (essentially) output variables that are global to PRINTER and are expected to retain their integrity. Usually, page count is set to 1 at the beginning of each report and only "read" thereafter. The end-of-page flag is provided in the calling program in case some special processing is to be done on page overflow.

```
02  W-STABLE-WORK-DATA.
    05  W-PAGE-NUMBER                         PICTURE 9(4) COMP.
    05  W-PAGE-END                            PICTURE X.
```

Perishable working data represent storage required internally by PRINTER during its processing. Typically, this consists of local flags, indices, and intermediate results. Internally to PRINTER this interface appears as:

```
01  WX-PERISHABLE-WORK-DATA.
    05  WX-PRINTER-INDEX                      PICTURE 9(4) COMP.
    05  WX-HEADER-INDEX                       PICTURE 9(4) COMP.
    05  WX-SPACE-INDEX                        PICTURE 9(4) COMP.
    05  WX-SPACE-LIMIT                        PICTURE 9(4) COMP.
    05  WX-NUMBER-LINES                       PICTURE 9(4) COMP.
```

With this interface structure the CALL . . . USING for the "PRINTER" subprogram appears as follows:

```
CALL 'PRINTER' USING P-W-TOTAL-INTERFACE
                     WX-PERISHABLE-WORK-DATA.
```

The PRINTER subprogram appears in the Appendix in its entirety, using this style of data interface.

In the calling program the working interface need not be specific; in fact, it should not be (as is discussed in this chapter under multimodule linkage). The reason why the perishable structure is left discrete (at the 01 level) becomes clear in the discussion on multiple program-module interface.

Subroutine interface makes more clear the desirability of subdividing the interface into these distinct conceptual pieces. The generality of a given subprogram is dependent on the flexibility of control that may be applied to it. If a routine such as PRINTER is used for more than one report, by setting up separate control interface sets, one may quickly and efficiently change the mode in which PRINTER is to operate. Rather than have the headings for some number of reports embedded, and subject to recompilation, different headings may be obtained by staging alternate interfaces for each report.

When there are just two or three separate interfaces in a subprogram, one may choose to have a CALL . . .USING for each case and select from among them. When there is a great deal of volatility of interface, the alternate is to build each separate interface in a work area and execute a group MOVE to the interface area referenced in a single CALL . . . USING.

MULTIPLE PROGRAM MODULE LINKAGE

In a large multiple program module system, the interface problem may become a major one. If it does become a nuisance, a programmer may feel that modularity itself is intractable rather than properly attributing the blame to poor definition and control of the data interfaces.

Multiple program module system implies a hierarchic structure of subprograms rather than a sequential string of job steps. In the latter, interface between modules is dependent on files and, as a design model, is more typical of second-generation systems and their lack of large-scale random access storage and the overlay structures such storage makes possible.

The structure of a multiple program module system is basically the same as that of a single program module. The difference is that the scope of the applicational and procedural functions is broader. At this more macro level, it is still appropriate to identify levels of driver, housekeeping, input/output, process, and exception. Each individual program module also continues to exhibit these functions on the microlevel.

In a multiple program module system, the distinction between global and local data takes on more significance. It is now the responsibility of the mainline or executive module not only to schedule the uppermost drivers but also to contain all global data structures and allocate local working storage for the entire hierarchy of modules. The key to the successful use of multiple program module systems lies in careful management of the data.

Global and Local Variables

The first rule of data management should be that no subprograms contain local variables.[3] There should be no expectation that a data element resident in any subprogram will retain its value from one CALL to another. What this boils down to is that a subprogram should not MOVE any data to its WORKING-STORAGE-SECTION. Refer to the sample subprogram PRINTER and verify that the only WORKING-STORAGE entry consists of two constants placed there for the sake of visibility.

The no-local-variable rule has some useful side effects (which will be cited shortly), but the most important reason for it is that strict rein can be exercised over the variables that account for control in the system. The reasoning is similar to that behind the recommendation for carefully defining the scope of flags. No assumptions should be made about the state of a subprogram by the calling module, and it is the programmer's responsibility to make clear the task of setting and resetting interface data items.

SUBPROGRAM INTERFACE

Interface to a subprogram utilizes the same structure as interface within a module. Rather than being optionally grouped together in WORKING-STORAGE (to obtain good interface visibility), the interface data now must be grouped together in the LINKAGE SECTION. Interface with the subprogram then rests on providing either a single interface area, subject to alteration for a single CALL, or multiple CALLs, each with its own discretely named interface area. The former is more likely to be the effective choice, the strict logical interface model being:

1. Gather the interface data in a staging area which has a structure compatible with that of the interface.
2. Group MOVE the data to the interface area named in the CALL.

3. CALL the subprogram.
4. Redistribute the interface data as appropriate.

The multiple program module system may be generally structured as shown in Figure 26. An executive module is responsible for the same tasks as the mainline module within a program, that of scheduling the drivers and executing (CALLing in this case) whatever housekeeping needs to be done at that level. I have termed the

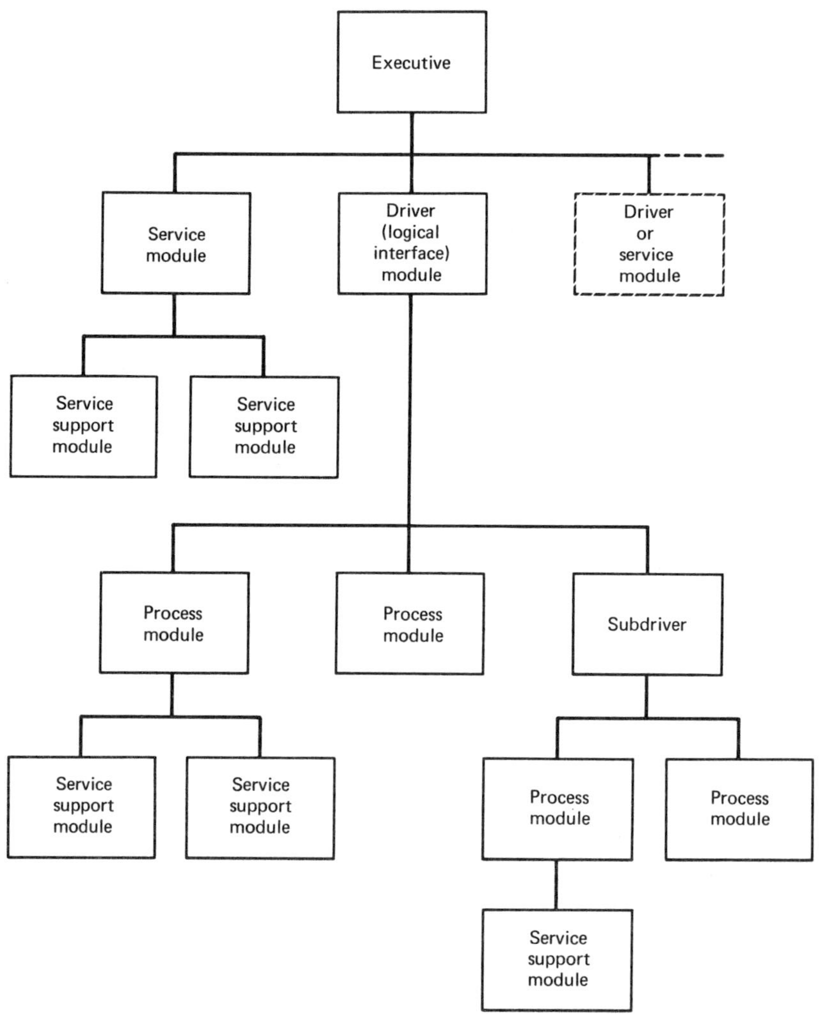

Figure 26 **Structure of general multiple program module system.**

housekeeping routines "service modules"; typically their job is to CALL a routine such as PRINTER to OPEN its file, or CALL on an input module to perform the required label checking prior to beginning processing. PRINTER or a disk input routine falls under the heading of service support module. Process modules are those that perform the code to solve the applicational job of the system. This is where the code to edit, extract, match, merge, update, and so on, resides. Service support routines to print, interface with files, make table searches, handle exceptions, and so on, are CALLed by the process modules. PRINTER would likely reappear again at this level.

SAMPLE PROGRAM STUDY

As an aid in evaluating interface methods, I have taken the sample accounts payable program of the Appendix and somewhat arbitrarily divided it into subprograms. Since the tasks being performed by the code are the same in the two programs, I have removed the documentation and most of the statements and left only the DATA DIVISION, paragraph names and EXIT names, PERFORM statements (without the VARYING part), and the newly added CALLs. Figure 27 shows the structure of the subroutinized AP503/4 program. Since it is a simple program, there is no driver separate from the executive.

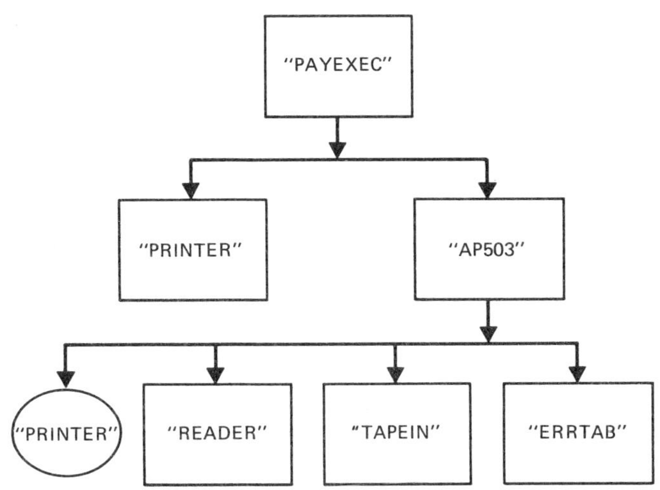

Figure 27 **Structure of subroutinized AP 503/4.**

It has only one process module and four service support modules. This structure has been devised here for illustrative purposes only; the focus of the discussion is the contents of the DATA DIVISION and the interfaces.

In looking first at the executive module, PAYEXEC, the presumption is that it requires "PRINTER" to issue a message signaling the beginning and end of the job. (I am ignoring DISPLAY for the sake of the example.) The contents of WORKING STORAGE, then, are the messages to be printed, P-PRINTER-INTERFACE for the "PRINTER" subprogram, and for the allocation of sufficient storage for the remainder of the system, WX-WORKING-STORAGE. Allocating all the storage to the executive is a point of style; on some machines it is easy, and on others impractical. Such allocation enforces the no-local-variable rule and provides a consistent model for storage management. For these two reasons this treatment of storage is recommended unless contradicted by an organization's machine environment.

The size of storage may be computed by adding the storage requirements for each module (which should be calculated once and placed in the logical interface portion of the program abstract) down each leg (limb?) of the structure and taking the largest sum as the total storage requirement. One of the side effects of this allocation method, which may be meaningful at times, is that it reuses working storage from one leg of the structure to another.

Although it is known that interfaces and likely initialization are required for the tape input, card input, and error-table subprograms, they are not needed on this level in this program, so definition of these interfaces can be left to a lower level. The situation would be different if "PAYEXEC" called more that a single driver and if these services modules needed to preserve the stable part of their interface down more than one leg of the structure. Allocating definitions only at the level at which they are no longer perishable can reduce the number of items in the CALL list. Execution of "AP503" by "PAYEXEC" appears as:

```
CALL "AP503" USING P-PRINTER-INTERFACE
                   WX-WORKING-STORAGE.
```

Definition of the other two interfaces would have necessitated two additional 01-group-level names in the argument list, for no gain. It is worth noting that one of the leading manufacturer's COBOL programmer's guide recommends defining all data in a given subprogram as a single 01-level group to facilitate the use of COPY.

This recommendation actually has more utility for those occasions when a checkpoint may be required at selected points in the execution of a system, in that all data may be written easily from the single structure. Note that a checkpoint of this kind usually can be taken only if there are no local variables to worry about lower down in the structure. (This is another beneficial side effect of the allocation recommendation.) For a system to be checkpointed, the executive module should do nothing but: (1) allocate all storage, (2) CALL one driver, and (3) execute the checkpoint module code (if required). In general, the data interfaces corresponding to reusable modules should be available as 01-level entries in a library; however, whether they are built into a multiple module system at the executive or main driver level is a matter of choice.

The WORKING-STORAGE SECTION of "AP503" contains only local constants. The LINKAGE SECTION contains the "PRINTER" interface, and the uncommitted space provided by QQ-WORKING-STORAGE (passed by "PAYEXEC" as WX-WORKING-STORAGE). "AP503" now takes this space and defines whatever structures are appropriate. Note in particular the interfaces being built for the service support modules "READER," "TAPEIN," and "ERRTAB" (RA-, SA-, and TA-). When compiling a CALLed subprogram, most COBOL compilers assume that the data names in the USING argument list are defined as 01-level in the CALLing program. For the sake of either success or efficiency, the programmer should take care of any boundary alignment or other requirement of an individual compiler. The statements

```
02  FILLER                              COMP-2 SYNC.
```

found in the example are for this purpose.

In "AP503," WX-WORKING-STORAGE is again defined and passed in the CALL . . . USING as uncommitted space for local use by the service support modules. Here it is apparent that the same storage is reused by "PRINTER," "ERRTAB," and so on. If one of the service modules CALLs still lower in the hierarchy, the same convention may be used at that level, as long as the space required has been allocated by the executive module.

Because of the requirement in many business-oriented systems for back-up files, audit trails, and more frequent checkpointing than other types of systems, it may be legitimate for these systems to be more linear than scientific or software systems; so, depending on local preferences, a systems group may seek to limit the depth of CALL in systems, but it should not be at the expense of modularity.

OVERLAY STRUCTURES

The final topic under the subject of linkage and multiple program module structures is overlay. The manner in which most systems or programs evolve is that the need to expand beyond available core or normally allocated partitioning comes about as a by-product of the unanticipated realities of implementation or by the addition of capability beyond the original design specifications. In short, the need to overlay may not have been planned for.

Whether planned for or not, the best way to prepare a system for overlay is to follow the recommendations already given for micro-modular segmentation and the executive resident and module-related allocation and structuring of data.

The classic overlay structure is shown in Figure 28. A root phase remains core-resident throughout the execution of a multiple program module system. It occupies only part of the total available user core or partition and consists of the executive (which now has the primary task of phasing the overlay segments), service support modules used in common by the overlay segments (typically input/output mod-

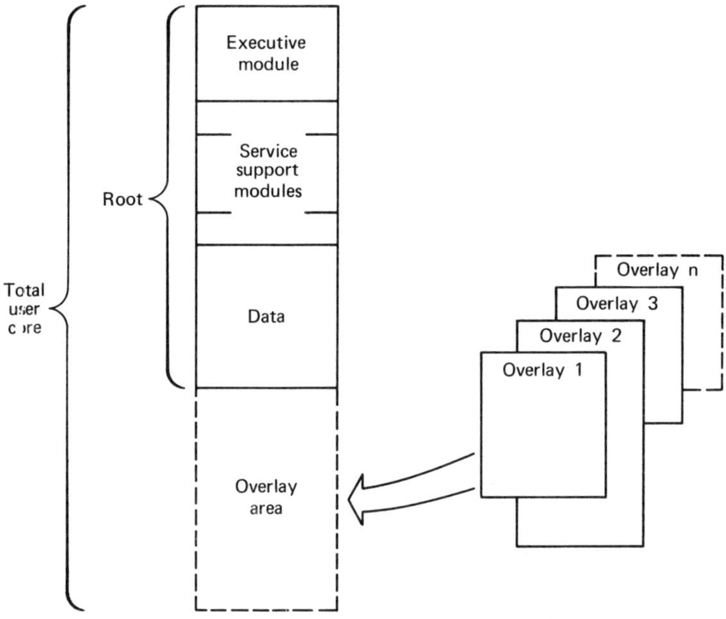

Figure 28 **Classic overlay structure.**

ules), and the data for the system. Overlay segments contain the housekeeping, process, and exception modules and are loaded into core and overwritten on demand. The rule of no local variables scores an additional few points for the indifference with which a module may be brought into core or overlaid by another module, since the code is "neutralized" by the fact that a module is always in the same "state."

The design problem in decomposing a large program into an overlay structure may come when the large program is structured as in Figure 29. Let us assume that the code for performing each of the functions of housekeeping, edit, matching, and update is too extensive for a single core load and so must be overlaid as shown. (It is as if the sample program in the Appendix were to be run in a 4k partition.) The initial and final housekeeping is no problem, but the processing of a single transaction using a single input and a single output file requires three separate overlays. This results in the phenomenon called "thrashing" or "running the program by the data." In this case

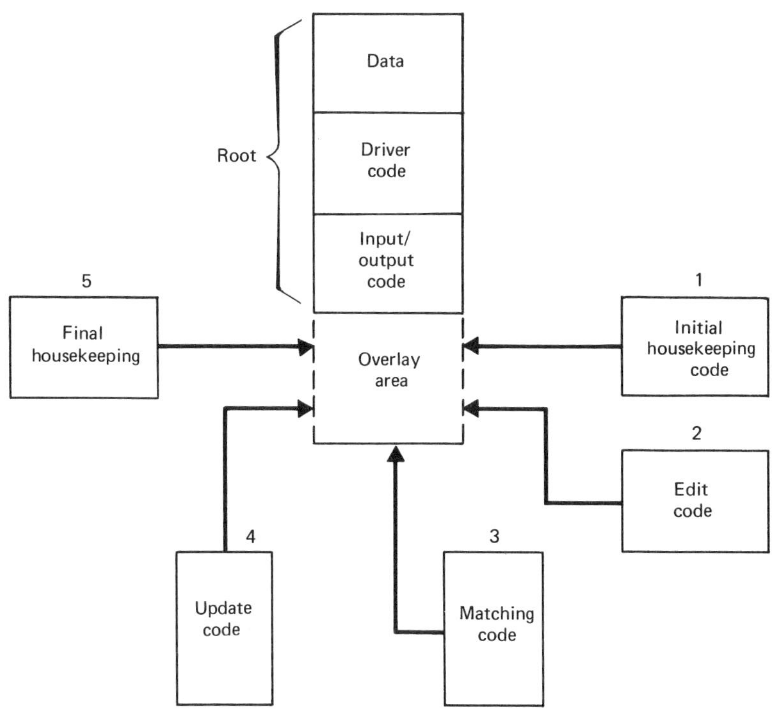

Figure 29 **Overlay decomposition of program.**

intermediate files are required to hold the good data for the next phase and to spin off transactions with errors. Thus overlay 2 might perform editing on all, or a large block of the input data and place the successful transactions on tape or disk. Then overlay 3 would pass the intermediate file, retaining and rejecting as indicated, and so forth.

More than a single level of overlay may be considered; exception processing (especially if the exceptions are reasonably infrequent) is a good candidate. Overlay is then performed from the process modules into a third overlay area as exceptions are encountered in the data stream. Most operating systems support this type of processing; otherwise, the systems software group of an organization can likely provide support.

Even in systems that support "virtual memory" (automatic peripheral-to-core allocation), the intelligent segmentation of code aids in assigning meaningful priority levels to modules. If, in addition, the data are carefully structured, the amount of unseen and costly thrashing that can occur in virtual systems can be avoided.

SUMMARY

Unless the data interface problem is well-controlled, the benefits of modularity may be lost. Grouping the data for a given paragraph-group or subprogram interface together in a functionally significant structure can result in greatly improved data management. Subprograms are a useful tool and, if the global/local variable relationships are controlled, then less difficulty is encountered when multiple program-module systems are used. These recommendations also facilitate the use of overlay structures in a multiple program module system.

REFERENCES

1. CALL is a nonstandard COBOL verb. For those readers who lack CALL in their COBOL environment I suggest they give special attention to this chapter's guidelines on interface requirements within a module. For those readers working in a virtual environment without CALL (such as are to be found in Xerox ANS COBOL for the Sigma series of computer) the discussion on interface data organization should be helpful.
2. LINKAGE SECTION is an IBM/360-370 nonstandard COBOL convention. Its function is merely to identify the structures associated with the USING

variables to the complier so that no local storage is allocated for these structures. Since it also enhances the visibility of the interface data, I must basically approve of LINKAGE SECTION, in spite of its not being standard. See International Business Machines, *IBM System/360 Disk Operating System American National Standard COBOL,* S360-24 GC28-6394-2, New York, 1968, 1969.

3. The Hoskyns Systems Research literature has always made this point. See Jackson, Michael, and Swanwick, Anthony B., "Segmented Level Programming," *Computers and Automation,* February 1969.

CHAPTER 8

Developing Standard Constructs

Chapter 6 described the use of PERFORM in designing micromodular programs. Chapter 7 discussed CALL and demonstrated the importance of cleanly defined interfaces between both the module and program levels of modularity. In these discussions standardized groupings of various COBOL language facilities were recommended. These groupings may be called constructs.

There are several other COBOL facilities for which constructs need to be defined, either because they are naturally troublesome in themselves, or because their misuse tends to violate modularity. If a programmer gets into difficulty because of some complexity, especially in the control structure, there is a strong temptation to patch the problem, often with a few GO TOs.

Standard constructs may be developed on any level of modularity. This chapter deals with the microlevel, for that is where it all begins; the macrolevel is built from the microlevel. Chapter 9 continues with some larger constructs. One guideline should underlie the development of constructs: increasing the simplicity of the code.

DEFINING THE COBOL LANGUAGE SUBSET

Distinction should be made rather sharply between a production subset of a language and the set of facilities a language contains as it comes from a vendor.

Language facilities were originally influenced by local hardware considerations which have been carried, by tradition, into the compiler languages COBOL, FORTRAN, and ALGOL. Not all these language facilities are "good" for the programmer. The level of complexity arising from the use of these facilities may exceed what is a tolerable working level. Programming languages provide only some primitive capabilities, after all, and it is the responsibility of the programmer to select and combine these primitives into civilized constructs. It is important to remember that it is not that a given facility or construct cannot be made to work; the question is how much difficulty a given construct causes on a day-to-day basis.

The most successful programming seems to take place when the solution to the problem we are trying to solve can be totally contained in the mind. Success comes when one can turn over in the mind all the conditions and branches and somehow "see" the complete implications of the solution in the data, the code, and the branching control. Obviously, for most of us, it does not take a very complex set of relationships for this kind of complete grasp to elude us. The strategy, if one is to deal with complexity, is to subdivide the complex into the simple. If one can determine the degree of complexity with which one can deal (on "bad" days, not "good" or even "average" days) and maintain this throughout a solution (program or system), then one can expect more success.

There are some facilities that repeatedly cause difficulty. For every computing language one could (and should) make a checklist of the statements or constructs that account for most of the trouble programmers have. In COBOL the most likely culprits are:

1. Mixing GO TO and PERFORM for the same paragraph name.
2. Branching out of PERFORMed paragraphs.
3. Use of the ALTER verb.
4. Indexing incorrectly.
5. The use of complex conditionals in IF statements.
6. Use of multiple IF constructs.
7. Nesting IF statements.
8. Missing the setting or resetting of a flag value (so that its value is unexpected).

9. Using a flag for multiple purposes.
10. Misusing loops.
11. Using a more complex facility (such as SEARCH) without fully understanding it.

The defense against these culprits may involve one of two strategies, namely, elimination of the construct or facility. This is appropriate in the case of 1, 2, 3, 7, 9 and, perhaps, 11, but the remainder are useful or mandatory for normal data processing. For these one must define better and more reliable constructs by maximizing their clarity, either by logical arrangement or by better documentation.

The proper use of PERFORM and GO TO was covered in Chapter 6. The remaining troublesome facilities are discussed here as follows.

1. Misuse of ALTER and substitution of PERFORM or GO TO . . . DEPENDING ON.
2. Problems involving the use of program loops and indices.
3. The use of flags for maximum control structure visibility.
4. The IF statement and its correct use, table-driven code.
5. Other COBOL facilities.

ALTER AND GO TO . . . DEPENDING ON

The ALTER verb is one of those language facilities that should be dropped from the production COBOL repertory. The meta-language construct is:

```
ALTER paragraph-name-1 TO (PROCEED TO) paragraph-name-2.
```

Paragraph-name-1 must be a paragraph containing a single statement, a GO TO, or GO TO <paragraph-name>. The DEPENDING ON option may not be used with the GO TO.

The machine language implementation of ALTER is simply the replacement of an address in a branch instruction with an alternative address at the required step during execution.

A simple and typical example of the use of ALTER is the following.

```
                    .
                    .
                    .
SLI-BRANCH.
   GO TO SLK-ONE-TIME-READ.
SLK-ONE-TIME-READ.
```

```
    READ A-INPUT-FILE INTO A-REC-AREA
       AT END MOVE "Y" TO W-EOF-FLAG.
    ALTER SLI-BRANCH TO PROCEED TO SLM-NORMAL.
SLM-NORMAL.
                .
                .
                .
```

On the first execution of SLI-BRANCH, the GO TO will proceed to SLK-ONE-TIME-READ and then, because of the ALTER, all subsequent executions will skip over the READ to SLM-NORMAL.

In this example it is quite easy to discern the conditions that affect the control structure: execute it once and it is all over. Frequently, programmers who use ALTER in this manner claim that this demonstrates its legitimacy. The concern is, however:

1. The narcotic effect; if using it once "won't hurt," the user is tempted to repeat in other circumstances.
2. The fact that any program segment containing such a construct is, under present operating systems design, normally prevented from being a candidate for overlay and refresh. In other words, say the ALTER has been executed in a segment (A) which the programmer overlays with another segment (B), and then reoverlays with the original (A). The programmer will obtain a fresh copy of A in which the ALTER has not been executed. In the foregoing example the "one-time" code might be executed more than one time. This violates the neutrality of a module's control structure.

ALTER violates our rule of maximizing the visibility of the control structure, making it precisely invisible, in fact, since knowledge of the action of the control structure becomes dependent on a knowledge of prior data and program flow. What this means is that in looking at a COBOL program source listing which contains ALTERs, one cannot believe what one reads. The control structure may not be as it appears, and it is much more difficult to debug such a program. While the same might be said for the values of flags, it seems easier for the mind to keep track of changing data values than to allow the control logic itself to change dynamically.

An alternative to this use of ALTER may be achieved by rearranging the code. Most one-time functions may be considered housekeeping and PERFORMed one time at the beginning of the program or job step.

For those cases in which process execution must take place before the one-time action, the creation of an ordinary flag and an IF statement test is the obvious alternative. In the following example it is presumed that the RIGHT-HERE paragraph is to be executed on and off during the processing of a program module.

```
JUMP-IN.
    GO TO SKIP-OVER.
RIGHT-HERE.
    MOVE MOUNT-AIN TO MO-HAMMED.
    PERFORM ACRO-BATICS.
    ALTER JUMP-IN TO PROCEED TO SKIP-OVER.
SKIP-OVER.
    ADD MOLE-HILL TO MOUNT-AIN GIVING HEART-BURN.
```

Paragraph RIGHT-HERE must be activated during processing by an ALTER which is triggered by the IF evaluation of some conditional.

```
IF A-INPUT-FLAG=90
    ALTER JUMP-IN TO PROCEED TO RIGHT-HERE.
```

The conditional must be evaluated in any case to find out when to execute the process, and the above ALTER construct shuffles the branch address in the same way most COBOL compilers implement the PERFORM. So there is no essential difference (in microefficiency), and considerably more clarity, in the following alternative construct.

```
IF A-INPUT-FLAG=90
    PERFORM RA-RIGHT-HERE THRU RZ-RIGHT-HERE-X.
                              .
                              .
                              .
RA-RIGHT-HERE.
    MOVE MOUNT-AIN TO MO-HAMMED.
    PERFORM ACRO-BATICS.
RZ-RIGHT-HERE-X.
    EXIT.
```

Some programmers make an even more extensive use of ALTER. A bit of reflection on such use reminds us, however, that in order to use very many ALTERs there must be numerous GO TOs in the program. Further, these GO TOs must make fairly dramatic changes in control not to be superfluous. What these two ingredients must add up to in program structure is an all too familiar product—spaghetti; extensive use of ALTER violates the principle of a hierarchic structure of closed modules.

A final example of how ALTER is (mis)used and a description of the proper use of GO TO . . . DEPENDING ON should properly bury ALTER for purposes of this monograph.

This example is based upon my knowledge of a program in current use in a system which is my personal candidate for the National Worst Systems Contest. (Nearly every systems person I talk to has a candidate. Such a contest might be a competitive one indeed.)

Let us presume several paragraphs which edit input data fields. We have six different input formats such that there is considerable overlap in the editing requirements. None of the input formats are the same, but there are several paragraphs of code that apply to more than one of the input formats.

The scheme chosen, using ALTER, is to find out which one of the formats has been read and then to ALTER the control structure to "visit" each of the applicable paragraphs and have it operate on the data, as follows.

```
                                   .
                                   .
A-VALUE-EDIT.
    MOVE . . .
    IF . . .
                                   .
                                   .
A-VALUE-EDIT-X.
    GO TO B-NAME-EDIT.
*
B-NAME-EDIT.
    IF . . .
    MOVE . . .
                                   .
                                   .
B-NAME-EDIT-X.
    GO TO F-MASTER-FILE-EDIT.
*
C-INV-CODE-EDIT.
                                   .
                                   .
                                   .
C-INV-CODE-EDIT-X.
    GO TO D-TIMEVAL-EDIT.
```

The code permitting the "visits" is.:

```
IF B-INPUT-TYPE="A"
    ALTER A-VALUE-EDIT-X TO PROCEED TO
    C-INV-CODE-EDIT
    ALTER C-INV-CODE-EDIT-X TO PROCEED TO
    I-OLDCODE-EDIT
    ALTER M-MIDVAL-EDIT-X TO PROCEED TO
    R-CUSTOMER-EDIT
    ALTER S-TAGFIELD-EDIT-X TO PROCEED TO
```

```
 9.    X-END-OF-EDIT-X.
10. IF B-INPUT-TYPE="B"
11.    ALTER A-VALUE-EDIT-X TO PROCEED TO
12.    D-TIMEVAL-EDIT
13.    ALTER D-TIMEVAL-EDIT-X TO PROCEED TO
14.    F-MASTER-FILE-EDIT
15.    ALTER F-MASTER-FILE-EDIT-X TO PROCEED TO
16.    J-NEWCODE-EDIT
17.    ALTER J-NEWCODE-EDIT-X TO PROCEED TO
          and so on.
```

So for each input the programmer needs to refer to a "map" of what code is to be used and set all the "road signs" to effect the branching. For any single journey this might seem to be a reasonable method, but a serious problem has been posed. Each time a pass is made through the set of paragraphs, the control structure is set in a different state. Before any decision can be made on how to ALTER for the next input visit, the effect of the prior visit must be known. In the example, before any input disturbs the structure, the A-VALUE-EDIT paragraph "falls through" to B-NAME-EDIT. After the "A" input has gone through, A-VALUE-EDIT is ALTERed to proceed to C-INV-CODE-EDIT. After a "B" input, A-VALUE-EDIT branches to D-TIMEVAL-EDIT. It is only safe, then, to *make no assumptions about the structure.* The frequent difficulty in the use of ALTERs is that programmers do make assumptions about the state of control structure. They tend to be wrong because they do not plan and draw the careful diagrams necessary to help them make the control structure visible. Since it is easy for such diagrams, even if they are produced, to become separated from the code, it is better to exclude this use of ALTER together. This is especially true in that there is a better alternative solution for this problem. In the example lines 11 to 17 represent an attempt to avoid assumptions about the control structure. Note that in each case of proceeding to a given paragraph the next ALTER defines the exit branch for that paragraph. If a given paragraph (D-TIMEVAL-EDIT) is referenced, its EXIT paragraph (D-TIMEVAL-EDIT-X) is also referenced, so that integrity is maintained on the path through the ALTER structure. The reliability of the control structure is increased by treating each paragraph as an independent entity. This suggests that the following construct can solve our problem in a more reliable way.

The following example of GO TO . . . DEPENDING ON is typical of how it should be used. In order to keep the example simple (and adhere to the recommended simplicities of this monograph), one-dimensional tables are used.

For each input type that defines a journey through the editing paragraphs, a table is defined which corresponds to an entry in a GO TO . . . DEPENDING ON list of paragraph names.*

First determine the type of record:

```
IF B-INPUT-TYPE="A"
```

Then obtain the number of paragraphs to be visited for this type:

```
MOVE WA-TYPE-LENGTH TO WC-LOOP-LIMIT.
```

Move a "visitation table" for input type "A" to an area to be referenced by a GO TO . . . DEPENDING ON. This eliminates the requirement for either a two-dimensional table or multiple GO TO . . . DEPENDING ON statements.

```
MOVE TA-A-TYPE-VISIT TO WA-DRIVER-TABLE.
PERFORM NA-TABLE-LOOP THRU NX-TABLE LOOP-X
   VARYING WN-LOOP-INDEX FROM 1 BY 1 UNTIL
   WN-LOOP-INDEX>WC-LOOP-LIMIT.
.
.
NA-TABLE-LOOP.
   GO TO
      A-VALUE-EDIT
      B-NAME-EDIT
      C-INV-CODE-EDIT
      F-MASTER-FILE-EDIT
         and so on
   DEPENDING ON
   WA-DRIVER TABLE (WN-LOOP-INDEX).
NX-TABLE-LOOP-X.
   EXIT.
```

The values in the table are evaluated by successive passes through the loop (NA-TABLE-LOOP). Suppose the length of the table as contained in WA-TYPE-LENGTH were 7 and the table TA-A-TYPE-VISIT contained the values:

```
2 3 5 7 8 12 13
```

Each paragraph in the GO TO list has the following structure.

```
A-VALUE-EDIT.
              .
              .
  (Editing statement and local branching)
```

*The format is GO TO *paragraph-name 1 [paragraph-name-2 . . . paragraph-name-n]* DEPENDING ON *identifier*. If the value of *identifier* is 1, control will pass to *paragraph-name-1*; if *n* to *paragraph-name-n*; and so on.

```
          .
          .
AX-VALUE-EDIT-X.
    GO TO NX-TABLE-LOOP-X.
```

Each paragraph terminates in a GO TO the EXIT paragraph of the PERFORM controlling the DEPENDING ON loop. In the example given, control would be passed to the second (B-NAME-TEST), third (C-INV-CODE-EDIT), fifth (F-MASTER-FILE-EDIT), seventh, eighth, twelfth, and thirteenth paragraphs, (whatever their label names might be in a complete example). Note how much more visible this structure is than the foregoing ALTER example. It requires less coding and is more flexible. The paragraphs may be visited in any order required by simply altering the index values in the table. Adding a new paragraph simply means adding its name to the GO TO list and using its indexes in the tables of visits. (The table sizes may also have to be adjusted.)

LOOP CONTROL AND INDEXING

The most natural and visible loop in COBOL is obtained through use of PERFORM with the VARYING option. The meta-language construct of the standard form is:

```
PERFORM paragraph-name THRU paragraph-exit name
    VARYING index-name FROM identifier-1 TO identifier-2
    UNTIL condition-statement.
```

A typical problem in looping is underflow or overflow of the index; either its value is zero or less, or it becomes greater in size than the table being indexed, or some process being controlled by an index is not executed the proper number of times. Some compilers generate coding to check on the range; others do not. The solution to these problems is first to maximize the visibility of the index. The index-name should be uniquely identified for each PERFORM . . . VARYING, assuring that it can be simply documented. If care has been taken to define most tables simply and one-dimensionally, identifier-1 (initial value) and identifier-2 (the stepping value) can usually both have a value of 1, and the condition statement merely tests the index for its having satisfied a predetermined limit set as a constant in working storage.* An example is:

*Compilers differ in when the test for loop termination is executed, in some it occurs before and in some after the PERFORM is executed.

```
WORKING-STORAGE-SECTION.
                         .
                         .
                         .
   05 W-ERROR-LOOP-LIMIT      PICTURE 9(4)     VALUE 100 COMP.
                         .
                         .
                         .
PROCEDURE DIVISION.
                         .
                         .
                         .
PERFORM NA-ERROR-LOOP THRU NAX-ERROR-LOOP-X
   VARYING W-ERR-INDEX FROM 1 BY 1
   UNTIL W-ERR-INDEX>W-ERROR-LOOP-LIMIT.
```

With the limit clearly defined in working storage as 100, the initial and stepping values are defined in the PERFORM itself. This maximizes the clarity. It cannot be overstressed that a great deal of difficulty may be avoided by designing a program so that this most simple construct can be used in most cases.

There are some instances in which it is awkward or infeasible to use either PERFORM . . . VARYING, or at least the simple construct cited above.

In these cases, the following tasks associated with every implementation of a loop should be clearly separated and identified.

1. Setting the index value.
2. Setting the limiting value.
3. Setting the increment value.
4. Incrementing the index value.
5. Testing the condition and branching.
6. Resetting the index value.

This is why the index and flag directory (see Chapter 4) is important to aid in clearly identifying where these functions are performed. Take, for example, the implied loop in TN-TABLE-LOOP in the sample program AP503/4.

```
TN-TABLE-LOOP.
   ADD 1 TO WI-INDEX-ERR.
   IF WI-INDEX-ERR GREATER THAN WI-ERRTAB-LIMIT
      MOVE "Y" TO W2-TABLE-FLUSH
      PERFORM ZN-FLUSH-LOOP THRU ZNX-FLUSH-LOOP-X
      MOVE 1 TO WI-INDEX-ERR.
TNX-TABLE-LOOP-X.
```

Here the functions of incrementing (ADD 1), testing and branching (IF, PERFORM), and resetting (MOVE 1) are together in this paragraph. Referring to the index and flag directory shows that WI-INDEX-ERR is set to 1 in working storage and that its value is limited by WI-ERRTAB-LIMIT which has a value of 100 in working storage. The increment is set by the literal 1 in the ADD statement. Making it simple to find the whereabouts of the six tasks involved in implementing a loop is the secret of increased success. If there is a good reason why these functions must be separated, then careful structural arrangement of the program in the detailed design phase can help increase the clarity. If some fairly involved processing is required to obtain each of the values to be assigned to an index, a loop limit, and the increment value, PERFORM the module(s) to determine these parameters just prior to PERFORMing the process module. The programmer may lose track of what is happening when intervening code is allowed to intrude between loop functions. With the loop functions spread over several modules, it becomes easier to insert a logical path which varies some loop parameters (index, limit, etc.) from what is expected.

Processes that might be defined as loops with an irregular increment should be treated as table-driven constructs. These are covered at the end of this chapter.

USING FLAGS

The term "flags" refers to the use of data items for control purposes. Typically, flags have a value of "Y", "N", 0, 1, or some small range of low-valued integers. A possible synonym for "flags" might be "switches," however, the latter has a second-generation-computer holdover connotation of toggles on the console of the computer.

An example of the use of a flag is as follows. Somewhere in the program a MOVE statement sets the value of the flag:

```
MOVE "Y" TO W-TEST-FLAG.
```

Elsewhere in the program, usually dependent on a condition, the flag may or may not be reset:

```
IF A-INPUT NOT EQUAL W-GOOD-VALUE
   MOVE "N" TO W-TEST-FLAG.
```

Finally, the program tests the value of the flag and takes some action depending on its value:

```
IF W-TEST-FLAG="N"
   PERFORM SA-EDIT-ERROR THRU SAX-EDIT-ERROR-X
   GO TO DAX-TEST-X.
        .
        .
        .
```

Data items having a range of numeric values should be treated as indexes and controlled by PERFORM . . . VARYING loops as discussed previously. Flags, however, may be considered binary, with two values: on or off. "Y" for "yes" and "N" for "no" are reasonably communicative of the action desired and, since the IF conditionals should largely be restricted to EQUAL or NOT EQUAL, the "Y" and "N" should be paired with the IFs in that order. See the above example.

Problems occur in the use of flags as follows.

1. The programmer loses track of where in the chain of logic the flag was last set or reset, and the results are unexpected.
2. The same flag is used for multiple purposes, and the programmer loses track of which use has last affected the flag's value.

The cure for the above is to make as visible as possible the three functions:

1. Set the flag.
2. Conditionally reset the flag.
3. Test the flag.

This may be achieved through documentation and program structure. Chapter 4 specifies a format for the data dictionary entry in the source code listing to identify these functions of flags. Structurally, the most dependable construct is to set the flag just before performing down through the hierarchy of modules in which the flag will be conditionally reset and then executing the test as soon after returning from the PERFORM as possible. For example:

```
MOVE "Y" TO W-GOOD-EDIT-FLAG.
PERFORM EA-EDIT THRU EAX-EDIT-X.
IF W-GOOD-EDIT-FLAG="N"
   PERFORM SA-BAD-DATA THRU . . .
       .
       .
       .
EA EDIT.
       .
       .
```

```
IF W-ERROR-VALUE NOT EQUAL SPACES
   MOVE "N" TO W-GOOD-EDIT-FLAG.
          .
          .
EAX-EDIT-X.
   EXIT.
```

Refer to the sample program in the Appendix for numerous examples, easily identified by the "Y" and "N" values.

Do not use a flag for multiple purposes. Not only will this scatter the three functions and cause structural difficulties, but it will prove much harder to document in the data dictionary.

There are cases in which it may be infeasible to bracket precisely and contiguously the PERFORM with setting and testing. In the sample program the END OF FILE (EOF) flags are set in WORKING STORAGE and reset only once, by the READ statement for that file, but are tested numerous times. The important point in these matters is to develop consistency. If in a system of programs the same construct is treated in the same manner each time, a high level of clarity and dependability will result. The overriding guideline is to keep the flag constructs as simple, compact, and visible as possible.

IF STATEMENTS AND TABLE-DRIVEN CODE

There are several ways in which the use of the IF statement can be abused:

1. Using complex conditionals, particularly those that may be ambiguously defined in a given compiler implementation.
2. Using too many IFs in a single dense construct of logic, especially when other less opaque constructs could be substituted.
3. Nesting IF statements, logically one within the scope of another.
4. All of the above combined.

These are discussed in turn here, except number four for which the recommendation is the converse, "none of the above."

Using Conditionals in IF Statements

COBOL permits a violation of the normal logic of connectives. For what seems to be for notational convenience, an IF statement may read as follows, where the repetition of the initial identifier is implied.

```
IF A-INPUT-VALUE=17 or 23 or ZEROS
   GO TO AND-SO-FORTH
```

The implied meaning of the above is:

```
IF A-INPUT-VALUE=17
   OR
A-INPUT-VALUE=23
   OR
A-INPUT-VALUE=ZEROS
   GO TO AND-SO-FORTH
```

Difficulty (subject to possible variation from compiler to compiler) may arise when the programmer uses a construct such as the following, in which the relational operator is also implied.

```
IF A-INPUT-VALUE NOT=18
   OR                 24
   OR                 ZEROS
   GO TO AND-SO-FORTH.
```

While the intended meaning may be:

```
IF A-INPUT-VALUE NOT=18
   OR
   A-INPUT-VALUE NOT=24
   OR
   A-INPUT-VALUE NOT=ZEROS
   GO TO AND-SO-FORTH.
```

Its meaning may actually be:

```
IF A-INPUT-VALUE NOT=18
   OR
   A-INPUT-VALUE=24
   OR
   A-INPUT-VALUE=ZEROS
   GO TO AND-SO-FORTH.
```

More complex examples may be given in which more than one identifier or more than one relational operator has been omitted. Suffice it to say that if difficulty can arise from simple cases (and it can), the difficulty that can arise from more complex cases increases at some geometric rate. A word of caution: It is precisely these kinds of "challenges" that stimulate programmers to try to use complex constructs. Programmers may walk where angels fear to tread, but their programs may not run there.

It will pay dividends to spell out IF statements simply and precisely. In cases similar to the above example, it may prevent errors. When a conversion to another language (e.g., PL/I) is in a system's future, it may also help prevent mistranslation.

Even when IF statements are spelled out precisely, errors may result from using complex strings of conditions:

```
IF A-INPUT-VALUE NOT LESS THAN C-CODE-TARGET OR
A-CONTROL+A-ADJUSTMENT EQUAL TO W-CONTROL-TOTAL
AND A-FLAG NOT="S"
```

At the very least such conditionals should be (1) laid out for maximum visual clarity, and (2) parenthesized. The COBOL compiler processes statements in a logical fashion, in discrete pieces, and according to a formal order. To gain a good understanding of how precisely the compiler will treat one's statements, one should do likewise. For the above example:

```
IF A-INPUT-VALUE NOT LESS THAN C-CODE-TARGET
   OR
(A-CONTROL+A-ADJUSTMENT EQUAL TO W-CONTROL-TOTAL
   AND
A-FLAG NOT EQUAL TO "S")
```

Obviously, the more simple the conditionals, the better the chances are of logically dependable programs.

The nesting of IF statements is another problem arèa. Nesting refers to a construct such as the following in which the scope of one IF statement lies within the scope of another:

```
1. IF WA-FATAL-FLAG="Y"
2.    IF WN-TRAP-FLAG="Y"
3.       MOVE "Y" TO WN-FINI-FLAG
4.    ELSE
5.    PERFORM MA-RECOVER THRU MZ-RECOVER-X
6.    MOVE "Y" to W-PERMIT-FLAG.
7. PERFORM UA-UPDATE THRU UN-UPDATE-X.
   and so on.
```

The TRUE branch of the first IF statement causes the second IF statement to be executed. Its TRUE branch is to the MOVE statement on line 3 and then to the PERFORM on line 7. The FALSE branch from the IF on line 2 will be to whatever follows the ELSE on line 4, here the PERFORM on line 5. The FALSE branch of the IF on line 1 is to the PERFORM on line 7.

A common problem in nesting is that the programmer often intends something other than the branching structure he has coded. In the foregoing example the intent might have been that the FALSE branch of line 2 execute first the MOVE on line 3 and then the code following the ELSE, as well.

Straightforward coding of the above example is:

```
IF WA-FATAL-FLAG="Y"
AND
WN-TRAP-FLAG="Y"
   MOVE "Y" TO WN-FINI-FLAG
   GO TO KZ-EDIT-TEST.
IF WN-TRAP-FLAG="Y"
   PERFORM MA-RECOVER THRU MZ-RECOVER-X
   MOVE "Y" TO W-PERMIT-FLAG.
KZ-EDIT-TEST.
PERFORM UA-UPDATE THRU UN-UPDATE-X.
and so on.
```

The difference in coding for the nested example and the straightforward recording is minimal. Even in this simple example it can be seen that less evaluation is needed to comprehend clearly what the straightforward version is doing as contrasted with the nested version. In cases in which avoiding nesting seems to require a significant amount of repetitive coding, use a PERFORM to execute the common code to reduce the repetition. It is easy to construct a nested IF example that defies quick comprehension and reliable desk checking, and indeed is only amendable to machine checking:

```
IF T-TOGGLE-SWITCH="Y"
   MOVE A-ELEMENT TO B-LINE
   IF RN-TEST-VALUE=31 OR 71
      AND A-INPUT-FLAG="A"
         IF RN-TEST-VALUE=42 OR 44
            AND B-INPUT-FLAG="B"
            PERFORM RA-COMPUTE THRU RAX-COMPUTE-X
         ELSE
         MOVE WN-LOCATER-TAG TO WX-INDEX-FLAG
      ELSE
      PERFORM NA-INDEX-GET THRU NAX-INDEX-GET-X
      IF A-NEST-FLAG=0
         IF WZ-LAST-FLAG="Y"
            PERFORM WA-RECOVER-CHK THRU WAX-RECOVER-CHK-X
         ELSE
         PERFORM EA-ERROR-ANALYSIS THRU EAX-ERROR-ANALYSIS-X
         PERFORM ZA-ALSO-RAN THRU ZAX-ALSO-RAN-X.
```

The above code is a paraphrase of an example of nested IFs given in a leading computer manufacturer's ANS COBOL manual.[1] Two flow diagrams are provided in the manual to aid in the programmer's understanding. If one also turns to the topic of nested IFs in the same manufacturer's COBOL programmer's guide,[2] the recommendation is that IFs, either nested or with complex conditionals, be avoided as too difficult to debug. Good advice.

At any rate the programmer who loves to generate and play with such code under the constraints of deadlines, cost, and the probability that someone else will inherit this code to maintain should be given the Don Quixote Award.

Table-Driven Code

Even with the use of simple IF statements, complexity may be introduced into a program by dense passages of code in which many consecutive IF statements appear. The solution to this is to consider seriously substituting table-driven code.

Table-driven code refers to a tabular array of datum which is tested and used as the basis for branching. In this case data are used to determine the control function. In the general interest of simplicity, one should use one-dimensional arrays, so a more precise description of this type of construct might be "vector-driven" code. Consider the following.

Working storage contains definitions of the following codes, each of which identifies a particular type of transaction in the input data stream. Each separate transaction type requires its own editing, processing, and so on.

```
01  W-TRANSACTION-CODES.
    05  W-ORDER-CODE          PIC 99 VALUE 33.
    05  W-SHIP-CODE           PIC 99 VALUE 77.
    05  W-CANCEL-CODE         PIC 99 VALUE 99.
    05  W-MFG-CODE            PIC 99 VALUE 44.
    05  W-CHANGE-CODE         PIC 99 VALUE 88.
01  WR-TABLE-CODES REDEFINES W-TRANSACTION-CODES.
    05  WR-T-CODES OCCURS 5 TIMES.
        10 WR-T-C PIC 99.
```

To evaluate the input stream to determine what type of transaction is current, the following code may be used.

```
MOVE ZEROES TO W-TRANS-INDEX.
PERFORM CA-CODE-CHECK-THRU CAX-CODE-CHECK-X
   VARYING W-TLOOP-INDEX
   FROM 1 BY 1 UNTIL
   W-TRANS-INDEX NOT EQUAL TO ZEROES
   OR
   W-TLOOP-INDEX GREATER THAN W-T-LIMIT.
IF W-TRANS-INDEX EQUAL TO ZEROES
   PERFORM SA-ERROR-TYPE THRU SAX-ERROR-TYPE-X
   GO TO AFX-DRIVER-X.
   .
   .
   .
```

The paragraph being PERFORMed is:

```
CA-CODE-CHECK.
    IF WR-T-CODES (W-TLOOP-INDEX) EQUAL TO A-INPUT-CODE
        MOVE W-TLOOP-INDEX TO W-TRANS-INDEX.
CAX-CODE-CHECK-X.
        EXIT.
```

The value of W-T-LIMIT is assumed to be 5 in the example.

A zero means no match was encountered, probably an error condition. On a successful type-code match a nonzero index value is assigned to W-TRANS-INDEX. The index may be used throughout the remainder of the processing of this transaction in GO TO . . . DEPENDING ON and other constructs. This simple example is the essence of table-driven code.

The utility of table-driven code lies in its simplicity, its maintainability, and its compactness. The maintainability of table-driven code is obvious. When properly used, a change in application requires only some change in the control values in working storage, and with properly identifying documentation such tables clearly reflect their function. Compactness occurs as a result of fewer statements, typically statements that perform one function repetitively. Such code has the virtue of either working correctly or most definitely incorrectly. This reduces the number of errors that can lie quietly in the midst of complex IF logic until some inopportune time.

Everything that can be done with multidimensional tables can be done with one-dimensional tables, and designing a solution so that linear, non-overlapping, unRENAMED tables are used may greatly increase its clarity. A systems organization that has a class of problems clearly calling for two- or multidimensional tables should develop a standard approach, including a specification of the documentation needed for further clarification. As soon as complex tables are used, significant documentation will be required to describe the technique to a maintainer or prospective modifier of the system. In every case it may be demonstrated that the easier, more direct way to solve the problem is as a series of vectors, each searched by the simple construct just described. Simple REDEFINEs to reuse storage or to facilitate initializing the values in a table should create no problem.

When the processing of complex cross-field relationships is required, table-driven techniques greatly simplify both the processing and the code reader's perception of it. Chapter 9 describes a method of handling complex decision situations with a table-driven technique.

CONSTRUCTS WITH OTHER COBOL FACILITIES

Most systems could easily be built with only the COBOL verbs discussed thus far. IF, PERFORM, and MOVE are the workhorses; all one needs additionally is an occasional READ, WRITE, GO TO, and COMPUTE. The remaining verbs are, in a purist's sense, parsley around the potatoes. However, they do represent extended capability over the basic required verbs and are frequently useful.

Since this chapter is not intended to be a COBOL tutorial but is concerned with trouble-free style, the following discussion of some of the other verbs is brief.

EXAMINE, SEARCH, and SORT

The principal method for more complex language facilities in general is to isolate them in a paragraph-group, treating them the same way one would any other procedural construct. More complex verbs or other language facilities often have side effects not found in the more simple basic language, which can create problems. By isolating the complex verbs, and so on, a structured approach may be taken in managing loose ends.

In EXAMINE a potential loose end is the TALLY register. Since TALLY is, in a sense, "invisible" and is typically used as a control variable, a programmer should equate a visible index or flag data name to TALLY immediately after execution of EXAMINE. The data name may then be controlled in the same manner as recommended for flags or indices in general. In this way the scope or contents of TALLY need never be in doubt.

The SEARCH verb may be treated in a similar manner, with the associated SET verb(s) being kept visibly and closely related to the paragraph-group that contains the SEARCH.

An ideal justification for procedural isolation may be made from the example of SEARCH . . . ALL (the binary search). If this verb were not available in a COBOL compiler, it would certainly be appropriate to isolate the paragraph-group of basic code that implemented the same job. The setting, testing, and utilization of the indices would clearly need to be well controlled. The same treatment is appropriate for SEARCH and SET in any of its modes; it should not be an exception.

SORT should also be treated discretely. My usual recommendation is to use a utility sort package and make sorting a separate job step rather than use the internal COBOL SORT verb. This provides two advantages: (1) it is easier to take a checkpoint in a system run, and (2) more flexibility can be provided with less developmental overhead and error if a systems group has a variety of utility sort routines available for the several sort requirements that exist. Too many systems groups use a single utility sort and let it go at that, overhead apparently not being a concern in spite of the extensive amount of sorting done in most organizations.

However, there are instances in which the SORT verb is a perfectly useful facility. In these cases it is best isolated in a subprogram with the associated procedures to communicate the data from the application to the SORT. Do not try to do more in this subprogram than: (1) obtain the input data; (2) sort it; and (3) place the sorted data where appropriate. The programmer should not combine the task of extracting, editing, or reporting with the task of sorting.

READ, WRITE, Report Writer

READ and WRITE are discussed here and there in this monograph as especially deserving of modular isolation. One READ or one WRITE per file is all that should be found in a single program. Any associated activity such as controlling the line and page overflow for a printer output or calculating a disk address should be isolated logically close to the READ or WRITE.

The Report Writer feature included in many compilers (it is an ANS standard feature) is consistent with modular concerns. Reports using this facility should be defined as separate simple subprograms with minimal PROCEDURE DIVISION entries. Dependable alterations to report parameters are made simple as a result of the high visibility of REPORT DESCRIPTION entries.[3]

For other COBOL facilities, either standard or peculiar to a given vendor's COBOL, the same principles delineated here apply: isolate, keep the structure logically tight, simplify, and document.

SUMMARY

A systems organization should identify the troublesome areas in a given language and replace, refine, or avoid them. In COBOL the ALTER verb should be eliminated, a clean GO TO . . . DEPENDING ON structure used, loops and indices controlled, IF statements kept simple, and the use of flags controlled. Simple table-driven code should be developed, and more complex facilities should be treated as separate independent modules.

REFERENCES

1. International Business Machines, IBM System/360 Disk Operating System American National Standard COBOL, S360-24 GC28-6394-2, New York, 1968, 1969.
2. International Business Machines, *IBM System/360 Disk Operating System Full American National Standard COBOL Programmers Guide,* S360-24 GC28-C398-2. Several of the recommendations in this book may be found, very condensed, in this guide. Apparently, hardly anyone seems to have read these recommendations and taken them seriously enough to extrapolate on the advice given.
3. Hicks, Harry T., Jr., "Using the COBOL Report Writer", *Datamation,* September 1972. This is a good introduction to the Report Writer feature.

CHAPTER **9**

Developing Reusable Capability

At various places throughout this book, I have mentioned the desirability of developing reusable capability. In discussing reusability it is useful to separate it into a few categories, as the following illustrates.

1. A construct or method of solving a particular problem may be standardized and so become a reusable model.
2. A paragraph-group and its associated data interface may be usable in another program.
3. A subprogram may be usable in its entirety.
4. A preprocessor or package may be developed.
5. A system may be generalized to serve several cases for a given application.

Since the next step up in reusability is to a generalized MIS system or a universal problem solver, the above five categories are probably sufficient. While an organization would like to achieve several generalized systems, it is likely to have difficulty obtaining and keeping a timeless set of specifications. Also, if a reasonable generalized definition can be obtained for a given system, nothing about aiming for a lesser degree of generalization contradicts it. (Recall the differentiation between flexibility and generality discussed in Chapter 1.) The emphasis in this book, and in this chapter specifically, is on achieving reusability in the manner of the first three of the above five categories, although some mention is made of the fourth.

These four categories of reusability (model, paragraph-group, subprogram, and preprocessor) are discussed in turn, along with their minor variants.

REUSABLE MODELS

A reusable model is a method description or procedural guideline for solving a problem. It may be in the form of a narrative description, a generalized flow diagram, or skeleton coding.

Several reusable models have already been presented in this book, among them: the model of the GO TO . . . DEPENDING ON construct; the protocol for setting, resetting, and testing flags; and the structure of a paragraph-group. These could be described as being on the microprocedural level. Although the definition of constructs at this level as representing reusable capability may seem an academic point, this is definitely not the case. Having a set of predetermined responses for a variety of expected problems permits one to take care of the familiar quickly and to concentrate on responding more effectively to the unfamiliar. During the famous 1972 Bobby Fisher–Boris Spassky World Championship Chess Match, many people became aware for the first time that players of this caliber have a broader frame of reference than do novice players. Not only single moves, but familiar groups of moves (openings, attacks, and defenses) have names. This allows the players to group possibilities together in a more macroscopic manner so that they need not reconstruct the possible consequences of every gambit but can focus on variations. A programmer who has a repertory of responses has a similar advantage and is much more efficient and more effective in solving problems of program design.

Standardized constructs should permit a program to be implemented with more inherent reliability. As the strength and weakness of a construct become familiar, corrective action may be taken to control the weakness.

As an example of a reusable model, I will describe a method of handling a complex decision situation. The following problem narrative serves as an introduction to the kind of requirements that would necessitate its use. This is an artifically constructed example but illustrates realistically a frequently encountered level of complexity.

A given input data stream contains data from three locations: Boston, Chicago, and Los Angeles. The transactions may be of three types: inquiry, order, or change. Further, a given transaction may refer to one of three product lines: integrated circuits, scientific ceramics, or wristwatches. Boston and Chicago can originate error changes, but Los Angeles cannot. Los Angeles or Boston may process integrated circuits, but Boston cannot have any wristwatch input, and Los Angeles cannot have any ceramic input. Chicago can have either of the other two but no integrated circuits.

All inquiries may be processed by the same edit logic. Orders are edited in the same way for integrated circuits and ceramics but not for wristwatches. The same is true of changes; integrated circuits and ceramics use the same logic, but watches are different.

The possible permutations of the above conditions, and the name of a paragraph-group driving each process, are tabulated in Figure 30.

1.	Boston, inquiry, IC	INQ-EDIT
2.	Chicago, inquiry, IC	IC-ERROR
3.	LA, inquiry, IC	INQ-EDIT
4.	Boston, order, IC	ORDER-EDIT
5.	Chicago, order, IC	IC-ERROR
6.	LA, order, IC	ORDER-EDIT
7.	Boston, change, IC	CHANGE-EDIT
8.	Chicago, change, IC	IC-ERROR
9.	LA, change, IC	C-ERROR
10.	Boston, inquiry, ceramics	INQ-EDIT
11.	Chicago, inquiry, ceramics	INQ-EDIT
12.	LA, inquiry, ceramics	CP-ERROR
13.	Boston, order, ceramics	ORDER-EDIT
14.	Chicago, order, ceramics	ORDER-EDIT
15.	LA, order, ceramics	CP-ERROR
16.	Boston, change, ceramics	CHANGE-EDIT
17.	Chicago, change, ceramics	CHANGE-EDIT
18.	LA, change, ceramics	CP-ERROR, C-ERROR
19.	Boston, inquiry, wristwatches	W-ERROR
20.	Chicago, inquiry, wristwatches	INQ-EDIT
21.	LA, inquiry, wristwatches	INQ-EDIT
22.	Boston, order, watches	W-ERROR
23.	Chicago, order, watches	WATCH-ORDER-EDIT
24.	LA, order, watches	WATCH-ORDER-EDIT
25.	Boston, change, watches	W-ERROR
26.	Chicago, change, watches	WATCH-CHANGE-EDIT
27.	LA, change, watches	C-ERROR

Figure 30.

Obviously, to construct 27 IF statements would not only be laborious coding but would lend itself to error and probably encourage some spaghetti in the structure. Figure 31 shows the previous tabular

```
INQ-EDIT 1, 3, 10, 11, 20, 21
ORDER-EDIT 4, 6, 13, 14
CHANGE-EDIT 7, 16, 17
WATCH-ORDER-EDIT 23, 24
WATCH-CHANGE-EDIT 26
IC-ERROR 2, 5, 8
C-ERROR 9, 18, 27
CP-ERROR 12, 15, 18
W-ERROR 19, 22, 25
```

Figure 31.

depiction with each of the 27 option numbers assigned to the target module.

There is a great deal of asymmetry in the assignments in Figure 31. Proceeding first to a "city paragraph" and then to the possibilities within each city choice would create a difficult structure, and the same is true of a hierarchy in which transaction type or product line might be uppermost. A table is suggested as the appropriate solution, and it may be constructed as follows: Figure 32 shows a matrix with the parameters of the problem in three rows of three elements each.[1] There is a number in each of the cells in the matrix, associated with each choice. If the input stream is tested for the row-1 possibilities (city code), either 1, 2, or 3 is assigned to a counter. Next, the second-row entries are tested to establish the transaction type, and either 0, 3, or 6 is added to the counter. Similarly, evaluate for product line, and add 0, 9, or 18 to the counter.

	Element 1	Element 2	Element 3
Row 1	1 Boston	2 Chicago	3 Los Angeles
Row 2	0 Inquir	3 Order	6 Change
Row 3	0 Integrated circuits	9 Scientific ceramics	18 Wristwatches

Figure 32 **Decision matrix.**

For example, if a transaction contained the codes indicating Chicago (MOVE 2), inquiry (ADD 0), and wristwatch (ADD 18), the result is 20, and a branch would be executed to INQ-EDIT. Each discrete possibility in Figure 32 results in the assignment of a unique number which ranges from 1 to 27 without interruption. A GO TO . . . DEPENDING ON construct could then be executed which would appear as:

```
GO TO
   INQ-EDIT
   IC-ERROR
   INQ-EDIT
   ORDER-EDIT
   IC-ERROR
        .
        .
        .
   C-ERROR
DEPENDING ON W-MATRIX-INDEX.
```

For the one case, option 18 in Figure 30, in which more than one action is indicated, a paragraph name may be inserted in the GO TO . . . DEPENDING ON list that PERFORMS the two actions.

The structure of the GO TO . . . DEPENDING ON should be the same as that recommended in Chapter 8. Most realistic applications require more processing than a single paragraph. In these cases the paragraphs referenced in the GO TO should control a hierarchy of PERFORMed paragraphs. Treat this GO TO . . . DEPENDING ON construct as a single logical control module.

The table technique just described may be generalized. For a case similar to the previous example (with the same number of elements in each row), the formula is as follows. *N* is the number of elements in each row. *M* is the number of rows.

Row 1	1	2	3 . . .	N
Row 2	$0n^1$	$1n^1$	$2n^1$ . . .	$(n-1)\ n^1$
Row 3	$0n^2$	$1n^2$	$2n^2$ . . .	$(n-1)\ n^2$
Row M	$0n^{m-1}$	$1n^{m-1}$	$2n^{m-1}$. .	$(n-1)\ n^{m-1}$

Appling the above formula to the case of four elements in three rows, one may construct the following matrix:

1	2	3	4
0	4	8	12
0	16	32	48

This matrix provides a series of sums from 1 through 64 (the sum of column 4).

Since most of the applications in the real world may not be as symmetric as the above example, a narrative description of the general method for this problem may be more useful and applies equally to the previous example.

Let the choice be from combinations of two cities, four transaction types, three product lines, and four priority codes. Place the two cities on row 1:

1	2		

Row 2 starts with the usual zero. (Having zeroes in every column-1 position except row 1 is the only way that final values 1,2, . . . N can occur.) Bring down the last element in row 1 (2) as the second element in row 2. Finish row 2, multiplying this second element (2) by 2 then 3, 4, . . ., $(n-1)$. So for four transactions types:

1	2		
0	2	4	6

For the next row start with a zero but choose as the second element what the nth (next element of the previous row) would have been. For three product lines:

1	2		
0	2	4	6
0	8	16	

Repeat the last step for all remaining rows.

For four priority codes the completed matrix is:

1	2		
0	2	4	6
0	8	16	
0	24	48	72

This will provide 1 thru 96 unique indices. Certainly, in this case one might want to further structure the program to avoid a long GO TO . . . DEPENDING ON. The general solution may be diagrammed as follows:

Row 1	1	2	3 . . .	N	
Row 2	0	N	$2N$ . . .	$(n-1)N$	$n(N)=M$
Row 3	0	M	$2M$ . . .	$(n-1)N$	$n(M)=P$
Row 4	0	P	$2P$ . . .	$(n-1)P$	
and so on					

where n is the number of elements in each row.

This is an example of the type of model that may be formalized, documented, and made available for the solution of a specific set of problems in a systems organization. Even if code is developed and made available to implement a construct similar to this one, documentation explaining the methodology should also be available along with the code.

REUSABLE PARAGRAPH-GROUPS

Frequently, whole paragraph-groups represent usable code for more than one program. If a given paragraph-group represents code that is frequently executed, it may be more desirable to include it in-line with existing code rather than embed it in a subprogram. The COPY facility in COBOL permits such reuse and even provides the programmer with the capability to replace data names in the library entry with data names local to the using program. Here again a SECTION name is required to identify the paragraph-group for the COPY verb. COPY is an excellent tool, of which too few installations take advantage. A certain amount of foresight in building library entries and preplanning data name usage in the program that copies the data facilitate the process. The grouping of the interface data by paragraph-group discussed in Chapter 7 pays off again here. Each paragraph-group (SECTION) entry in the library can also have an entry for its corresponding data-group. Although not mentioned previously, because in general programmers naturally avoid the extra writing, the use of qualified data names could be used to reduce the amount of REPLACING required. For example, if there is a data description:

```
01  L-VENDOR-GROUP
    05  PLACEMENT-CODE          PICTURE 9(8)
    05  NAME                    PICTURE X(30)
    05  ADDRESS                 PICTURE X(45)
                 .
                 .
                 .
```

Then COPY statements could change the 01-level name in both the data division and procedure division. However, this maintains the proper identification of data names only as long as qualified names are used for every procedure division reference:

```
MOVE NAME OF L-VENDOR-GROUP TO LA-OUTPUT-NAME.
```

The use of qualified data names is more appropriate if a group finds itself reusing driver sections of code rather than just process modules. In general, better data base control may be exercised by using the paragraph-group/data-group recommendations of Chapter 7.

To illustrate the construction of reusable paragraph-groups, a convenient example is the coded implementation of the model table-handling technique cited previously. The problems of reuse really solve themselves by following the now-familiar recommendations for modular isolation and interface structure.

The main difference between the reuse of paragraph-group code and the implementation of a similar capability in a subprogram is that in the former case the library entry for the DATA DIVISION interface is bound to a given application. For each reuse a DATA DIVISION entry is constructed, cataloged in the library, and incorporated into each particular application, either by the COPY verb or other means. Another alternative of course is to build the interface in a working structure and execute group MOVEs.

For sake of brevity the problem narrative is presumed unnecessary in light of the previous method description. First the data interface:

```
01  CC-TABLE-INTERFACE.
    05  CCC-CONTROL.
        10 CCC-TOTAL-NUMBER-ENTRIES       PICTURE 9(4) COMP.
        10  CCC-NUMBER ROWS               PICTURE 9(4) COMP.
    05  CCP-PROCESS.
        10  CCP-OUTPUT-VALUE               PICTURE 9(4) COMP.
        10  CCP-ERROR-FLAG                 PICTURE X.
        10  CCP-INPUT-CODES OCCURS
              9 TIMES.
            15  CCP-INPUT-REC              PICTURE X(2).
    05  CCW-STABLE WORK.
        10  CCW-COMP-VALUES.
            15  CCW-CVAL-1 PICTURE X(2) VALUE 'C1'.
            15  CCW-CVAL-2 PICTURE X(2) VALUE 'C2'.
            15  CCW-CVAL-3 PICTURE X(2) VALUE 'T1'.
            15  CCW-CVAL-4 PICTURE X(2) VALUE 'T2'.
            15  CCW-CVAL-5 PICTURE X(2) VALUE 'T3'.
            15  CCW-CVAL-6 PICTURE X(2) VALUE 'T4'.
            15  CCW-CVAL-7 PICTURE X(2) VALUE 'P1'.
            15  CCW-CVAL-8 PICTURE X(2) VALUE 'P2'.
            15  CCW-CVAL-9 PICTURE X(2) VALUE 'P3'.
        10  CCWR-COMPS REDEFINES CCW-COMP-VALUES
              OCCURS 9 TIMES.
            15  CCWR-COMP-REC              PICTURE X(2).
        10  CCW-MATRIX-VALUES.
            15  CCW-MVAL-1 PICTURE 9(4) COMP. VALUE 1.
            15  CCW-MVAL-2 PICTURE 9(4) COMP. VALUE 2.
            15  CCW-MVAL-3 PICTURE 9(4) COMP. VALUE 0.
```

```
            15   CCW-MVAL-4 PICTURE 9(4) COMP. VALUE 2.
            15   CCW-MVAL-5 PICTURE 9(4) COMP. VALUE 4.
            15   CCW-MVAL-6 PICTURE 9(4) COMP. VALUE 6.
            15   CCW-MVAL-7 PICTURE 9(4) COMP. VALUE 0.
            15   CCW-MVAL-8 PICTURE 9(4) COMP. VALUE 8.
            15   CCW-MVAL-9 PICTURE 9(4) COMP. VALUE 16.
        10   CCWR-MATRIX REDEFINES CCW-MATRIX-VALUES
               OCCURS 9 TIMES.
            15   CCWR-MAT-REC                 PICTURE 9(4) COMP.
    05   CCX-PERISHABLE-WORK.
        10   CCX-TOTAL-COUNTER                PICTURE 9(4) COMP.
        10   CCX-MATCH-LOOP                   PICTURE 9(4) COMP.
        10   CCX-MATCH-FLAG                   PICTURE X.
```

And the paragraph-group code:

```
CT-TABLE SECTION.
CTA-NOTE.
   NOTE    CLEAR OUTPUT AREA
           INITIALIZE INDEX
           SET ERROR FLAG
           PERFORM CODE-VECTOR-MATCHING
              AND ADDING-MATRIX-VALUE-INTO-OUTPUT-AREA
           IF MISMATCH OCCURS SET OUTPUT AREA TO
           MATRIX INDEX OF ELEMENT ON WHICH ERROR OCCURRED.
CTE-EVAL-TABLE.
   MOVE ZEROES TO CCP-OUTPUT-VALUE.
   MOVE 1 TO CCX-TOTAL-COUNTER.
   MOVE "N" TO CCP-ERROR-FLAG.
   PERFORM CTM-VECTOR-MATCH THRU CTMX-VECTOR-MATCH-X.
      VARYING CCX-MATCH-LOOP FROM 1 BY 1 UNTIL
      CCX-MATCH-LOOP GREATER THAN CCC-NUMBERS-ROWS
      OR
      CCP-ERROR-FLAG='Y'.
CTE-EVAL-TABLE-X.
   EXIT.
CTM-NOTE.
   NOTE    SET MATCH FLAG
           PERFORM COMPARISON, ON MATCH SET MATCH FLAG AND
           ADD MATRIX VALUE TO OUTPUT VALUE
           INCREMENT COUNTER/INDEX
           IF TOTAL ENTRIES VISITED AND NO MATCH: ERROR
           IF TOTAL ENTRIES VISITED AND MATCH: EXIT
           IF END OF ROW AND MATCH: EXIT
           IF END OF ROW AND NO MATCH: ERROR
           IF WITHIN ROW AND NO MATCH: COMPARE
           IF WITHIN ROW AND MATCH: INCREMENT INDEX ONLY
           TRICKY CODE WARNING: ZERO ELEMENT IN CONTROL
              MATRIX IS USED TO DEFINE BEGINNING OF NEW ROW.
CTM-VECTOR-MATCH.
   MOVE 'N' TO CCX-MATCH-FLAG.
```

```
CTM-COMPARE
   IF CCP-INPUT-REC (CCX-MATCH-LOOP)=CCWR-COMP-REC
   (CCX-TOTAL-COUNTER)
      MOVE 'Y' TO CCX-MATCH-FLAG
      ADD CCWR-MAT-REC (CCX-TOTAL-COUNTER) TO CCP-OUTPUT-
      VALUE.
CTMH-INCREMENT.
   ADD 1 TO CCX-TOTAL-COUNTER.
   IF CCX-TOTAL-COUNTER NOT GREATER THAN CCR-TOTAL-NUMBER-
   ENTRIES
      GO TO CCML-CYCLE.
   IF CCX-MATCH-FLAG='N'
      GO TO CTMR-ERROR-SET.
   GO TO CTMX-VECTOR-MATCH-X.
CCML-CYCLE.
   IF CCWR-MAT-REC (CCX-TOTAL-COUNTER) NOT=ZERO
      GO TO CTMP-NOT-ZERO.
CTMN-ZERO.
   IF CCX-MATCH-FLAG='Y'
      GO TO CTMX-VECTOR-MATCH-X.
   GO TO CTMR-ERROR-SET.
CTMP-NOT-ZERO.
   IF CCX-MATCH-FLAG='N'
      GO TO CTMC-COMPARE.
   GO TO CTMH-INCREMENT.
CTMR-ERROR-SET.
   MOVE 'Y' TO CCP-ERROR-FLAG.
   COMPUTE CCP-OUTPUT-VALUE=CCX-TOTAL-COUNTER-1.
CTMX-VECTOR-MATCH-X.
   EXIT.
```

Note that the perishable data have also been included in the structure. REDEFINES is used to obtain the indexability of the tables containing the matrix and comparison values.

The tables here contain the input codes for transactions with two cities ("C1," "C2") of four types ("T1," "T2," "T3," 'T4"), and three products ("P1," "P2," "P3").

If the input area were loaded with the three transaction values "C2," "T4," and "P1," the output value would be computed as 8, to be used to index a table, to be mapped to a disk record, or to drive a GO TO . . . DEPENDING ON construct.

To convert this paragraph-group to a subprogram simply requires removing the specific values from the working storage tables. It is then the responsibility of a hierarchically superior module to initialize these tables in the interface. Coincidentally, this method lends itself to "automatic" checking of its procedural integrity (the mathematics of the matrix).

DETERMINE TYPE

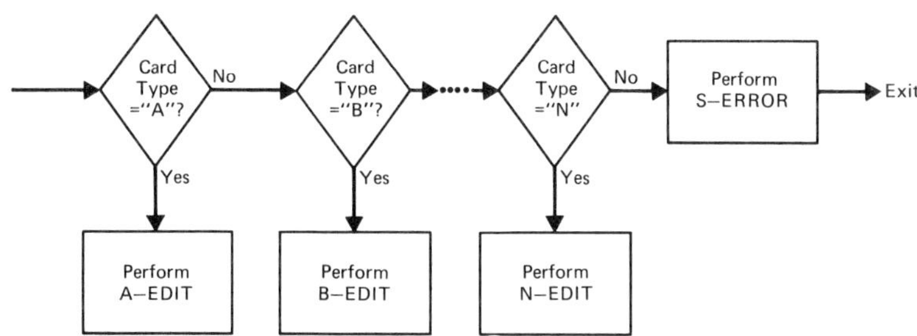

EDIT

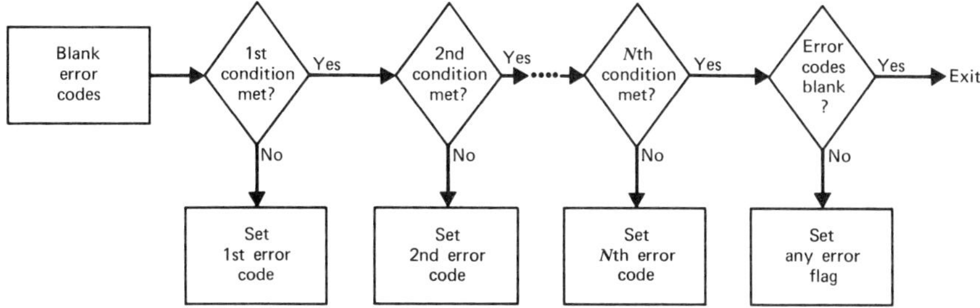

Figure 33 **Editing by input record.**

Some code is not easily reused; an example is the following construct for implementing the edit function.

The usual manner in which the task of editing is structured is to modularize it by input record format. A diagrammatic model of this process appears in Figure 33, and a sample of representative coding is as follows.

```
IF A-CARD-TYPE='A'
   PERFORM EA-EDIT THRU EAX-EDIT-X.
          .
          .
          .
EA-EDIT.
   MOVE SPACES TO E-ERROR-CODES.
   IF A-PART-NUMBER NOT NUMERIC
      MOVE 'N' TO E-PN-CLASS-ERROR.
   IF A PART-NUMBER LESS THAN 10000
      OR GREATER THAN 99999
      MOVE 'R' TO E-PN-RANGE-ERROR.
```

```
IF A-VENDOR-IDENT NOT NUMERIC
        .
        .
        .
and so on.
```

This is very "straight-line" coding and is somewhat laborious and repetitive. This method does have the advantages that an edit module A, B, . . ., *N* can be easily matched one to one with an input requirement, and that to add, delete, or change a module is a simple process. The data associated with each edit module are likely to be REDEFINES of the input buffer area. One improvement would be to implement the determination of type as a table-look-up, GO TO . . . DEPENDING ON construct.

While the model of this method is useful in the sense of a standard, the code implementing the method does not lend itself to reuse, since particular applicational logic is very much embedded in the coding. Neither could this method reasonably convert into a reusable subroutine, since it has no generality. This is not to say that in a system this code could not or should not be segmented for the sake of general clarity.

At this point it is worth discussing two aids that greatly facilitate both program design and development and the data naming problems that arise in reusing modules. The first of these is applicable in a terminal environment in which programmers may develop their programs in either a time-shared or interactive batch mode.

Terminal Text Editors

One of the attractive features of terminal systems is the facility for change provided by a text editor. If a programmer wishes to use a predeveloped module and there are data name conflicts, these conflicts can be quickly resolved by the text editor. For example, using the recommended alphabetic prefixing convention, the only likely name conflicts that can arise are in the prefixes. Using an editing command (the verbs and formats differ widely from one editor to another) such as

```
REPLACE ALL " WP-" BY " EP-".
```

could resolve the naming problem. Text editors facilitate changes in the data name or DATA DIVISION restructuring and the construction of REDEFINES and LINKAGE SECTIONs. Additionally, a terminal/batch interface capability may have even more significance for documentation. For all the steps in Chapter 4 in which it was recommended that a coding sheet be used for a scratch pad, the terminal could be used even more easily. To make this documentation more palatable, a menu could be displayed of the items desired at various stages, with blank spaces for each required entry. With such a system documentation could be built in a professional manner by analysts, designers, and finally programmers.

Abbreviational COBOL Preprocessors

Some way is needed to reduce the verbosity required in preparing COBOL programs. Many decisions of program structure, documentation, and data base control are made simply to avoid a lot of writing.

Abbreviational preprocessors for COBOL are available for many machines and their purpose is to reduce the amount of code-writing and key-punching or terminal input for coding COBOL programs.[2] Thus abbreviations are either predefined:

PD	Procedure division
WS	Working-storage section
AMR	Access mode is random
C3P	Computational picture
VZ	Value zero
AA	After advancing
GT	Greater than
M	Move
WR	Write

or defined by the programmer dynamically in the source code input or from a library. Programmers may define their own abbreviations for data names, paragraph names, verbs, and phrases in addition to those predefined. The preprocessor expands abbreviations into their full-length form for input to the COBOL compiler and subsequent program listings.

Thus A-VENDOR-CODE could be abbreviated A-V-C. For KA-WRITE-TEST, one could substitute KA-WT or just KA-. Such packages do not violate any good rules of programming since the expansion returns the documentary value and meaningfulness to the source listing. Abbreviational preprocessors are indisputable time savers, and if an organization has access to one it should be used. One of the advantages is that documentation may also be made easier as abbreviations can be assigned to standard documentation phrases. The following abbreviations could be useful for describing the flags or indices in a program.

FUN	Function
IXS	Indexes
STT	Set to
INC	Incremented by
RS	Reset to

Care should be taken in purchasing these packages; some impose restrictions on the length and total number of abbreviations allowed. Either obtain a package to meet your needs or plan on modification or development by your software staff. Such a package may be used either in a batch or terminal environment.

Reusable Subprograms

The third method of capturing or containerizing reusable capability is in a subprogram. A subprogram designed to be reused is likely to include some generalizations; this may not only be unnecessary but is frequently undesirable. Systems groups often make the mistake of overgeneralizing every subprogram. It is better to maintain several variations of a given procedural or applicational theme than to attempt a single comprehensive subprogram. The discrete variations will prove easier to use and maintain and are more easily modified into yet another variation, if one is needed. (Naturally, control should be exercised to prevent overproliferation of routines with bells, whistles, or arabesques which do not enhance either basic capability or responsiveness to user requirements.)

To a large extent one could regard reusable subprograms (and paragraph-groups of code as well) as extensions of the COBOL language. It helps of course if these extensions have been thoroughly tested; they should give as little (or less, in some cases) difficulty as using a COBOL verb in a given manufacturer's compiler implementation. In general, the way to enhance a function-poor language (such as COBOL) is to add functions that are CALLable or otherwise easily executed.

The subject of the technical implementation of subprograms has been dealt with in sufficient detail in Chapter 7. It is appropriate here to discuss some of the procedural and applicational functions an organization should have packaged, ready for reuse, in subprograms.

Many reusable subprograms should be in the category of system support modules. Examples of modules an organization should have on the shelf are:

Input/output	
Random access disk module(s)	This capability should include separate modules for physical, single-key, or multiple-key retrieval and storage as dictated by local needs.
Secondary-level access disk modules	In so far as possible there should be the same interface requirement as above for a particular manufacturer's access or data management methods (indexed sequential, IDS, IMS, DMS, etc.)
Printer output modules	Variations on the "PRINTER" subprogram from Chapter 7, with provision for driving the printer control tape.
Data manipulation	
Sort	I have already, in the previous chapter, alluded to the need for alternatives to one or two system utility sorts (one of which is usually used to implement the SORT verb.) For frequently reoccuring problems an organization can do much better. For example, for the case in which there is a high probability that the data are already ordered, a method that will detect this should be used. Perhaps there are particular cases of partial orderings which also provide an opportunity for an improved method.
Merge	"*N*-way" merges may also be implemented for a given class of problems; they have a great advantage over system routines, simply because the organization is able to match their problems more precisely than is the vendor's software.
Core-to-peripheral managers	This category includes modules to handle pseudobuffering or to map between linear and nonlinear data structures.
List or tree-structure processing	Combined with the above this can provide powerful handling of data base problems.
Table searches	As recommended in the discussion of the SEARCH verb, the more elaborate but frequently used constructs may be standardized.

The foregoing examples have been, with the possible exception of SORT, procedural extensions of the COBOL facilities. Implementation of these capabilities into subprograms presents no unsurpassable difficulty. For input/output, to select one, the problem is to bind the descriptive data names from the calling module positionally with the data names in the subroutine code (thru the CALL . . . USING) and then to COPY the file definition in terms of the data names in the subprogram. For the lowest applicational level, there are varying degrees of difficulty. Such functions as extraction and update are relatively easy and involve adding key-matching code on top of the file access methods. (If the key-matching code is separate, there is more flexibility in the choice of a primary or secondary access method.) The REPLACING option of COPY may aid in the identification and binding of file keys.

In some cases there may be problems involving data interface that are best solved through file-to-file translation, converting the data structures of one system into compatible structures for another. There is a tendency for systems groups to develop separate systems for separate structures rather than translate, probably because of efficiency. While efficiency may be a concern, file conversion is a mundane task for which the computer is well suited.

More comprehensive functions require more elaborate capability and may not lend themselves to easy subroutinization, partly because of the extent of the interface required. This is particularly true when one steps up the ladder of applicational complexity to what was defined in Chapter 5 as the program level. To define a general check-writing subprogram is not too difficult, but any more complex a task may easily become a project of very different scope. Having several building blocks at the procedural level makes the process of creating new applicational material much easier.

PREPROCESSORS AND PACKAGES

There are cases in which COBOL does not provide ideal facilities for a problem, and in which additional aids may be indicated. Although this book is about COBOL, I have no hesitation recommending such aids as decision table preprocessors or report generators. Even with such aids (and there should be more of them), there will still be a significant amount of COBOL writing to be done.

Decision table preprocessors for COBOL form a subject that has adequate coverage in the literature[2] and is, in any case, outside the purview of this monograph. The available preprocessors, both commercial and public (DETAB), are highly useful and desirable. Their use in no way contradicts modularity or any of the peripheral concerns we have discussed here. As a matter of fact, the COBOL code generated by a decision table package may be highly modular, especially if the user establishes a hierarchy or network of tables of reasonable simplicity (long and complex tables should be avoided).

Increased clarity will be attained in decision tables if a conceptual distinction is made between applicational and procedural modularity, if control is made highly visible, and if, in using hierarchies, the distinctions among interface, process, exception, housekeeping, and input/output are heeded.

Report generators, especially those that encompass some data base management capability, are very desirable. These packages should not be treated as a totally separate entity, as in some organizations, but their files may be made compatible with other capability, accessible to COBOL subprograms in general.

An example of the kind of package capability an organization can (should) develop is an edit processing package. First, defining the basic edit requirements, one may edit for:

1. A precise single value, such as "EQUAL TO 53", or special cases of precise match, such as SPACES or ZEROES.
2. A set of precise values, as in a vector or table. "EQUAL TO 51 OR 55 OR 62", or calculated, "EQUAL TO PREVIOUS-ELEMENT +1.2".
3. A range of values, either singly bound, "LESS THAN 42", "GREATER THAN ZERO", "GREATER THAN 19", or bound with both an upper and lower limit, "GREATER THAN 18 OR LESS THAN 35".
4. Membership in a class, NUMERIC, ALPHABETIC.
5. Negations and exclusions of the above using NOT.
6. Combinations of the above using the logical connectives AND or OR.

Edit is a significantly more complex applicational function than update or extract, although they are conceptually on the same level. An examination of a possible implementation of a subprogram to service the general edit problem reveals the difficulties and points to the greater feasibility of an alternative approach.

A method for implementing generalized reusable editing code is to employ a table-driven construct. An input format can be described in terms of the number of entries, the number of characters in each entry, and a table of specifications as to how each entry is to be edited. The input entry can be moved to a staging area and a GO TO . . . DEPENDING ON can drive the choice of code to perform the required tests on the entry. Further tables are required to contain the values for the precise single-value edit, a vector of values for the vector edit, or the low and high values for a range check. Additionally, some method of providing for cases of negations and exclusions (NOT), and a way to introduce the code for complex and unique combinations of edits, must be found.

A few problems arise. The tables would be potentially very asymmetrical. Figure 34 shows all the tables to be of variable length, some also with variable-length entries. The implementation of code to use these tables requires that either several limit values or pointers be provided for the edit routine, or all tables be of fixed length and entries made only where they are needed. In either case the implementation, modification, and reuse of this construct risks being clumsy and error-prone. To further clutter the situation, a subprogram implementation does not lend itself to the need to supply special code for complex cross-field or logical connective cases. Finally, the execution of such code could be expensive. All this points to the

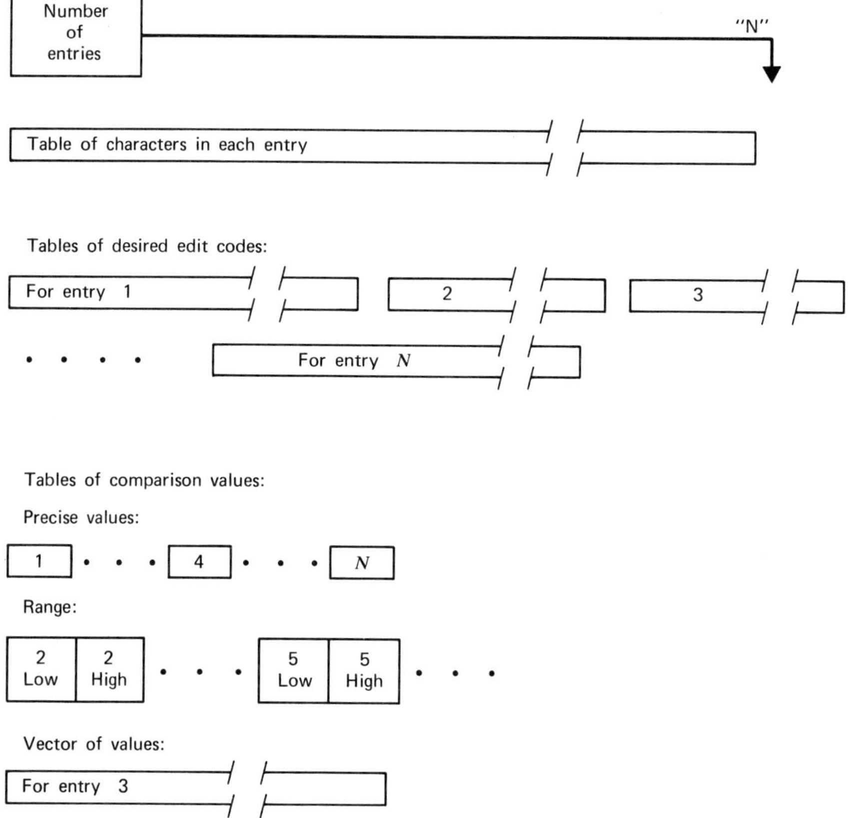

Figure 34 **Tables for general table-driven edit.**

desirability of implementing the edit program as preprocessor or separate package. Report generators have been useful to many organizations for some time; an edit generator seems to be equally appropriate. I leave the precise details of the implementation to the reader's imagination, but an example of what hypothetical input could be for a generator will illuminate its utility.

```
A-VENDOR-IDENT PICTURE 9(6)
   EDIT: NUMERIC ON ERROR 'VC'
      IN I-VEND-I-ERR, 'Y' IN T-FATAL-FLAG,
         RANGE   100001 to 999999
      ON ERROR 'VR' IN I-VEND-I-ERR,
      'Y' IN T-FATAL-FLAG.
A-DISCOUNT-VALUE PICTURE 99V9
   EDIT: NUMERIC ON ERROR 'DC'
      IN I-DISCT-ERROR, 'Y' IN T-FATAL-FLAG,
         VECTOR  0  5  10  15  ON ERROR
      'DR' IN I-DISCT-ERROR, 'Y' IN T-FATAL-FLAG,
      INCLUDE CODE.
      IF A-DISCOUNT-VALUE>A TERM-VALUE
         MOVE 'DTR' TO I-DISCT-TERM-ERR
         MOVE 'Y' TO T-FATAL-FLAG.
      END CODE.
```

Figure 35. **Edit generator input.**

Figure 35 shows two examples of possible input. In the first example the data name and its PICTURE are followed by requests for NUMERIC and RANGE checks and include the data names and the values to be MOVED if the edit test is failed. In the second example a VECTOR of precise values is supplied as well as the code for a cross-field edit test.

SUMMARY

Reusability ranges from a documented description of a method (a model) to a generalized application system. Most significant for an organization using COBOL is the development of reusable paragraph-groups and subprograms, for this provides instant capability, prefabricated parts for new systems. By employing the paragraph-group and interface recommendations, maximum advantage may be made of COPY or a text editor in building programs. An organization should seek to develop or acquire better tools for the systems building job.

REFERENCES

1. The use of a COBOL decision table preprocessor is also an appropriate tool for a problem of this nature but would result in less compact code. See Pollack, Solomon L., Hicks, Harry T., and Harrison, William J., *Decision Tables: Theory and Practice,* John Wiley, New York, 1971.
2. Naftaly, Stanley M., Johnson, Bruce G., and Cohen, Michael C., *COBOL Support Packages: Programming and Productivity Aids,* John Wiley, New York, 1972. Contains information on abbreviational COBOL preprocessors and, as well, on the important subject of Test Data Generators.

CHAPTER 10

Overall Summary

T his book has discussed the problems, environment, the documentation, design, interface, and trouble-free coding of COBOL application programs. These pages have recommended a strict style, with little compromise, more engineering than art. Yet, I do not feel that the style is a restrictive one but that, quite to the contrary, it frees a programmer to put more time and energy into better problem definition and increased responsiveness to the user's needs. Additionally, I am reminded that even art benefits from a structured environment.

An organization that currently uses COBOL can take the recommendations of this book and use them without fear of ideological obsolescence. I feel that the principles that underlie the book's recomendations are sound: modular division of tasks into applicational, procedural, and structural differentiation; the separation of data functions in interface design; the identification of critical documentation; the definition of reliable constructs; and the development of reusable capability. These principles are sufficiently broad and powerful to permit their extension into the areas of acquired software packages, data base management and yet higher or more macrolevels of language. There are strong tendencies in current research and development toward more and more applications-oriented capability.[1] The principles here defined for the COBOL language can aid an organization, even as they move away from strictly COBOL programming.

I hope that this book has a side effect; I hope that some vendor, university, government, and user research is applied to the development of a production-oriented language. To date the use of computers has grown so fast, and they have been marketed so aggressively that there has hardly been time to create a production environment for the creation of applications systems.

Just recently there has been a growing awareness of the definition and desirability of creating a systems production environment. One might legitimately expect that programming languages, a primary systems tool, should be reevaluated in terms of supporting a production need. A production language should enforce the concepts put forth in this volume.

1. One should not be able to produce anything but a modular system in the terms I have defined.
2. Neither applicational nor procedural modularity should be contradicted by the implementation.
3. Structural modularity, increased separation of data, and separation of the control functions should be supported.
4. Troublesome language features should be eliminated or isolated. (The idea of simple subsets which are not affected by the more complex superset of a language is a good idea, but it has yet to be successfully implemented, as in PL/I.)
5. Interfaces should be clearly defined in the language as functionally separate.

Such a language could be a variation of COBOL as we know it today, supplied by our friendly vendors for use on their machines. There should be ego-free (without regard to each vendor's hardware quirks) standardization, in other words, real standardization. Language designers should consider not just utility but production concerns. Universities should not only produce languages of elegant wildness but of sober (but not somber) usefulness.

In the meantime organizations creating a production environment should define their subset as I have recommended. Good luck, and don't neglect a good working environment.

REFERENCES

1. Teichroew, Daniel, and Sayani, Hassan, "Automation of System Building", *Datamation,* August 15, 1971, pp. 25–30. This article describes the University of Michigan ISDOS project. Some of the most important research on data base technology and higher-level languages for the building of applications systems is being done on this project.

APPENDIX:

Sample Programs

The sample programs have been provided with the aim of illustrating program structure and providing examples of documentation. As the astute COBOL programmer will easily observe, run-time efficiency has not been one of my concerns. On certain computers the expressed or implied USAGE of several of the data items or their alignment will result in behind-the-scenes conversion and extra data movement and alignment. What I wanted to avoid was unnecessary focus on the peculiarities of any particular vendor's implementation, although the predominance of IBM does reflect itself in a few of the details. The equally astute systems analyst will note that in the example from the accounts payable system some applicational niceties have been omitted, largely to reduce the size of the example. I feel no generality has been lost.

```
IDENTIFICATION DIVISION.
PROGRAM-ID. AP503.
REMARKS.     SYSTEM:     ACCOUNTS PAYABLE
             PROGRAM:    CHECK VOIDING AND UPDATE
             INPUT:      A-OLD-DISK DISK SEQUENTIAL
                            MAJOR SORT CHECK NUMBER
                            MINOR SORT INVOICE NUMBER
                         B-CARDS-IN SORTED CARD FILE
                           ON SEQUENTIAL DISK
                            MAJOR SORT CHECK NUMBER
             OUTPUT:     C-NEW-DISK DISK SEQUENTIAL
                         D-EDIT-LIST PRINTER
                            LISTING OF UPDATED DISK
                            RECORDS
                         ERROR LIST, PRINTER (CONDITIONAL)
                            LISTING OF EDIT FAILURES
                            CONDITION: ERROR IMAGES AND THEIR
                                       FAILURE CODES ARE ENTERED
                                       IN ERROR-TABLE. IF
                                       ERROR-TABLE FILLS IT IS
                                       FLUSHED ONTO A FILE CALLED
                                       PRINT-IMAGE FOR LATER PRINT
                         E-ERROR-DISK DISK SEQUENTIAL (CONDITIONAL
             PROCESS:    ANY CHECKS ISSUED IN ERROR MUST BE
                         FLAGGED BEFORE CHECKS ISSUED FILE IS
                         PRINTED.
                         FLAGS ARE 'S' FOR STOP PAYMENT AND 'H'
                         FOR HAND VOID.
                         INPUT CARD-IMAG IS EDITTED TO INSURE
                         CORRECT/COMPLETE DATA IS PRESENT.


    ************************************************************

                      SECTION DIRECTORY

    ************************************************************

                  AA-MAINLINE         MAINLINE
                  AB-INITIALIZE       HOUSEKEEPING
                  AF-DRIVER           MAIN CONTROL LOOP
                  DA-DUP-CHECK        TEST FOR AND SERVICE
                                         DUPLICATE CHECK NUMBER
                                         ON SUCCESSIVE INPUT
                  DD-DETAIL-MATCH     DOES DETAILED COMPARISON
                                       OF INPUT TO MASTER
                                       RECORD
                  EA-EDIT-INPUT       EDIT INPUT RECORD
                  EN-DRIVER           PROCESS DRIVER
                  MA-MATCH-CHECKS     CYCLES OLD MASTER FILE
                                       UNTIL A MATCH IS MADE
                                       DETAIL EDITS
                  NM-FETCH-MASTER     MOVE MASTER RECORD TO
                                         WORK AREA
                  NN-FETCH-INPUT      MOVE INPUT RECORD TO WORK
                                         AREA
                  RA-READ-MASTER      READ MASTER FILE
```

RB-READ-INPUT	READ INPUT FILE
SA-EDIT-EXCPT	SERVICE EDIT ERRORS
SD-PREMATURE-EOF	REPORT ERROR IN FILES
SF-BAD-FILE	SETS SWITCHES TO ABORT ON BAD FILE MATCH; REPORTS ERROR
TA-ERR-TAB	SERVICES TABLE OF ERROR MESSAGES
TN-TABLE-LOOP	SERVICES ERROR TABLE OVER FLOW
TP-END-PAGE	FIND PAGE END IF ERROR TABLE IS TO BE PRINTED
TQ-ERROR-HEADS	WRITE HEADINGS FOR ERROR LISTING REPORT
TR-TABLE-LOOP	PERFORMED VARYING TO PRINT ERROR TABLE
TS-BLANK-LOOP	PLACES BLANK LINES IN ERROR TABLE AS DESIRED
TT-WRITE-BLANKS	PLACE BLANK LINES IN PRINTER OUTPUT FOR HEADINGS AND END OF PAGE
UA-UPDATE	WRITES UPDATED NEW MASTER AFTER MOVING FIELDS LISTS RECORD ON PRINTER CYCLES UPDATING ALL MASTER RECORDS WITH CURRENT CHECK NUMBER NEW MASTER FILE
UN-UPDATE-WRITE	WRITES NEW MASTER RECORD
WA-PAGE-HEADING	WRITE NEW MASTER LISTING HEADINGS
WD-WRITE-OUT	MOVE AND CONTROL ERROR TABLE WRITE
WE-WRITE-E	WRITE ERROR TABLE
WP-PRINT	CONTROLS OUTPUT TO LINE PRINTER
WQ-WRITE-LOOP	CONTROL PAGE HEADINGS FOR PRINTER ROUTINE WP-PRINT
WY-WRITE	WRITE EDIT LIST FOR PRINT ING, ALSO USED FOR ERROR LISTING FOR PRINTING
ZA-FLUSH-OLD	CYCLE OLD TO NEW FILE WRITES.
ZD-END-JOB	DUMP OUT ERROR TABLE AS REQUIRED; CLOSE FILES; FINAL HOUSEKEEPING.
ZL-FLUSH-LOOP	CYCLE REMAINING MASTER AT REQUEST OF ZA-FLUSH-OLD
ZN-FLUSH-LOOP	CONTROL ERROR TABLE DUMP
ZZ-CLOSE	CLOSE FILES HOUSEKEEPING

****

PROGRAM NARRATIVE

****

THE PROGRAM WILL ACCEPT, EDIT AND UPDATE A SORTED INPUT STREAM OF CORRECTIONS TO A MASTER FILE CONTAINING RECORDS OF CHECKS TO BE PRINTED. WHILE THERE SHOULD BE ONLY ONE INPUT PER CHECK NUMBER THERE MAY BE A NUMBER OF RECORDS ON THE MASTER FILE TO BE UPDATED, SINCE A SINGLE CHECK MAY APPLY TOWARDS PAYING SEVERAL INVOICES. THE MASTER FILE HAS BEEN EDITED PREVIOUSLY SO THERE ARE: (1) NO GAPS IN THE CHECK NUMBERS; ALL CHECK NUMBERS ARE SEQUENTIAL AND HAVE BEEN ACCOUNTED FOR; ALL RECORDS FOR DIFFERENT INVOICES FOR THE SAME CHECK NUMBER AGREE IN DETAIL. THERE ARE TWO CATEGORIES OF CORRECTIONS, "HAND VOIDED " WHICH WILL BE NOTED ON THE MASTER RECORD BY AN "H" AND "STOP PAYMENT" WHICH WILL BE NOTED BY AN "S". THE INPUT TO THIS PROGRAM WILL HAVE BEEN SORTED BY CHECK-NUMBER. VENDOR-IDENTIFICATION (A NUMERIC CODE) , ISSUE DATE AND THE AMOUNT-PAID ON THE CHECK MAY BE COMPARED AS A SAFETY MEASURE TO INSURE THAT THE PROPER DELETION HAS BEEN MADE. THE MASTER FILE INPUT IS ALSO IN SORTED ORDER BY CHECK-NUMBER (MAJOR) AND INVOICE-NUMBER (MINOR). PROCESSING OF THIS FILE IS TO PROCEED AS FOLLOWS: READ THE INPUT FILE AND EDIT IT FOR NON-NEGATIVE NUMERIC DATA. READ THE OLD MASTER FILE UNTIL A MATCH IS FOUND BETWEEN THE CHECK NUMBERS ON THE TWO FILES. READ THE NEXT INPUT RECORD TO INSURE THAT THERE IS NO DUPLICATION OF CHECK NUMBERS. IF A DUPLICATE IS DISCOVERED DO NOT PROCESS ANY INPUT RECORDS WITH THAT CHECK NUMBER. REPORT ERRORS. CONTINUE TO READ UNTIL A NEW NUMBER IS ENCOUNTERED. REPEAT THE MATCH AND DUPLICATE CHECKING PROCEDURE. RECORDS ON THE OLD FILE FOR WHICH THERE IS NO MATCH CONDITION ARE WRITTEN TO THE NEW MASTER FILE AS THEY ARE ENCOUNTERED. PREPARE A LISTING OF THE NEW MASTER FILE. WHEN A VALID MATCH OCCURS FURTHER COMPARE THE VENDOR CODES AND THE ISSUE DATES. IF THERE IS A NO-MATCH CONDITION WRITE OUT AN ERROR REPORT AND REPEAT THE PROCESS. ON A MATCH OF THE ABOVE FIELDS UPDATE THE FLAG FIELD IN THE OLD MASTER RECORD AND WRITE THE RECORD TO THE NEW MASTER FILE. THE MASTER FILE WILL BE CYCLED, UPDATING, UNTIL A NEW CHECK NUMBER IS ENCOUNTERED. IF THE OLD MASTER FILE GOES TO END OF FILE BEFORE THE UPDATE INPUR FILE THIS WILL INVALIDATE THE NEW MASTER AND THE PROGRAM WILL HAVE TO BE RERUN. AT THE NORMAL END OF THE PROGRAM CYCLE ANY OF THE OLD MASTER REMAINING UNREAD TO THE NEW MASTER FILE.

THE PROGRAM WILL BE RUN IN A SMALL SHOP ENVIORNMENT. WHEN AN ERROR IS ENCOUNTERED, PLACE AN IMAGE OF THE INPUT ALONG WITH AN ERROR MESSAGE IN AN

```
IN-CORE TABLE.  PRINT THE ERROR TABLE AT THE END OF
THE PROGRAM SO AS NOT TO CONFLICT WITH THE LISTING OF
THE NEW MASTER FILE.  IF THERE ARE MORE ERRORS THAN
THE TABLE WILL HOLD DUMP THE ERROR TABLE INTO A FILE
, BOTH ON THE FULL CONDITION AND AT THE END OF THE
JOB, FOR SUBSEQUENT DUMPING ONTO THE PRINTER.  ISSUE
A MESSAGE THAT THIS HAS BEEN DONE.


*************************************************************

                DATA DICTIONARY

*************************************************************


A-CHECK                 INPUT RECORD OLD MASTER FILE
                        FILE IS PRE-EDITED
  A-VENDOR-IDENT        VENDOR NUMERIC CODE
  A-VENDOR-NAME         VENDOR NAME FROM VENDOR REGISTER
  A-CHECK-NUMBER        SEQUENTIAL CHECK NUMBER, FILE
                        HAS NO GAPS, MAJOR SORT FIELD
  A-ISSUE-DATE          DATE CHECK WRITTEN: MMDDYY
  A-INVOICE-NUMBER      IN SEQUENCE WITHIN CHECK NUMBER
                        MINOR SORT FIELD
  A-AMOUNT-PAID         DOLLAR VALUE OF CHECK
  A-VOID-FLAG           UPDATE FIELD FOR THIS PROGRAM
                        CONTAINS CODE FOR STOP PAYMENT
                        OR CODE FOR HAND PAYMENT
B-CARD                  INPUT RECORD, PROPOSED UPDATE FILE
  B-CHECK-NUMBER        SEE A-CHECK-NUMBER
                        RANGE 1 TO 99999999
                        FATAL IF NOT NUMERIC OR NEGATIVE
                        FATAL TO JOB IF NO MATCH WITH
                        INPUT MASTER FILE
  B-VENDOR-IDENT        SEE A-VENDOR-IDENT
                        RANGE 1 TO 999999
                        FATAL IF NOT NUMERIC OR NEGATIVE
                        FATAL IF NO MATCH WITH MASTER
                        FILE
  B-ISSUE-DATE          SEE A-ISSUE-DATE
                        FATAL IF NOT NUMERIC OR NEGATIVE
                        FATAL IF NO MATCH WITH MASTER
                        FILE
  B-AMOUNT-PAID         SEE A-AMOUNT-PAID
                        IGNORED FOR EDIT
  B-VOID-CATEGORY       SEE A-VOID-CATEGORY
                        FATAL IF NOT PRECISE VALUE
C-CHECK                 OUTPUT RECORD NEW MASTER FILE
  C-CHECK-REC           DATA NAME
D-PRINT-LINE            OUTPUT RECORD PRINTER LISTING OF
                        NEW MASTER FILE, ERROR LISTING
  D-PRINT-REC           DATA NAME
E-ERROR-IMAGE           OUTPUT RECORD DISK DUMP OF ERROR
                        TABLE LISTING
  E-ERROR-REC           DATA NAME
I-PRINTER-MESSAGES      REPORT HEADINGS AND ERROR
                        MESSAGES
```

```
  I-ERR-DUMP-MSG      ON TABLE OVERFLOW NOTE THAT ERROR
                      FILE DUMPED TO DISK
  I-REPORT-HEADING    HEADING FOR LISTING OF NEW MASTER
  I-INPUT-EDIT-MSG    FLAGS THAT LINE CONTAINING IMAGE
                      OF BAD IMPUT AND ERROR CODES
                      FOLLOWS
  ID-ERROR-MSG        ABORT MESSAGE ON BAD FILE
                      SORT SEQUENCE PROBLEM
  IC-ERROR-HEADING    HEADING FOR ERROR TABLE LISTING
  ID-PREMAT-ERROR     ABORT MESSAGE ON PREMATURE
                      TERMINATION OF MASTER FILE
J-PRINT-LINE          INPUT AREA FOR LOADING A LINE
                      IN ERROR TABLE
  J-PRINT-DATA        DATA NAME
K-ERROR-TABLE         SEE TABLE DIRECTORY
  K1-ERROR-REC        OCCURS DATA NAME
  K-REC-DEF           DATA NAME
L-CARD-WORK           WORK AREA FOR B-CARD INPUT
  L-CHECK-NUMBER      *  SEE CORRESPONDING ENTRY IN
  L-VENDOR-IDENT      *   B-CARD GROUP
  L-ISSUE-DATE        *
  L-AMOUNT-PAID       *
  L-VOID-CATEGORY     *
L-ERROR-NOTES         ERROR CODES LOADED BY EDIT
                      MODULES IN OUTPUT LINES
  L-CARD-REC          GROUP-NAME
L-ERROR-MSG           CONTAINS LITERAL "ERRORS" TO
                      PREFIX ERROR CODES IN EDIT LIST
L-ERROR-CODES         GROUP NAME OF SPACE TO LOAD CODES
  L-CHK-ERR           BAD EDIT,CHECK NUMBER "N"
  L-VEN-ERR           BAD EDIT, VENDOR-IDENT "V"
                      MISMATCH TO MASTER "R"
  L-DATE-ERR          BAD EDIT, ISSUE-DATE "I"
                      MISMATCH TO MASTER "S"
  L-AMOUNT-ERR        UNUSED
  L-CATEGORY-ERR      BAD EDIT, VOID-CATEGORY "C"
  L-DUPLICATE-ERR     ON DUPLICATE SUCCESSIVE CHECK
                      NUMBERS "D"
M-MASTER-WORK         WORK AREA FOR A-CHECK MASTER
                      INPUT
  M-MASTER-REC        GROUP NAME
  M-VENDOR-IDENT      *    SEE CORRESPONDING ENTRY
  M-VENDOR-NAME       *    IN A-CHECK GROUP FOR
  M-CHECK-NUMBER      *  DEFINITION
  M-ISSUE-DATE        *
  M-INVOICE-NUMBER    *
  M-AMOUNT-PAID       *
  M-VOID-FLAG         *
Q-CATEGORY-CODES      CODES FOR UPDATING MASTER CHECK
                      FILE
  Q-STOP-PAY-CODE       STOP PAYMENT ON CHECK "S"
  Q-HAND-PAY-CODE       HAND PAYMENT OF CHECK "H"
S-ERROR-CODES         CODES TO INDICATE DETAIL MISMATCH
                      BETWEEN INPUT AND MASTER FILE
  S-VEN-MATCH-CODE      VENDOR-IDENT MISMATCH "R"
  S-DATE-MATCH-CODE     ISSUE-DATE MISMATCH "S"
T-ERROR-CODES         DUPLICATION ERROR CODES
  T-DUPLICATE-CODE      SUCCESSIVE INPUT WITH SAME
```

```
                    CHECK NUMBERS "D"
V-ERROR-CODES      INPUT EDIT ERROR INDICATORS
  V-CHK-CODE         BAD CHECK NUMBER   "N"
  V-VEN-CODE         BAD VENDOR-IDENT   "V"
  V-DATE-CODE        BAD ISSUE DATE     "I"
  V-CATEGORY-CODE    BAD VOID CODE      "C"
```

```
*************************************************************

                  INDEX - FLAG DIRECTORY

*************************************************************
```

```
W-ANY-ERROR          INITIAL VALUE "N" IN W-S
                     RESET TO "Y" UPON ENTERING TA-ERR
                     -TAB;
                     USED TO DECIDE TO PROCESS ERROR
                     TABLE AT END OF JOB
W-BLANK-LINES        INITIAL VALUE 0 IN W-S
                     SET TO THE NUMBER OF BLANK LINE
                       IMAGES DESIRED AFTER A TRANSFER
                       OF A LINE OF DATA TO ERROR
                       TABLE
                     RESET TO 0 AFTER EACH USE IN TA-
                       ERR-TAB
W-BLOOP-INDEX        NO INITIAL VALUE
                     SET BY LOOP IN TS-BLANK-LOOP TO
                      PLACE BLANK LINES IN ERROR TABLE
W-DUP-LOOP           NO INITIAL VALUE
                     SET BY LOOP IN DA-DUP-CHECK TO
                      CONTROL READING NEW RECORDS
                      LIMITED BY W-SAFE-VALVE
W-ERR-LOOP           NO INITIAL VALUE
                     SET BY LOOP IN ZD-END-JOB
                     TO CONTROL TABLE PRINTING
                     LIMITED BY WI-INDEX-ERR.
W-GOOD-EDIT-FLAG     NO INITIAL VALUE
                     SET TO "Y" IN EN-DRIVER
                     RESET TO "N" IN EA-EDIT INPUT
                     IF FATAL ERROR FOUND IN EDITING
                        INPUT RECORD
W-HEADER-INDEX       INITIAL VALUE 0 IN W-S
                     SET TO 1 IN ACA-READ-LOAD TO
                     DESIGNATE MASTER LIST HEADINGS
                     SET TO 2 IN ZD-END-JOB TO
                     DESIGNATE ERROR LISTING HEADINGS
                     USED IN WQ-WRITE-LOOP TO CHOOSE
                      HEADER ROUTINE ON PAGE OVERFLOW
W-HEADING-LOOP       NO INITIAL VALUE
                     SET BY LOOP IN TQ-ERROR-HEADS
                     LIMITED BY W-PAGE-END
W-INPUT-EOF          INITIAL VALUE "N" IN W-S
                     SET TO "Y" IN RB-READ-INPUT
                     ON EOF CONDITION
W-LINE-CONTROL       INITIAL VALUE 1 IN W-S
```

	SET BEFORE A CALL TO WP-PRINT TO
	DESIRED NUMBER OF LINES TO
	CONTROL SPACING;
	SPACES WILL BE PROVIDED IRREGARD-
	LESS OF INTERVENING HEADERS;
	TO IGNORE REMAINING SPACING AT
	PAGE END PLACE < OR W-PAGE-END =
	PAGE END PLACE ' OR W-PAGE-END =
	"Y" ' AT END OF WP-LOOP
W-MASTER-EOF	INITIAL VALUE "N" IN W-S
	RESET TO "Y" ON MASTER FILE EOF
	IN RA-READ-MASTER
W-MATCH-FLAG	NO INITIAL VALUE
	SET TO "Y" IN MA-MATCH-CHECKS
	RESET TO "N" IN DD-DETAIL-MATCH
	IF NO MATCH HAS BEEN FOUND TO A
	MASTER RECORD CHECK NUMBER
W-MATCH-LOOP	NO INITIAL VALUE
	SET BY LOOP IN MA-MATCH-CHECKS
	CONTROL FINDING MASTER RECORDS
	LIMITED BY EOF ON MASTER FILE
W-PAGE-END	INITIAL VALUE "N" IN W-S
	SET TO "Y= IN WY-WRITE
	RESET TO "N" IN TP-END-PAGES
	RESET TO "N" IN TT-WRITE-BLANKS
	RESET TO "N" IN WQ-WRITE-LOOP
	INDICATES END OF PRINTER PAGE
W-NO-DUP-FLAG	NO INITIAL VALUE
	SET TO "Y" IN EN-DRIVER
	RESET TO "N" IN DA-DUP-CHECK
	IF DUPLICATE CHECK NUMBERS FOUND
	ON SUCCESSIVE INPUT CARDS
W-PRINTER-LOOP	NO INITIAL VALUE
	SET BY LOOP IN WP-PRINT TO
	CONTROL PRINTING OF DATA AND
	BLANK LINES WHICH FOLLOW
W-UPDATE-FLAG	INITIAL VALUE "N" IN W-S
	SET TO "Y" IN MA-MATCH-CHECKS
	WHEN UPDATE IS BEING EXECUTED
	WITH VOID OR STOP RATHER THAN
	CYCLE OF OLD TO NEW MASTER
	RESET TO "N" IN MA-MATCH-CHECKS
	USED BY UA-UPDATE
W-WRITE-SPACES	INITIAL VALUE 0 IN W-S
	SET TO NUMBER OF SPACED
	LINES DESIRED IN OUTPUT
	SET IN TQ-ERROR-HEADS
	TP-END-PAGE
	WA-PAGE-HEADING
	TESTED IN TT-WRITE-BLANKS
	RESET TO 0 IN TT-WRITE-BLANKS
WI-DUMP-INDEX	NO INITIAL VALUE
	SET BY LOOP IN ZN-FLUSH-LOOP TO
	CONTROL DUMP OF ERROR TABLE
	LIMITED BY CURRENT VALUE OF
	WI-INDEX-ERROR (100 AT TABLE
	OVERFLOW, LESS AT END OF JOB)
WI-ERRTAB-LIMIT	CONTROLS LOOP FOR ERROR TABLE IN

```
                      TA-TABLE-LOAD TO SIZE OF TABLE
W-ZLOOP               NO INITIAL VALUE
                      SET BY LOOP IN ZA-FLUSH-OLD
                       TO CONTROL CYCLING OF OLD TO NEW
                       MASTER
WI-INDEX-ERR          INITIAL VALUE 1 IN W-S
                      USED TO POINT TO NEXT AVAILABLE
                       SPACE IN ERROR TABLE IN TA-ERR-
                       TAB; INCREMENTED BY 1
                       VALUE LIMITED BY WI-ERRTAB-LIMIT
                       USED BY ZD-END-JOB TO EMPTY
                       ERROR TABLE
WZ-TABLE-FLUSH        INITIAL VALUE "N" IN W-S
                      RESET TO "Y" IF TABLE OVERFLOWS
                       DURING PROCESSING
                      USED TO DETERMINE ACTION TO BE
                       TAKEIN IN ZD-END-JOB


***********************************************************

                  TABLE DIRECTORY

***********************************************************


K-ERROR-TABLE  ACCOMODATES ERROR IMAGES. SIZE IS 132
               OCCURS 100 TIMES.


***********************************************************



ENVIRONMENT DIVISION.
CONFIGURATION SECTION.
SOURCE-COMPUTER. IBM-360-F40.
OBJECT-COMPUTER. IBM-360-F40.
INPUT-OUTPUT SECTION.
FILE-CONTROL.
    SELECT A-OLD-DISK   ASSIGN TO SYS005-UT-2400-S.
    SELECT B-CARDS-IN   ASSIGN TO SYS010-UR-2540R-S.
    SELECT C-NEW-DISK   ASSIGN TO SYS006-UT-2400-S.
    SELECT D-EDIT-LIST  ASSIGN TO SYS012-UR-1403-S
    RESERVE NO ALTERNATE AREA.
    SELECT E-ERROR-DISK ASSIGN TO SYS011-UR-2540P-S.


DATA DIVISION.
FILE SECTION.
FD  A-OLD-DISK
    BLOCK CONTAINS 5 RECORDS
    RECORD CONTAINS 80 CHARACTERS
    LABEL RECORDS ARE OMITTED
    DATA RECORD IS A-CHECK.
```

```
01  A-CHECK.
   05 A-VENDOR-IDENT       PICTURE X(6).
   05 A-VENDOR-NAME        PICTURE X(30).
   05 A-CHECK-NUMBER       PICTURE X(8).
   05 A-ISSUE-DATE         PICTURE X(6).
   05 A-INVOICE-NUMBER     PICTURE X(10).
   05 A-AMOUNT-PAID        PICTURE X(6).
   05 A-VOID-FLAG          PICTURE X.
   05 FILLER               PICTURE X(13).


FD  B-CARDS-IN
    LABEL RECORDS ARE OMITTED
    DATA RECORD IS B-CARD.
01  B-CARD.
   05 B-CHECK-NUMBER       PICTURE X(8).
   05 FILLER               PICTURE X.
   05 B-VENDOR-IDENT       PICTURE X(6).
   05 FILLER               PICTURE X.
   05 B-ISSUE-DATE         PICTURE X(6).
   05 FILLER               PICTURE X(2).
   05 B-AMOUNT-PAID        PICTURE X(6).
   05 FILLER               PICTURE X(2).
   05 B-VOID-CATEGORY      PICTURE X.
   05 FILLER               PICTURE X(47).


FD  C-NEW-DISK
    BLOCK CONTAINS 5 RECORDS
    RECORD CONTAINS 80 CHARACTERS
    LABEL RECORDS ARE OMITTED
    DATA RECORD IS C-CHECK.
01  C-CHECK.
   05 C-CHECK-REC          PICTURE X(80).


FD  D-EDIT-LIST
    LABEL RECORDS ARE OMITTED
    DATA RECORD IS D-PRINT-LINE.
01  D-PRINT-LINE.
   05 D-PRINT-REC          PICTURE X(132).


FD  E-ERROR-DISK
    LABEL RECORDS ARE OMITTED
    DATA RECORD IS E-ERROR-IMAGE.
01  E-ERROR-IMAGE.
   05 E-ERROR-REC          PICTURE X(80).


WORKING-STORAGE SECTION.

01  I-PRINTER-MESSAGES.
```

```
 05  I-ERR-DUMP-MSG       PICTURE X(132)  VALUE " ERRORS HAVE BEEN
-    "DUMPED TO DISK.  RUN PROGRAM AP111 TO OBTAIN ERROR REPORT
-    "                                                        ".
 05  I-REPORT-HEADING     PICTURE X(132)  VALUE " AP503 VOIDED CHEC
-    "K UPDATE REPORT.  ACCOUNTS PAYABLE SUB-SYSTEM
-    "                                                        ".
 05  I-INPUT-EDIT-MSG     PICTURE X(132)  VALUE " EDIT ERROR IN INP
-    "UT RECORD.
-    "                                                        ".
 05  IB-ERROR-MSG         PICTURE X(132)  VALUE " FILE MIS-MATCH JO
-    "B IS ABORTED.  DO NOT USE NEW MASTER.  EXAMINE DATA AND RE-R
-    "UN JOB.                                                 ".
 05  IC-ERROR-HEADING     PICTURE X(132)  VALUE " ERROR REPORT FOR
-    "CHECK VOIDING PROGRAM AP504.  ACCOUNTS PAYABLE SUB-SYSTEM.
-    "                                                        ".
 05  ID-PREMAT-ERROR      PICTURE X(132)  VALUE " PREMATURE END OF
-    "OLD MASTER FILE - ABORT JOB - EXAMINE DATE AND RE-RUN. DO NO
-    "T USE NEW MASTER FILE                                   ".

 01  J-PRINT-LINE.
     05  J-PRINT-DATA     PICTURE X(132).


 01  K-ERROR-TABLE.
     05 K1-ERROR-REC OCCURS 100 TIMES.
       10 K-REC-DEF       PICTURE X(132).


 01  L-CARD-WORK.
     05 L-CARD-REC.
        10 L-CHECK-NUMBER           PICTURE X(8).
        10 FILLER                   PICTURE X.
        10 L-VENDOR-IDENT           PICTURE X(6).
        10 FILLER                   PICTURE X.
        10 L-ISSUE-DATE             PICTURE X(6).
        10 FILLER                   PICTURE X(2).
        10 L-AMOUNT-PAID            PICTURE X(6).
        10 FILLER                   PICTURE X(2).
        10 L-VOID-CATEGORY          PICTURE X.
        10 FILLER                   PICTURE X(47).
     05 L-ERROR-NOTES.
        10 L-ERROR-MSG              PICTURE X(6).
        10 FILLER                   PICTURE X.
        10 L-ERROR-CODES.
           15 L-CHK-ERR             PICTURE X.
           15 L-VEN-ERR             PICTURE X.
           15 L-DATE-ERR            PICTURE X.
           15 L-AMOUNT-ERR          PICTURE X.
           15 L-CATEGORY-ERR        PICTURE X.
           15 L-DUPLICATE-ERR       PICTURE X.
        10 FILLER                   PICTURE X(39).
 01  M-MASTER-WORK.
     05 M-MASTER-RECORD.
        10 M-VENDOR-IDENT           PICTURE X(6).
        10 M-VENDOR-NAME            PICTURE X(30).
        10 M-CHECK-NUMBER           PICTURE X(8).
        10 M-ISSUE-DATE             PICTURE X(6).
        10 M-INVOICE-NUMBER         PICTURE X(10).
```

```
        10 M-AMOUNT-PAID            PICTURE X(6).
        10 M-VOID-FLAG              PICTURE X.
        10 FILLER                   PICTURE X(13).
     05 FILLER                      PICTURE X(52).


 01  Q-CATEGORY-CODES.
     05 Q-STOP-PAY-CODE    PICTURE X        VALUE "S".
     05 Q-HAND-PAY-CODE    PICTURE X        VALUE "H".

 01  S-ERROR-CODES.
     05 S-VEN-MATCH-CODE   PICTURE X        VALUE "R".
     05 S-DATE-MATCH-CODE  PICTURE X        VALUE "S".

 01  T-ERROR-CODES.
     05 T-DUPLICATE-CODE   PICTURE X        VALUE "D".

 01  V-ERROR-CODES.
     05 V-CHK-CODE         PICTURE X        VALUE "N".
     05 V-VEN-CODE         PICTURE X        VALUE "V".
     05 V-DATE-CODE        PICTURE X        VALUE "I".
     05 V-CATEGORY-CODE    PICTURE X        VALUE "C".


 01  W-WORKING-STORAGE.
 05  W-ANY-ERROR           PICTURE X        VALUE "N".
 05  W-BLANK-LINES         PICTURE 99       VALUE 00.
 05  W-BLOOP-INDEX         PICTURE 99.
 05  W-DUP-LOOP            PICTURE 9999.
 05  W-ERR-LOOP            PICTURE 999.
 05  W-GOOD-EDIT-FLAG      PICTURE X.
 05  W-HEADER-INDEX        PICTURE 99       VALUE 00.
 05  W-HEADING-LOOP        PICTURE 99.
 05  W-INPUT-EOF           PICTURE X        VALUE "N".
 05  W-LINE-CONTROL        PICTURE 99       VALUE 01.
 05  W-MATCH-FLAG          PICTURE X.
 05  W-MASTER-EOF          PICTURE X        VALUE "N".
 05  W-MATCH-LOOP          PICTURE 99999.
 05  W-NO-DUP-FLAG         PICTURE X.
 05  W-PAGE-END            PICTURE X        VALUE "N".
 05  W-PRINTER-LOOP        PICTURE 99.
 05  W-UPDATE-FLAG         PICTURE X        VALUE "N".
 05  W-WRITE-SPACES        PICTURE 99       VALUE 00.
 05  W-ZLOOP               PICTURE 999.
 05  WI-DUMP-INDEX         PICTURE 999.
 05  WI-ERRTAB-LIMIT       PICTURE 999      VALUE 100.
 05  WI-INDEX-ERR          PICTURE 999      VALUE 001.
 05  WZ-TABLE-FLUSH        PICTURE X        VALUE "N".


 PROCEDURE DIVISION.


 AA-NOTE.
     NOTE              IF END-OF-FILE FOUND DURING
                       INITIALIZATION, TERMINATE RUN.
```

```
AA-MAIN-LINE.
    PERFORM AB-INITIALIZE THRU ABX-INITIALIZE-X.
    IF W-MASTER-EOF = "Y"
        OR
        W-INPUT-EOF = "Y"
        PERFORM SD-PREMATURE-EOF THRU SDX-PREMATURE-EOF-X
        GO TO AAN-LAST-TASK.
    PERFORM AF-DRIVER THRU AFX-DRIVER-X.
AAN-LAST-TASK.
    PERFORM ZD-END-JOB THRU ZDX-END-JOB-X.
AAX-MAINLINE-X.
    STOP RUN.



AB-NOTE.
    NOTE            OPEN FILES
                    READ FIRST INPUT RECORD
                    READ FIRST MASTER RECORD
                    PRINT PAGE HEADINGS FOR NEW MASTER LISTING
                    CLEAR STORAGE.

AB-INITIALIZE.
    OPEN INPUT A-OLD-DISK, B-CARDS-IN.
    OPEN OUTPUT C-NEW-DISK, D-EDIT-LIST, E-ERROR-DISK.
ABA-LOAD-READ.
    PERFORM RA-READ-MASTER THRU RAX-READ-MASTER-X.
    PERFORM RB-READ-INPUT THRU RBX-READ-INPUT-X.
ABD-HEADING.
    PERFORM TP-END-PAGE THRU TPX-END-PAGE-X.
    MOVE 1 TO W-HEADER-INDEX.
    PERFORM WA-PAGE-HEADING THRU WAX-PAGE-HEADING-X.
ABF-CLEAR-WORK.
    MOVE SPACES TO L-CARD-WORK.
    MOVE SPACES TO M-MASTER-WORK.
ABX-INITIALIZE-X.
    EXIT.



AF-NOTE.
    NOTE            IF BOTH FILES HAVE REACHED EOF
                       INPUT PROCESSING IS TERMINATED
                    IF ONLY THE INPUT FILE HAS TERMINATED
                       CYCLE THE REMAINING OLD MASTER TO THE NEW
                    IF ONLY THE MASTER FILE HAS TERMINATED
                       SOME ERROR HAS OCCURRED
                       DECLARE THE RUN INVALID
                       ABORT THE RUN --- GRACEFULLY
                    IF THE INPUT EOF FLAG IS SET TO "Y" HERE THE
                    LAST RECORD HAS BEEN PROCESSED.

AF-DRIVER.
    IF W-INPUT-EOF = "Y"
       AND W-MASTER-EOF = "Y"
       GO TO AFX-DRIVER-X.
    IF W-INPUT-EOF = "Y"
       PERFORM ZA-FLUSH-OLD THRU ZAX-FLUSH-OLD-X
```

```
          GO TO AFX-DRIVER-X.
      IF W-MASTER-EOF = "Y"
          PERFORM SD-PREMATURE-EOF THRU SDX-PREMATURE-EOF-X
          GO TO AFX-DRIVER-X.
      PERFORM EN-DRIVER THRU ENX-DRIVER-X.
      GO TO AF-DRIVER.
 AFX-DRIVER-X.
      EXIT.


 DA-NOTE.
     NOTE                CHECK FOR EOF FLAG
                         CHECK FOR DUPLICATE CHECK NUMBERS IN
                         SUCCESSIVE INPUT CARDS
                          COMPARISON IS MADE BETWEEN INPUT AND WORK
                           AREAS;
                           IF A DUPLICATE IS FOUND
                                 SET ERROR FLAG IN RECORD
                                 RESET W-NO-DUP-FLAG
                                 CYCLE INPUT UNTIL A RECORD IS FOUND
                                  WITH A DIFFERENT CHECK NUMBER
                         EXIT ON END OF FILE.

 DA-DUP-CHECK.
      IF W-INPUT-EOF = "Y"
           GO TO DAX-DUP-CHECK-X.
      IF B-CHECK-NUMBER = L-CHECK-NUMBER
          MOVE T-DUPLICATE-CODE TO L-DUPLICATE-ERR
           MOVE "N" TO W-NO-DUP-FLAG
           PERFORM RB-READ-INPUT THRU RBX-READ-INPUT-X
                VARYING W-DUP-LOOP FROM 1 BY 1 UNTIL
                B-CHECK-NUMBER NOT = L-CHECK-NUMBER
                OR
                W-INPUT-EOF = "Y".
 DAX-DUP-CHECK-X.
      EXIT.


 DD-NOTE.
     NOTE                MATCH OTHER FIELDS BETWEEN INPUT AND OLD
                          MASTER; IF NO MATCH SET FLAG FOR REJECT .

 DD-DETAIL-MATCH.
      MOVE SPACES TO L-ERROR-CODES.
      IF M-VENDOR-IDENT NOT = L-VENDOR-IDENT
          MOVE S-VEN-MATCH-CODE TO L-VEN-ERR.
      IF M-ISSUE-DATE NOT = L-ISSUE-DATE
          MOVE S-DATE-MATCH-CODE TO L-DATE-ERR.
      IF L-ERROR-CODES NOT = SPACES
           MOVE "N" TO W-MATCH-FLAG.
 DDX-DETAIL-MATCH-X.
      EXIT.


 EA-NOTE.
```

```
    NOTE              EDIT THE INPUT RECORD FOR NUMERIC
                                               POSITIVE
                      IN THE CASE OF B-VOID CATEGORY SPECIFICALLY
                                             "S" OR "H"
                      IGNORE AMOUNT FIELD CURRENTLY
                      ON ANY ERROR RESET W-GOOD-EDIT-FLAG
                      NN-FETCH-INPUT HAS PLACED THE RECORD IN
                            L-CARD-WORK.
*
 EA-EDIT-INPUT.
     MOVE SPACES TO L-ERROR-CODES.
     IF L-CHECK-NUMBER NOT NUMERIC
        OR
        L-CHECK-NUMBER LESS THAN ZERO
        MOVE V-CHK-CODE TO L-CHK-ERR.
     IF L-VENDOR-IDENT NOT NUMERIC
        OR
        L-VENDOR-IDENT LESS THAN ZERO
        MOVE V-VEN-CODE TO L-VEN-ERR.
     IF L-ISSUE-DATE NOT NUMERIC
        OR
        L-ISSUE-DATE LESS THAN ZERO
        MOVE V-DATE-CODE TO L-DATE-ERR.
     IF L-VOID-CATEGORY = Q-STOP-PAY-CODE
        OR
         L-VOID-CATEGORY = Q-HAND-PAY-CODE
         GO TO EAD-CHECK-FLAGS.
     MOVE V-CATEGORY-CODE TO L-CATEGORY-ERR.
 EAD-CHECK-FLAGS.
     IF L-ERROR-CODES NOT = SPACES
        MOVE "N" TO W-GOOD-EDIT-FLAG.
 EAX-EDIT-INPUT-X.
     EXIT.



 EN-NOTE.
     NOTE             OBTAIN AN INPUT RECORD
                          GET IT EDITED AND
                          CHECKED FOR DUPLICATES
                      IF NO ERROR TRY FOR MATCH TO MASTER FILE
                          ELSE REPORT ERRORS AND EXIT
                      INPUT-EOF MAY BE RESET IN DA
                      MASTER-EOF MAY BE RESET IN MA.

 EN-DRIVER.
     PERFORM NN-FETCH-INPUT THRU NNX-FETCH-INPUT-X.
     MOVE "Y" TO W-GOOD-EDIT-FLAG.
     PERFORM EA-EDIT-INPUT THRU EAX-EDIT-INPUT-X.
     MOVE "Y" TO W-NO-DUP-FLAG.
     PERFORM DA-DUP-CHECK THRU DAX-DUP-CHECK-X.
     IF W-NO-DUP-FLAG = "N"
        OR
        W-GOOD-EDIT-FLAG = "N"
        PERFORM SA-EDIT-EXCPT THRU SAX-EDIT-EXCPT-X
        GO TO ENX-DRIVER-X.
     PERFORM MA-MATCH-CHECKS THRU MAX-MATCH-CHECKS-X.
 ENX-DRIVER-X.
```

```
     EXIT.


MA-NOTE.
     NOTE               OBTAIN A MASTER RECORD
                        COMPARE CHECK NUMBER WITH CURRENT INPUT
                        IF EQUAL GO TO DETAIL CHECK
                            IF MASTER LESS THAN INPUT
                                UPDATE NEW MASTER WITH INTERVENING
                                RECORD AND RECYCLE IF INPUT FILE NOT
                                EOF;
                            IF MASTER GREATER THAN INPUT
                               REPORT ERROR AND ABORT RUN;
                        DETAIL CHECK:
                        GET A DETAILED MATCH
                            IF DETAIL FAILS
                            UPDATE NEW MASTER WITH INTERVENING
                            RECORD AND EXIT
                        IF DETAIL CHECK SUCCEEDS UPDATE
                        INDICATE VOID UPDATE WITH FLAG
                        SINCE NO DUPLICATE INPUT CHECK NUMBERS WILL
                            REACH THIS PARAGRAPH THE MASTER RECORDS
                            INVOICE NUMBER WILL BE PASSED.

MA-MATCH-CHECKS.
     PERFORM NM-FETCH-MASTER THRU NMX-FETCH-MASTER-X.
     IF M-CHECK-NUMBER = L-CHECK-NUMBER
          GO TO MAD-DETAIL.
     IF M-CHECK-NUMBER LESS THAN L-CHECK-NUMBER
          PERFORM UA-UPDATE THRU UAX-UPDATE-X
          GO TO MAF-EOF-CHECK.
     PERFORM SF-BAD-FILE THRU SFX-BAD-FILE-X.
          GO TO MAX-MATCH-CHECKS-X.
MAF-EOF-CHECK.
     IF W-MASTER-EOF = "Y"
          GO TO MAX-MATCH-CHECKS-X.
     GO TO MA-MATCH-CHECKS.
MAD-DETAIL.
     MOVE "Y" TO W-MATCH-FLAG.
     PERFORM DD-DETAIL-MATCH THRU DDX-DETAIL-MATCH-X.
     IF W-MATCH-FLAG = "N"
          PERFORM SA-EDIT-EXCPT THRU SAX-EDIT-EXCPT-X
          PERFORM UA-UPDATE THRU UAX-UPDATE-X
          GO TO MAX-MATCH-CHECKS-X.
     MOVE "Y" TO W-UPDATE-FLAG.
     PERFORM UA-UPDATE THRU UAX-UPDATE-X.
     MOVE "N" TO W-UPDATE-FLAG.
MAX-MATCH-CHECKS-X.
     EXIT.


NM-NOTE.
     NOTE               MOVE MASTER RECORD FROM READ AREA TO WORK
                            AREA;
                        READ NEXT RECORD.
```

```
NM-FETCH-MASTER.
    MOVE A-CHECK TO M-MASTER-RECORD.
    PERFORM RA-READ-MASTER THRU RAX-READ-MASTER-X.
NMX-FETCH-MASTER-X.
    EXIT.



NN-NOTE.
    NOTE               INPUT RECORD FETCH
                       MOVE RECORD FROM READ AREA TO WORK AREA
                       READ NEXT RECORD.

NN-FETCH-INPUT.
    MOVE B-CARD TO L-CARD-REC.
    PERFORM RB-READ-INPUT THRU RBX-READ-INPUT-X.
NNX-FETCH-INPUT-X.
    EXIT.



RA-NOTE.
    NOTE               READ MASTER-FILE INDICATING EOF.

RA-READ-MASTER.
    READ A-OLD-DISK
       AT END
       MOVE "Y" TO W-MASTER-EOF.
RAX-READ-MASTER-X.
    EXIT.



RB-NOTE.
    NOTE               READ INPUT-FILE INDICATING EOF.

RB-READ-INPUT.
    READ B-CARDS-IN
       AT END
       MOVE "Y" TO W-INPUT-EOF.
RBX-READ-INPUT-X.
    EXIT.



SA-NOTE.
    NOTE               SET "ERRORS" IN INPUT LINE, PLACE ERROR
                       MESSAGE AND BLANK LINE IN ERROR TABLE.

SA-EDIT-EXCPT.
    MOVE "ERRORS" TO L-ERROR-MSG.
    MOVE I-INPUT-EDIT-MSG TO J-PRINT-LINE.
    PERFORM TA-ERR-TAB THRU TAX-ERR-TAB-X.
    MOVE L-CARD-WORK TO J-PRINT-LINE.
    MOVE 1 TO W-BLANK-LINES.
    PERFORM TA-ERR-TAB THRU TAX-ERR-TAB-X.
SAX-EDIT-EXCPT-X.
    EXIT.
```

```
SD-NOTE.
    NOTE              MASTER-FILE HAS ENDED PREMATURELY, PLACE
                      ABORT ERROR IN ERROR TABLE AND ON PRINTER
                      USE SIGNIFICANT SPACING.

SD-PREMATURE-EOF.
    MOVE ID-PREMAT-ERROR TO J-PRINT-LINE.
    PERFORM TA-ERR-TAB THRU TAX-ERR-TAB-X.
    MOVE ID-PREMAT-ERROR TO D-PRINT-LINE.
    MOVE 4 TO W-LINE-CONTROL.
    PERFORM WP-PRINT THRU WPX-PRINT-X.
SDX-PREMATURE-EOF-X.
    EXIT.


SF-NOTE.
    NOTE              A SEQUENCE MIS-MATCH HAS BEEN FOUND BETWEEN
                      MASTER FILE AND INPUT FILE;
                      ABORT JOB BY TURNING ON ALL EOF FLAGS
                      REPORT ERROR ACTION IN ERROR TABLE AND ON
                      PRINTER WITH SIGNIFICANT SPACING.

SF-BAD-FILE.
    MOVE "Y" TO W-INPUT-EOF.
    MOVE "Y" TO W-MASTER-EOF.
    MOVE IB-ERROR-MSG TO J-PRINT-LINE.
    PERFORM TA-ERR-TAB THRU TAX-ERR-TAB-X.
    MOVE IB-ERROR-MSG TO D-PRINT-LINE.
    MOVE 4 TO W-LINE-CONTROL.
    PERFORM WP-PRINT  THRU WPX-PRINT-X.
SFX-BAD-FILE-X.
    EXIT.


TA-NOTE.
    NOTE              ERROR MESSAGES ARE HANDLED BY THIS ROUTINE;
                      NORMALLY THE ROUTINE WILL MOVE THE CONTENTS
                      OF J-PRINT-LINE TO THE NEXT AVAILABLE SLOT
                      (INDEXED BY WI-INDEX-ERR) BUT ON TABLE FULL
                      CONDITION TABLE IS DUMPED TO DISK AND THE
                      INDEX VALUES RESET;
                      IF NOT ZERO W-BLANK-LINES CONTROLS PLACING
                      BLANK LINES IN ERROR TABLE FOR INCREASED
                      READABILITY OF ERROR DUMP; RESET W-BLANK-LINE
                      TO ZERO AFTER EACH USE.

TA-ERR-TAB.
    MOVE "Y" TO W-ANY-ERROR.
    MOVE J-PRINT-LINE TO K1-ERROR-REC (WI-INDEX-ERR).
    PERFORM TN-TABLE-LOOP THRU TNX-TABLE-LOOP-X.
    IF W-BLANK-LINES NOT = ZERO
        PERFORM TS-BLANK-LOOP THRU TSX-BLANK-LOOP-X
            VARYING W-BLOOP-INDEX FROM 1 BY 1 UNTIL
```

```
          W-BLOOP-INDEX GREATER THAN W-BLANK-LINES
       MOVE 0 TO W-BLANK-LINES.
TAX-ERR-TAB-X.
    EXIT.



TN-NOTE.
    NOTE             CONTROL INDEXING AND OVERFLOW OF ERROR TABLE
                     RESET INDEX ON OVERFLOW TO DISK.

TN-TABLE-LOOP.
    ADD 1 TO WI-INDEX-ERR.
    IF WI-INDEX-ERR GREATER THAN WI-ERRTAB-LIMIT
        MOVE "Y" TO WZ-TABLE-FLUSH
       PERFORM  ZN-FLUSH-LOOP THRU ZNX-FLUSH-LOOP-X
       MOVE 1 TO WI-INDEX-ERR.
TNX-TABLE-LOOP-X.
    EXIT.



TP-NOTE.
    NOTE             FINDS END-OF-PAGE THEN ADVANCES TO TOP
                     OF NEXT PAGE.

TP-END-PAGE.
    MOVE SPACES TO D-PRINT-LINE.
    MOVE "N" TO W-PAGE-END.
    PERFORM WY-WRITE THRU WYX-WRITE-X
        VARYING W-HEADING-LOOP FROM 1 BY 1
        UNTIL W-PAGE-END = "Y".
    MOVE 4 TO W-WRITE-SPACES.
    PERFORM TT-WRITE-BLANKS THRU TTX-WRITE-BLANKS-X.
TPX-END-PAGE-X.
    EXIT.



TQ-NOTE.
    NOTE             WRITES ERROR LISTING HEADINGS WITH PROPER
                     SPACING.

TQ-ERROR-HEADS.
    MOVE IC-ERROR-HEADING TO D-PRINT-LINE.
    PERFORM WY-WRITE THRU WYX-WRITE-X.
    MOVE SPACES TO D-PRINT-LINE.
    MOVE 4 TO W-WRITE-SPACES.
    PERFORM TT-WRITE-BLANKS THRU TTX-WRITE-BLANKS-X.
TQX-ERROR-HEADS-X.
    EXIT.



TR-NOTE.
    NOTE             MOVE TABLE LINES TO PRINT OUTPUT AREA,
                     PERFORM PRINT.
```

```
TR-TABLE-LOOP.
    MOVE K1-ERROR-REC (W-ERR-LOOP) TO D-PRINT-LINE.
    PERFORM WP-PRINT THRU WPX-PRINT-X.
TRX-TABLE-LOOP-X.
    EXIT.



TS-NOTE.
    NOTE              LOAD BLANK LINE INTO TABLE.

TS-BLANK-LOOP.
    MOVE SPACES TO K1-ERROR-REC (WI-INDEX-ERR).
    PERFORM TN-TABLE-LOOP THRU TNX-TABLE-LOOP-X.
TSX-BLANK-LOOP-X.
    EXIT.



TT-NOTE.
    NOTE              WRITE NUMBER OF BLANK LINES ON PRINTER
                      SPECIFIED BY W-WRITE-SPACES UP TO PAGE-END.

TT-WRITE-BLANKS.
    MOVE "N" TO W-PAGE-END.
    PERFORM WY-WRITE THRU WYX-WRITE-X
        VARYING W-HEADING-LOOP FROM 1 BY 1 UNTIL
        W-HEADING-LOOP GREATER THAN W-WRITE-SPACES
        OR
        W-PAGE-END = "Y".
    MOVE ZERO TO W-WRITE-SPACES.
TTX-WRITE-BLANKS-X.
    EXIT.



UA-NOTE.
    NOTE              CHECK FOR UPDATE OF VOID-FIELD AND MOVE
                      UPDATE INFO IN, OTHERWISE GET NEW MASTER
                      IMAGE WRITTEN OF DISK, PRINTED ON PRINTER
                      IF END OF FILE NOT SET
                          CHECK READ AREA FOR REPEAT OF CHECK
                          NUMBER
                              IF REPEAT, CYCLE, WRITING OUT UNTIL
                               NO REPEAT OR EOF.

UA-UPDATE.
    IF W-UPDATE-FLAG = "Y"
        MOVE L-VOID-CATEGORY TO M-VOID-FLAG.
    MOVE M-MASTER-WORK TO C-CHECK.
    PERFORM UN-UPDATE-WRITE THRU UNX-UPDATE-WRITE-X.
    MOVE M-MASTER-RECORD TO D-PRINT-LINE.
    PERFORM WP-PRINT THRU WPX-PRINT-X.
UAC-CYCLE-LOOP.
    IF W-MASTER-EOF = "Y"
        GO TO UAX-UPDATE-X.
    IF M-CHECK-NUMBER = A-CHECK-NUMBER
        PERFORM NM-FETCH-MASTER THRU NMX-FETCH-MASTER-X
```

```
          GO TO UA-UPDATE.
UAX-UPDATE-X.
     EXIT.



UN-NOTE.
     NOTE               WRITE NEW MASTER FILE.

UN-UPDATE-WRITE.
     WRITE C-CHECK.
UNX-UPDATE-WRITE-X.
     EXIT.



WA-NOTE.
     NOTE               WRITE NEW MASTER FILE LISTING HEADING WITH
                        PROPER SPACING.

WA-PAGE-HEADING.
     MOVE I-REPORT-HEADING TO D-PRINT-LINE.
     PERFORM WY-WRITE THRU WYX-WRITE-X.
     MOVE SPACES TO D-PRINT-LINE.
     MOVE 4 TO W-WRITE-SPACES.
     PERFORM TT-WRITE-BLANKS THRU TTX-WRITE-BLANKS-X.
WAX-PAGE-HEADING-X.
     EXIT.



WD-NOTE.
     NOTE               MOVE TABLE LINE TO OUTPUT AREA.

WD-WRITE-OUT.
     MOVE K1-ERROR-REC (WI-DUMP-INDEX) TO E-ERROR-IMAGE.
     PERFORM WE-WRITE-E THRU WEX-WRITE-E-X.
WDX-WRITE-OUT-X.
     EXIT.



WE-NOTE.
     NOTE               WRITE DISK.

WE-WRITE-E.
     WRITE E-ERROR-IMAGE.
WEX-WRITE-E-X.
     EXIT.



WP-NOTE.
     NOTE               PRINTER CONTROL ROUTINE, PLACE LINES ON
                        PRINTER, PRINTING PAGE HEADINGS AS SPECIFIED
                        IN GO TO LIST UNDER CONTROL OF W-HEADER-INDEX
                        DETERMINE NUMBER OF BLANK LINES DESIRED AFTER
                        PRINTING; DEFAULT IS ONE;
```

```
                         W-LINE-CONTROL CONTAINS NUMBER OF LINES TO BE
                          SKIPPED;
                                    SPACES WILL BE PROVIDED IRREGARD-
                                     LESS OF INTERVENING HEADERS;
                                    TO IGNORE REMAINING SPACING AT
                                     PAGE END PLACE < OR W-PAGE-END =
                                     "Y" > AT END OF WP-LOOP
                         W-HEADER-INDEX IS SET GLOBALLY TO OBTAIN
                          DIFFERENT REPORT HEADERS.

WP-PRINT.
    IF W-LINE-CONTROL LESS THAN 1
        MOVE 1 TO W-LINE-CONTROL.
    PERFORM WQ-WRITE-LOOP THRU WQX-WRITE-LOOP-X
        VARYING W-PRINTER-LOOP FROM 1 BY 1 UNTIL
        W-PRINTER-LOOP GREATER THAN W-LINE-CONTROL.
WPX-PRINT-X.
    EXIT.

WQ-WRITE-LOOP.
    MOVE "N" TO W-PAGE-END.
    PERFORM WY-WRITE THRU WYX-WRITE-X.
    MOVE SPACES TO D-PRINT-LINE.
    IF W-PAGE-END = "Y"
        GO TO
            WQC-HEAD-1
            WQF-HEAD-2
            DEPENDING ON W-HEADER-INDEX.
    GO TO WQX-WRITE-LOOP-X.
WQC-HEAD-1.
    PERFORM WA-PAGE-HEADING THRU WAX-PAGE-HEADING-X.
    GO TO WQX-WRITE-LOOP-X.
WQF-HEAD-2.
    PERFORM TQ-ERROR-HEADS THRU TQX-ERROR-HEADS-X.
WQX-WRITE-LOOP-X.
    EXIT.



WY-NOTE.
    NOTE             WRITE PRINTER FLAGGING END-OF-PAGE CONDITION.

WY-WRITE.
    WRITE D-PRINT-LINE BEFORE ADVANCING 1 LINES
      AT END-OF-PAGE
      MOVE "Y" TO W-PAGE-END.
WYX-WRITE-X.
    EXIT.



ZA-NOTE.
    NOTE             END OF INPUT
                      CYCLE OLD MASTER RECORDS REMAINING TO
                      NEW MASTER.

ZA-FLUSH-OLD.
    PERFORM ZL-FLUSH-LOOP THRU ZLX-FLUSH-LOOP-X
```

```
           VARYING W-ZLOOP FROM 1 BY 1 UNTIL
           W-MASTER-EOF = "Y".
ZAX-FLUSH-OLD-X.
    EXIT.



ZD-NOTE.
    NOTE               END OF JOB PROCESSING
                       CHECK TO SEE IF ERROR OCCURRED
                           CHECK TO SEE IF TABLE OVERFLOWED
                           CHECK INDEX TO SEE IF ANY ENTRIES IN
                           ERROR TABLE
                           IF SO DUMP REMAINING ERROR TABLE TO SAME
                           MEDIA
                       REPORT EVENT ON PRINTER
                       OTHERWISE PRINT ERROR TABLE
                       CLOSE FILES.

ZD-END-JOB.
    IF W-ANY-ERROR NOT = "Y"
        GO TO ZDR-CLOSE-FILES.
    IF WZ-TABLE-FLUSH NOT = "Y"
        GO TO ZDP-PRINT-TABLES.
    IF WI-INDEX-ERR NOT GREATER THAN 1
        GO TO ZDR-CLOSE-FILES.
    PERFORM ZN-FLUSH-LOOP THRU ZNX-FLUSH-LOOP-X.
    MOVE I-ERR-DUMP-MSG TO D-PRINT-LINE.
    MOVE 2 TO W-LINE-CONTROL.
    PERFORM WP-PRINT THRU WPX-PRINT-X.
    GO TO ZDR-CLOSE-FILES.
ZDP-PRINT-TABLES.
    MOVE 2 TO W-HEADER-INDEX.
    PERFORM TP-END-PAGE THRU TPX-END-PAGE-X.
    PERFORM TQ-ERROR-HEADS THRU TQX-ERROR-HEADS-X.
    PERFORM TR-TABLE-LOOP THRU TRX-TABLE-LOOP-X
        VARYING W-ERR-LOOP FROM 1 BY 1
        UNTIL W-ERR-LOOP = WI-INDEX-ERR.
ZDR-CLOSE-FILES.
    PERFORM ZZ-CLOSE THRU ZZX-CLOSE-X.
ZDX-END-JOB-X.
    EXIT.



ZL-NOTE.
    NOTE               CYCLE REMAINING OLD MASTER-FILE RECORDS
                       TO NEW MASTER FILE.

ZL-FLUSH-LOOP.
    PERFORM NM-FETCH-MASTER THRU NMX-FETCH-MASTER-X.
    MOVE M-MASTER-WORK TO C-CHECK.
    PERFORM UN-UPDATE-WRITE THRU UNX-UPDATE-WRITE-X.
ZLX-FLUSH-LOOP-X.
    EXIT.
```

```
ZN-NOTE.
    NOTE              CYCLE REMAINING ERROR TABLE ENTRIES TO DISK.

ZN-FLUSH-LOOP.
    PERFORM  WD-WRITE-OUT THRU WDX-WRITE-OUT-X
         VARYING WI-DUMP-INDEX FROM 1 BY 1 UNTIL
         WI-DUMP-INDEX = WI-INDEX-ERR.
ZNX-FLUSH-LOOP-X.
    EXIT.



ZZ-NOTE.
    NOTE              CLOSE FILES.

ZZ-CLOSE.
    CLOSE  A-OLD-DISK, B-CARDS-IN
    CLOSE  C-NEW-DISK, D-EDIT-LIST, E-ERROR-DISK.
ZZX-CLOSE-X.
    EXIT.
ZZZ-END.
    STOP RUN.
```

```
IDENTIFICATION DIVISION.
PROGRAM-ID. PAYEXEC.
REMARKS.    SYSTEM:
            END OF REMARKS.
ENVIRONMENT DIVISION.
CONFIGURATION SECTION.
SOURCE-COMPUTER. IBM-360-F40.
OBJECT-COMPUTER. IBM-360-F40.
DATA DIVISION.


WORKING-STORAGE SECTION.
01  A-PRINTER-LINES.

    05 A-START-MSG          PICTURE X(24) VALUE 'BEGIN WORKING STORAG
-     'E    '.

    05 A-BANNER-LINE        PICTURE X(132)  VALUE ' BEGINNING AP503/5
-     '04 SUB-SYSTEM
-     '                                                              '.
    05 A-TRAILER-LINE       PICTURE X(132)  VALUE ' ENDING AP503/504
-     'SUB-SYSTEM
-     '                                                              '.


01  P-PRINTER-INTERFACE.
    05 PA-PROCESS.
      10 PA-PRINT-LINE      PICTURE X(132).
      10 PA-HEADINGS OCCURS 5 TIMES.
         15 PA-HEAD         PICTURE X(132).
    05 PC-CONTROL.
      10 PC-OP-CODE         PICTURE 9(4) COMP.
      10 PC-NUMBER-LINES    PICTURE 9(4) COMP.
      10 PC-HEAD-LINES      PICTURE 9(4) COMP.
    05 PW-STABLE-WORK.
      10 PW-PAGE-END        PICTURE X.
      10 PW-PAGE-NUMBER     PICTURE 9(4) COMP.


01  WX-WORKING-STORAGE.
    05 WX-STORE OCCURS 80 TIMES.
      10 WX-REC             PICTURE X(100).

    05 WX-END-MSG           PICTURE X(24) VALUE 'END OF WORKING STORA
-     'GE  '.


PROCEDURE DIVISION.


AA-MAINLINE.
     PERFORM HA-HOUSEKEEP THRU HAX-HOUSEKEEP-X.
     CALL 'AP503' USING P-PRINTER-INTERFACE
                        WX-WORKING-STORAGE.
     PERFORM ZA-CLEAN-UP THRU ZAX-CLEAN-UP-X.
AAX-MAINLINE-X.
```

```
     STOP RUN.


 HA-HOUSEKEEP.
     MOVE 0 TO PC-OP-CODE.
     CALL 'PRINTER' USING P-PRINTER-INTERFACE
                          WX-WORKING-STORAGE.
     MOVE A-BANNER-LINE TO PA-PRINT-LINE.
     MOVE 1 TO PC-OP-CODE.
     MOVE 2 TO PC-NUMBER-LINES.
     MOVE 0 TO PC-HEAD-LINES.
     CALL 'PRINTER' USING P-PRINTER-INTERFACE
                          WX-WORKING-STORAGE.
 HAX-HOUSEKEEP-X.
     EXIT.


 ZA-CLEAN-UP.
     MOVE A-TRAILER-LINE TO PA-PRINT-LINE.
     MOVE 1 TO PC-OP-CODE.
     MOVE 0 TO PC-NUMBER-LINES.
     MOVE 0 TO PC-HEAD-LINES.
     CALL 'PRINTER' USING P-PRINTER-INTERFACE
                          WX-WORKING-STORAGE.
     MOVE 2 TO PC-OP-CODE.
     CALL 'PRINTER' USING P-PRINTER-INTERFACE
                          WX-WORKING-STORAGE.
 ZAX-CLEAN-UP-X.
     EXIT.
```

```
IDENTIFICATION DIVISION.
PROGRAM-ID. PAYMAIN.
REMARKS.     SYSTEM:
             END OF REMARKS.
ENVIRONMENT DIVISION.
CONFIGURATION SECTION.
SOURCE-COMPUTER. IBM-360-F40.
OBJECT-COMPUTER. IBM-360-F40.
INPUT-OUTPUT SECTION.
    SELECT C-NEW-DISK   ASSIGN TO SYS006-UT-2400-S.
DATA DIVISION.
FILE SECTION.
FD  C-NEW-DISK
    BLOCK CONTAINS 5 RECORDS
    RECORD CONTAINS 80 CHARACTERS
    LABEL RECORDS ARE OMITTED
    DATA RECORD IS C-CHECK.
01  C-CHECK.
   05 C-CHECK-REC       PICTURE X(80).
WORKING-STORAGE SECTION.
01  I-PRINTER-MESSAGES.
05  I-ERR-DUMP-MSG      PICTURE X(132)  VALUE " ERRORS HAVE BEEN
-    "DUMPED TO DISK.  RUN PROGRAM AP111 TO OBTAIN ERROR REPORT
-    "                                                          ".
05  I-REPORT-HEADING    PICTURE X(132)  VALUE " AP503 VOIDED CHEC
-    "K UPDATE REPORT.  ACCOUNTS PAYABLE SUB-SYSTEM
-    "                                                          ".
05  I-INPUT-EDIT-MSG    PICTURE X(132)  VALUE " EDIT ERROR IN INP
-    "UT RECORD.
-    "                                                          ".
05  IB-ERROR-MSG        PICTURE X(132)  VALUE " FILE MIS-MATCH JO
-    "B IS ABORTED.  DO NOT USE NEW MASTER.  EXAMINE DATA AND RE-R
-    "UN JOB.                                                   ".
05  IC-ERROR-HEADING    PICTURE X(132)  VALUE " ERROR REPORT FOR
-    "CHECK VOIDING PROGRAM AP504.  ACCOUNTS PAYABLE SUB-SYSTEM.
-    "                                                          ".

01  Q-CATEGORY-CODES.
   05 Q-STOP-PAY-CODE   PICTURE X       VALUE "S".
   05 Q-HAND-PAY-CODE   PICTURE X       VALUE "H".

01  S-ERROR-CODES.
   05 S-VEN-MATCH-CODE  PICTURE X       VALUE "R".
   05 S-DATE-MATCH-CODE PICTURE X       VALUE "S".

01  T-ERROR-CODES.
   05 T-DUPLICATE-CODE  PICTURE X       VALUE "D".

01  V-ERROR-CODES.
   05 V-CHK-CODE        PICTURE X       VALUE "N".
   05 V-VEN-CODE        PICTURE X       VALUE "V".
   05 V-DATE-CODE       PICTURE X       VALUE "I".
   05 V-CATEGORY-CODE   PICTURE X       VALUE "C".


LINKAGE SECTION.
01  PA-PRINTER-INTERFACE.
   05 PA-PROCESS.
```

```
     10 PA-PRINT-LINE       PICTURE X(132).
     10 PA-HEADINGS OCCURS 5 TIMES.
        15 PA-HEAD          PICTURE X(132).
   05 PC-CONTROL.
     10 PC-OP-CODE          PICTURE 9(4) COMP.
     10 PC-NUMBER-LINES PICTURE 9(4) COMP.
     10 PC-HEAD-LINES       PICTURE 9(4) COMP.
   05 PW-STABLE-WORK.
     10 PW-PAGE-END         PICTURE X.
     10 PW-PAGE-NUMBER      PICTURE 9(4) COMP.


01  QQ-WORKING-STORAGE.


02  RA-READER-INTERFACE.
  05 RA-PROCESS.
    10 RA-CARD-LINE         PICTURE X(80).
  05 RC-CONTROL.
    10 RC-EOF-FLAG          PICTURE X.
    10 RC-OP-CODE           PICTURE 9(4) COMP.
10  RAR-CARDS REDEFINES RA-CARD-LINE.
   15 RAR-CHECK-NUMBER                 PICTURE X(8).
   15 FILLER                           PICTURE X.
   15 RAR-VENDOR-IDENT                 PICTURE X(6).
   15 FILLER                           PICTURE X.
   15 RAR-ISSUE-DATE                   PICTURE X(6).
   15 FILLER                           PICTURE X(2).
   15 RAR-AMOUNT-PAID                  PICTURE X(6).
   15 FILLER                           PICTURE X(2).
   15 RAR-VOID-CATEGORY                PICTURE X.
   15 FILLER                           PICTURE X(47).

   02 FILLER                COMP-2 SYNC.

02  SA-ERROR-TABLE-INTERFACE.
   05 SA-PROCESS.
     10 SA-LINE             PICTURE X(132)
   05 SC-CONTROL.
     10 SC-OP-CODE          PICTURE 9(4) COMP.
     10 SC-NUMBER-SPACES PICTURE 9(4) COMP.
   05 SW-STABLE-WORK.
     10 SW-ERRTAB-LIMIT PICTURE 9(4) COMP.
     10 SW-ERROR-INDEX   PICTURE 9(4) COMP.
     10 SW-NUMBER-ERRORS PICTURE 9(4) COMP.
     10 SW-NUMBER-DUMPS  PICTURE 9(4) COMP.
     10 SW-ERROR-TABLE OCCURS 1 TO 100 TIMES
              DEPENDING ON SW-ERRTAB-LIMIT.
        15 SW-ERROR-REC  PICTURE X(132).

   02 FILLER                COMP-2 SYNC.

02  TA-TAPE-IN-INTERFACE.
   05 TA-PROCESS.
    10 TA-TAPE-LINE         PICTURE X(80).
   05 TC-CONTROL.
    10 TC-MASTER-EOF        PICTURE X.
    10 TC-OP-CODE           PICTURE 9(4) COMP.
```

```
10 TAR-TAPES REDEFINES TA-TAPE-LINE.
   15 TAR-VENDOR-IDENT            PICTURE X(6).
   15 TAR-VENDOR-NAME             PICTURE X(30).
   15 TAR-CHECK-NUMBER            PICTURE X(8).
   15 TAR-ISSUE-DATE              PICTURE X(6).
   15 TAR-INVOICE-NUMBER          PICTURE X(10).
   15 TAR-AMOUNT-PAID             PICTURE X(6).
   15 TAR-VOID-FLAG               PICTURE X.
   15 FILLER                      PICTURE X(13).

 02 FILLER               COMP-2 SYNC.

02  WL-CARD-WORK.
  05 WL-CARD-REC.
     10 WL-CHECK-NUMBER       PICTURE X(8).
     10 WL-VENDOR-IDENT       PICTURE X(6).
     10 WL-ISSUE-DATE         PICTURE X(6).
     10 WL-AMOUNT-PAID        PICTURE X(6).
     10 WL-VOID-CATEGORY      PICTURE X.
  05 WL-ERROR-NOTES.
     10 WL-ERROR-MSG.         PICTURE X(6).
     10 WL-ERROR-CODES.
        15 WL-CHK-ERR              PICTURE X.
        15 WL-VEN-ERR              PICTURE X.
        15 WL-DATE-ERR             PICTURE X.
        15 WL-AMOUNT-ERR           PICTURE X.
        15 WL-CATEGORY-ERR         PICTURE X.
        15 WL-DUPLICATE-ERR        PICTURE X.


 02 FILLER               COMP-2 SYNC.

02  WM-MASTER-WORK.
  05 WM-MASTER-RECORD.
     10 WM-VENDOR-IDENT           PICTURE X(6).
     10 WM-VENDOR-NAME            PICTURE X(30).
     10 WM-CHECK-NUMBER           PICTURE X(8).
     10 WM-ISSUE-DATE             PICTURE X(6).
     10 WM-INVOICE-NUMBER         PICTURE X(10).
     10 WM-AMOUNT-PAID            PICTURE X(6).
     10 WM-VOID-FLAG              PICTURE X.


02  WW-FLAGS-AND-INDICES.


   05 WW-BLOOP-INDEX      PICTURE 9(4) COMP.
   05 WW-DUP-LOOP         PICTURE 9(4) COMP.
   05 WW-ERR-LOOP         PICTURE 9(4) COMP.
   05 WW-GOOD-EDIT-FLAG   PICTURE X.
   05 WW-HEADING-LOOP     PICTURE 9(4) COMP.
   05 WW-MATCH-FLAG       PICTURE X.
   05 WW-MATCH-LOOP       PICTURE 9(4) COMP.
   05 WW-NO-DUP-FLAG      PICTURE X.
   05 WW-PRINTER-LOOP     PICTURE 9(4) COMP.
   05 WW-UPDATE-FLAG      PICTURE X.
   05 WW-ZLOOP            PICTURE 9(4) COMP.
```

```
    02 WX-WORKING-STORAGE  COMP-2 SYNC.


 PROCEDURE DIVISION.
     ENTRY "AP503" USING PA-PRINTER-INTERFACE
                         QQ-WORKING-STORAGE.

 AA-MAINLINE.
     PERFORM AB-INITIALIZE THRU ABX-INITIALIZE-X.
     PERFORM AF-DRIVER THRU AFX-DRIVER-X.
     PERFORM ZD-END-JOB THRU ZDX-END-JOB-X.
 AAX-MAINLINE-X.
     EXIT PROGRAM.



 AB-INITIALIZE.
     MOVE SPACES TO PA-PRINT-LINE.
     MOVE I-REPORT-HEADING TO PA-HEAD (1).
     MOVE 1 TO PC-HEAD-LINES.
     MOVE 58 TO PC-NUMBER-LINES.
     MOVE 1 TO PC-OP-CODE.
     CALL "PRINTER" USING PA-PRINTER-INTERFACE
                          WX-WORKING-STORAGE.
     CALL 'READER' USING RA-READER-INTERFACE.
     CALL 'TAPEIN' USING TA-TAPE-IN-INTERFACE.
     CALL 'READER' USING RA-READER-INTERFACE.
     CALL 'TAPEIN' USING TA-TAPE-IN-INTERFACE.
     CALL "ERRTAB" USING SA-ERROR-TABLE-INTERFACE
                         WX-WORKING-STORAGE.
 ABX-INITIALIZE-X.
     EXIT.

 AF-DRIVER.
         PERFORM ZA-FLUSH-OLD THRU ZAX-FLUSH-OLD-X
          PERFORM SM-PREMATURE THRU SMX-PREMATURE-X.
     PERFORM EN-DRIVER THRU ENX-DRIVER-X.
 AFX-DRIVER-X.
     EXIT.



 DA-DUP-CHECK.
          PERFORM RB-READ-INPUT THRU RBX-READ-INPUT-X
 DAX-DUP-CHECK-X.
     EXIT.



 DD-DETAIL-MATCH.
 DDX-DETAIL-MATCH-X.
     EXIT.
```

```
EA-EDIT-INPUT.
EAX-EDIT-INPUT-X.
    EXIT.


EN-DRIVER.
    PERFORM NN-FETCH-INPUT THRU NNX-FETCH-INPUT-X.
    PERFORM EA-EDIT-INPUT THRU EAX-EDIT-INPUT-X.
    PERFORM DA-DUP-CHECK THRU DAX-DUP-CHECK-X.
       PERFORM SA-EDIT-EXCPT THRU SAX-EDIT-EXCPT-X
    PERFORM MA-MATCH-CHECKS THRU MAX-MATCH-CHECKS-X.
ENX-DRIVER-X.
    EXIT.


MA-MATCH-CHECKS.
    PERFORM NM-FETCH-MASTER THRU NMX-FETCH-MASTER-X.
        PERFORM UA-UPDATE THRU UAX-UPDATE-X
    PERFORM SF-BAD-FILE THRU SFX-BAD-FILE-X.
    PERFORM DD-DETAIL-MATCH THRU DDX-DETAIL-MATCH-X.
        PERFORM SA-EDIT-EXCPT THRU SAX-EDIT-EXCPT-X
        PERFORM UA-UPDATE THRU UAX-UPDATE-X
    PERFORM UA-UPDATE THRU UAX-UPDATE-X.
MAX-MATCH-CHECKS-X.
    EXIT.


NM-FETCH-MASTER.
    CALL 'TAPEIN' USING TA-TAPE-IN-INTERFACE.
NMX-FETCH-MASTER-X.
    EXIT.


NN-FETCH-INPUT.
    CALL 'READER' USING RA-READER-INTERFACE.
NNX-FETCH-INPUT-X.
    EXIT.


RB-READ-INPUT.
    CALL 'READER' USING RA-READER-INTERFACE.
RBX-READ-INPUT-X.
    EXIT.


SA-EDIT-EXCPT.
    CALL "ERRTAB" USING SA-ERROR-TABLE-INTERFACE
                        WX-WORKING-STORAGE.
SAX-EDIT-EXCPT-X.
    EXIT.
```

```
SF-BAD-FILE.
    CALL "ERRTAB" USING SA-ERROR-TABLE-INTERFACE
                        WX-WORKING-STORAGE.
    MOVE IB-ERROR-MSG TO PA-PRINT LINE.
    MOVE 4 TO PC-NUMBER-LINES.
    CALL "PRINTER" USING PA-PRINTER-INTERFACE
                         WX-WORKING-STORAGE.
SFX-BAD-FILE-X.
    EXIT.



SM-PREMATURE.
    CALL "ERRTAB" USING SA-ERROR-TABLE-INTERFACE
                        WX-WORKING-STORAGE.
    CALL "PRINTER" USING PA-PRINTER-INTERFACE
                         WX-WORKING-STORAGE.
SMX-PREMATURE-X.
    EXIT.



TP-END-PAGE.
    MOVE SPACES TO PA-PRINT-LINE.
    MOVE 58 TO PC-NUMBER-LINES.
    MOVE IC-ERROR-HEADING TO PA-HEAD (1).
    CALL "PRINTER" USING PA-PRINTER-INTERFACE
                         WX-WORKING-STORAGE.
TPX-END-PAGE-X.
    EXIT.



TR-TABLE-LOOP.
    CALL "PRINTER" USING PA-PRINTER-INTERFACE
                         WX-WORKING-STORAGE.
TRX-TABLE-LOOP-X.
    EXIT.



UA-UPDATE.
    PERFORM UN-UPDATE-WRITE THRU UNX-UPDATE-WRITE-X.
    CALL "PRINTER" USING PA-PRINTER-INTERFACE
                         WX-WORKING-STORAGE.
UAC-CYCLE-LOOP.
        PERFORM NM-FETCH-MASTER THRU NMX-FETCH-MASTER-X
UAX-UPDATE-X.
    EXIT.



UN-UPDATE-WRITE.
UNX-UPDATE-WRITE-X.
    EXIT.
```

```
ZA-FLUSH-OLD.
    PERFORM ZL-FLUSH-LOOP THRU ZLX-FLUSH-LOOP-X
ZAX-FLUSH-OLD-X.
    EXIT.


ZD-END-JOB.
    CALL "PRINTER" USING PA-PRINTER-INTERFACE
                         WX-WORKING-STORAGE.
    PERFORM TP-END-PAGE THRU TPX-END-PAGE-X.
    PERFORM TR-TABLE-LOOP THRU TRX-TABLE-LOOP-X
    PERFORM ZZ-CLOSE THRU ZZX-CLOSE-X.
ZDX-END-JOB-X.
    EXIT.


ZL-FLUSH-LOOP.
    PERFORM NM-FETCH-MASTER THRU NMX-FETCH-MASTER-X.
    PERFORM UN-UPDATE-WRITE THRU UNX-UPDATE-WRITE-X.
ZLX-FLUSH-LOOP-X.
    EXIT.


ZZ-CLOSE.
    CALL "ERRTAB" USING SA-ERROR-TABLE-INTERFACE
                        WX-WORKING-STORAGE.
ZZX-CLOSE-X.
    EXIT.

ZZZ-END.
    STOP RUN.
```

```
IDENTIFICATION DIVISION.
PROGRAM-ID.  RDSUB.
REMARKS.
ENVIRONMENT DIVISION.
CONFIGURATION SECTION.
SOURCE-COMPUTER. IBM-360-F40.
OBJECT-COMPUTER. IBM-360-F40.
INPUT-OUTPUT SECTION.
FILE-CONTROL.
    SELECT A-CARDS-IN   ASSIGN TO SYS010-UR-2540R-S.
DATA DIVISION.
FILE SECTION.
FD  A-CARDS-IN
    LABEL RECORDS ARE OMITTED
    DATA RECORDS IS A-CARD-REC.
01  A-CARD-REC.
   05 A-DATA                        PICTURE X(80).
LINKAGE SECTION.
01  R-READER-INTERFACE.
  05 RA-PROCESS.
    10 RA-CARD-LINE      PICTURE X(80).
  05 RC-CONTROL.
    10 RC-OP-CODE        PICTURE 9(4) COMP.
    10 RC-EOF-FLAG       PICTURE X.
PROCEDURE DIVISION.
    ENTRY 'READER' USING R-READER-INTERFACE.
A-MAINLINE.
AC-OPEN.
AH-READ.
AR-CLOSE.
AX-EXIT.
    EXIT PROGRAM.
```

```
IDENTIFICATION DIVISION.
PROGRAM-ID.  TPSUB.
REMARKS.
ENVIRONMENT DIVISION.
CONFIGURATION SECTION.
SOURCE-COMPUTER. IBM-360-F40.
OBJECT-COMPUTER. IBM-360-F40.
INPUT-OUTPUT SECTION.
FILE-CONTROL.
    SELECT A-TAPE-IN    ASSIGN TO SYS007-UT-2400-S.
DATA DIVISION.
FILE SECTION.
FD  A-TAPE-IN
    BLOCK CONTAINS 80 CHARACTERS
    LABEL RECORDS ARE OMITTED
    DATA RECORDS IS A-CARD-REC.
01  A-CARD-REC.
   05 A-DATA                    PICTURE X(80).
LINKAGE SECTION.
01  R-READER-INTERFACE.
  05 RA-PROCESS.
    10 RA-CARD-LINE      PICTURE X(80).
  05 RC-CONTROL.
    10 RC-EOF-FLAG       PICTURE X.
    10 RC-OP-CODE        PICTURE 9(4) COMP.
PROCEDURE DIVISION.
    ENTRY 'TAPEIN' USING R-READER-INTERFACE.
A-MAINLINE.
AC-OPEN.
AH-READ.
AR-CLOSE.
AX-EXIT.
    EXIT PROGRAM.
```

```
IDENTIFICATION DIVISION.
PROGRAM-ID. ERRORTABLE.
REMARKS.    SYSTEM:     UTILITY
            END OF REMARKS.
ENVIRONMENT DIVISION.
CONFIGURATION SECTION.
SOURCE-COMPUTER. IBM-360-F40.
OBJECT-COMPUTER. IBM-360-F40.
INPUT-OUTPUT SECTION.
FILE-CONTROL.
    SELECT E-ERROR-FILE ASSIGN TO SYS011-UR-2540P-S.
DATA DIVISION.
FILE SECTION.
FD  E-ERROR-FILE
    LABEL RECORDS ARE OMITTED
    DATA RECORD IS E-ERROR-IMAGE.
01  E-ERROR-IMAGE.
   05 E-ERROR-REC        PICTURE X(80).
LINKAGE SECTION.
01  T-INTERFACE.
   05 T-PROCESS-DATA.
     10 T-LINE           PICTURE X(132).
   05 C-CONTROL-DATA.
     10 C-OP-CODE        PICTURE 9(4) COMP.
     10 C-SPACE-LINES    PICTURE 9(4) COMP.
   05 W-STABLE-WORK-DATA.
     10 W-ERRTAB-LIMIT   PICTURE 9(4) COMP.
     10 W-ERROR-INDEX    PICTURE 9(4) COMP.
     10 W-NUMBER-ERRORS PICTURE 9(4) COMP.
     10 W-NUMBER-DUMPS   PICTURE 9(4) COMP.
     10 W-ERROR-TABLE OCCURS 1 TO 100 TIMES
           DEPENDING ON W-ERRTAB-LIMIT.
       15 W-ERROR-REC    PICTURE X(132).
01  WX-PERISHABLE.
   05 WX-LOOP-INDEX      PICTURE 9(4) COMP.
   05 WX-DUMP-INDEX      PICTURE 9(4) COMP.
   05 WX-BRANCH-INDEX    PICTURE 9(4) COMP.
PROCEDURE DIVISION.
    ENTRY 'ERRTAB' USING T-INTERFACE
                         WX-PERISHABLE.
AA-BEGIN.
AAB-INITIALIZE.
    PERFORM BA-INIT THRU BAX-INIT-X.
AAC-PROCESS.
    PERFORM TA-PROCESS THRU TAX-PROCESS-X.
AAD-CLEAN-UP.
    PERFORM ZA-CLEAN-UP THRU ZAX-CLEAN-UP-X.
AAX-BEGIN-X.
    EXIT PROGRAM.

BA-INIT.
BAX-INIT-X.
    EXIT.

TA-PROCESS.
    PERFORM TN-TABLE-LOOP THRU TNX-TABLE-LOOP-X.
        PERFORM TS-SPACE-LOOP THRU TSX-SPACE-LOOP-X
TAX-PROCESS-X.
```

```
    EXIT.

TN-TABLE-LOOP.
         PERFORM ZN-FLUSH-LOOP THRU ZNX-FLUSH-LOOP-X
TNX-TABLE-LOOP-X.
    EXIT.

TS-SPACE-LOOP.
    PERFORM TN-TABLE-LOOP THRU TNX-TABLE-LOOP-X.
TSX-SPACE-LOOP-X.
    EXIT.

WE-WRITE.
WEX-WRITE-X.
    EXIT.

ZA-CLEAN-UP.
    PERFORM ZN-FLUSH-LOOP THRU ZNX-FLUSH-LOOP-X
ZAP-CLOSE-FILE.
ZAX-CLEAN-UP-X.
    EXIT.

ZN-FLUSH-LOOP.
    PERFORM WE-WRITE THRU WEX-WRITE-X.
ZNX-FLUSH-LOOP-X.
    EXIT.
```

```
IDENTIFICATION DIVISION.
PROGRAM-ID. PRINT.
REMARKS.      SYSTEM:      UTILITY
              PROGRAM:     'PRINTER' USING P-W-DATA-INTERFACE
                                           WX-PERISHABLE-WORK-DATA
              PROCESS:     ON OPERATION CODE 0
                             OPEN FILE
                           ON OPERATION CODE OF 1
                           PRINTS CONTENTS OF P-PRINT-LINE
                             FOLLOWED BY NUMBER OF BLANK LINES
                             SPECIFIED IN C-NUMBER-LINES.
                             ON PAGE OVERFLOW WRITES ONE TO FIVE
                             LINES OF HEADINGS (IN P-HEADINGS)
                             SPECIFIED BY C-HEAD-LINES THEN SPACES
                             TO BELOW HEADER AREA
                             W-PAGE-NUMBER IS INCREMENTED BY 1 ON
                             PAGE OVERFLOW
                             W-PAGE-END'S LAST VALUE IS AVAILABLE TO
                             CALLING PROGRAM
                             TO FORCE HEADERS MOVE SPACES TO P-PRINT
                              -LINE AND SET C-NUMBER-LINES TO MORE
                             THAN 57
                             ON PAGE OVERFLOW ANY REMAINING BLANK
                             LINES ARE NOT PRINTED
                           ON OPERATION CODE OF 2
                             CLOSES FILE
              INTERFACES
              INPUT:
              ARGUMENT LIST
                      P-W-DATA-INTERFACE  GROUP NAME
                      P-PROCESS-DATA      GROUP NAME
                        P-PRINT-LINE      LINE TO BE PRINTED
                        P-HEADINGS        OCCURS NAME
                        P-HEAD-RECS       1 TO 5 LINES OF HEADINGS
                                            FOR THE TOP OF THE PAGE
                      C-CONTROL-DATA      GROUP NAME
                        C-OP-CODE         CONTROLS OPEN PROCESS OR
                                            CLOSE OPERATION
                        C-NUMBER-LINES    NUMBER OF BLANK LINES TO
                                            COME AFTER A PRINTED
                                            LINE
                        C-HEAD-LINES      NUMBER OF LINES OF HEAD-
                                            INGS, 1 TO 5
              WORK:   WX-PERISHABLE-WORK-DATA
                                          GROUP NAME
                        WX-BRANCH-CODE    C-OP-CODE PLUS 1 FOR
                                            GO TO DEPENDING
                        WX-HEADER-INDEX   NO INITIAL VALUE
                                          SET BY LOOP IN WO TO
                                            CONTROL HEADING LINES
                                            PRINTED
                                          LIMITED BY C-HEAD-LINES
                        WX-NUMBER-LINES   PRINT LINE PLUS BLANK
                                            LINES REQUESTED
                        WX-PRINTER-INDEX  NO INITIAL VALUE
                                          SET BY LOOP IN WA TO
                                            CONTROL NUMBER OF LINES
                                            PRINTED = PRINT LINE
```

```
                                              PLUS BLANK LINES
                                            LIMITED BY WX-NUMBER-
                                              LINES OR 'Y' W-PAGE-END
                                            AVAILABLE TO CALLING PRO-
                                              GRAM AFTER FIRST CALL
                           WX-SPACE-INDEX   NO INITIAL VALUE
                                            SET BY LOOP IN WO TO
                                              CONTROL SPACING BEYOND
                                              HEADER AREA
                                            LIMITED BY WX-SPACE-LIMIT
                           WX-SPACE-LIMIT   THE REMAINDER OF SPACE IN
                                              HEADING AREA ON FORM
                                              AFTER HEADINGS HAVE
                                              BEEN PRINTED
                         Z-CONSTANTS        GROUP NAME FOR LOCAL
                                              WORKING-STORAGE
                           Z-HEADLINES      NUMBER OF LINES IN
                                              HEADING AREA ON FORM
                                              MOORE 1412TRH
                            Z-HEADSPACE     NUMBER OF LINES TO SPACE
                                            FROM PAGE END TO TOP
                                            OF PAGE
                OUTPUT:
                ARGUMENT LIST
                         W-STABLE-WORK-DATA GROUP NAME
                           W-PAGE-END       FLAG SIGNALLING END OF
                                              PAGE
                                            NO INITIAL VALUE
                                            SET TO 'N' IN WA
                                            RESET TO 'Y' IN WY
                                              ON PAGE END SENSING
                                            TESTED IN WE TO DETERMINE
                                              IF HEADINGS ARE TO BE
                                              PRINTED
                                            TESTED IN WA TO PREVENT
                                              BLANK LINES FROM CONT-
                                              INUING OVER PAGE END
                           W-PAGE-NUMBER    CURRENT PAGE NUMBER
                                              SET TO 1 IN BA
                                              IF OTHER START VALUE
                                              DESIRED SET AFTER
                                              OPENING CALL
                                              PRINTER INCREMENTS IT
                                              BY 1 EACH PAGE END
                FILES
                             A-PRINT-LIST   PRINTER OUTPUT FILE
                LOGICAL:     NO SUB-PROGRAMS ARE CALLED
                             REQUIRES 6 HALF-WORDS PERISHIBLE STORAGE
                             USE  ASSGN SYS012,X'00E'
                             END OF REMARKS.
ENVIRONMENT DIVISION.
CONFIGURATION SECTION.
SOURCE-COMPUTER. IBM-360-F40.
OBJECT-COMPUTER. IBM-360-F40.
INPUT-OUTPUT SECTION.
FILE-CONTROL.
    SELECT A-PRINT-LIST ASSIGN TO SYS012-UR-1403-S
    RESERVE NO ALTERNATE AREA.
```

```
 DATA DIVISION.
*
 FILE SECTION.
 FD  A-PRINT-LIST
     LABEL RECORDS ARE OMITTED
     DATA RECORD IS A-PRINT-LINE.
 01  A-PRINT-LINE.
    05 A-REC                PICTURE X(132).
*
 WORKING-STORAGE SECTION.
 01  Z-CONSTANTS.
   05 Z-HEADLINES           PICTURE 9(4) COMP VALUE 5.
   05 Z-HEADSPACE           PICTURE 9(4) COMP VALUE 3.
*
 LINKAGE SECTION.
 01  P-W-DATA-INTERFACE.
 02  P-PROCESS-DATA.
     05  P-PRINT-LINE       PICTURE X(132).
     05  P-HEADINGS OCCURS 5 TIMES.
       10  P-HEAD-RECS      PICTURE X(132).
 02  C-CONTROL-DATA.
     05  C-OP-CODE          PICTURE 9(4) COMP.
     05  C-NUMBER-LINES     PICTURE 9(4) COMP.
     05  C-HEAD-LINES       PICTURE 9(4) COMP.
 02  W-STABLE-WORK-DATA.
     05 W-PAGE-END          PICTURE X.
     05 W-PAGE-NUMBER       PICTURE 9(4) COMP.
 01  WX-PERISHABLE-WORK-DATA.
     05 WX-BRANCH-CODE      PICTURE 9(4) COMP.
     05 WX-HEADER-INDEX     PICTURE 9(4) COMP.
     05 WX-NUMBER-LINES     PICTURE 9(4) COMP.
     05 WX-PRINTER-INDEX PICTURE 9(4) COMP.
     05 WX-SPACE-INDEX      PICTURE 9(4) COMP.
     05 WX-SPACE-LIMIT      PICTURE 9(4) COMP.
*
*
*
 PROCEDURE DIVISION.
     ENTRY 'PRINTER' USING   P-W-DATA-INTERFACE
                             WX-PERISHABLE-WORK-DATA.
*
 AA-NOTE.
     NOTE        INCREMENT OP CODE AND BRANCH TO PERFORM CODE
                 PROGRAM EXIT HERE.
 AA-BRANCH.
     ADD 1 C-OP-CODE GIVING WX-BRANCH-CODE.
     GO TO
         AAB-INITIALIZE
         AAC-PROCESS
         AAD-CLOSE
         DEPENDING ON WX-BRANCH-CODE.
*
 AAB-INITIALIZE.
     PERFORM BA-INIT THRU BAX-INIT-X.
     GO TO AAX-BRANCH-X.
*
 AAC-PROCESS.
     PERFORM WA-BEGIN THRU WAX-BEGIN-X.
```

```
     GO TO AAX-BRANCH-X.
*
 AAD-CLOSE.
     PERFORM ZA-CLOSE THRU ZAX-CLOSE-X.
*
 AAX-BRANCH-X.
     EXIT PROGRAM.
*
*
*
 BA-NOTE.
     NOTE           OPEN FILE.
 BA-INIT.
     OPEN OUTPUT A-PRINT-LIST.
 BAX-INIT-X.
     EXIT.
*
*
*
 WA-NOTE.
     NOTE           IF NO BLANKS REQUIRED SET LOOP CONTROL TO 1
                    OTHERWISE ADD 1 TO BLANKS REQUIRED
                    MOVE PRINT LINE TO OUTPUT BUFFER
                    SET PAGE END FLAG
                    PERFORM PRINT LOOP AND EXIT AFTER ALL LINES OR
                    END OF PAGE.
 WA-BEGIN.
     IF C-NUMBER-LINES LESS THAN 1
          MOVE 1 TO WX-NUMBER-LINES
          GO TO WAC-CONTINUE.
     ADD 1 C-NUMBER-LINES GIVING WX-NUMBER-LINES.
 WAC-CONTINUE.
     MOVE P-PRINT-LINE TO A-PRINT-LINE.
     MOVE 'N' TO W-PAGE-END.
     PERFORM WE-PRINT-LOOP THRU WEX-PRINT-LOOP-X
          VARYING WX-PRINTER-INDEX FROM 1 BY 1 UNTIL
          WX-PRINTER-INDEX GREATER THAN WX-NUMBER-LINES
          OR
          W-PAGE-END = 'Y'.
 WAX-BEGIN-X.
     EXIT.
*
*
*
 WE-NOTE.
     NOTE           WRITE LINE THAN FILL OUTPUT
                    BUFFER WITH SPACES
                    IF END OF PAGE ADD 1 TO PAGE COUNT AND PERFORM
                      END OF PAGE PROCESSING
                    OTHERWISE EXIT.
 WE-PRINT-LOOP.
     PERFORM WY-WRITE THRU WYX-WRITE-X.
     MOVE SPACES TO A-PRINT-LINE.
     IF W-PAGE-END = 'Y'
          ADD 1 TO W-PAGE-NUMBER
          PERFORM WO-PAGE-END THRU WOX-PAGE-END-X.
 WEX-PRINT-LOOP-X.
     EXIT.
```

```
*
*
*
 WO-NOTE.
     NOTE          SPACE TO TOP OF NEXT PAGE
                   PERFORM HEADINGS LOOP
                   COMPUTE REMAINING SPACE IN HEADER AREA
                   MOVE SPACES TO OUTPUT BUFFER
                   PERFORM SPACING LOOP AND EXIT.
 WO-PAGE-END.
     PERFORM WQ-TOP-PAGE THRU WQX-TOP-PAGE-X
         VARYING WX-HEADER-INDEX FROM 1 BY 1 UNTIL
         WX-HEADER-INDEX GREATER THAN Z-HEADSPACE.
     PERFORM WR-HEAD-LOOP THRU WRX-HEAD-LOOP-X
         VARYING WX-HEADER-INDEX FROM 1 BY 1 UNTIL
         WX-HEADER-INDEX GREATER THAN C-HEAD-LINES.
     SUBTRACT C-HEAD-LINES FROM Z-HEADLINES GIVING WX-SPACE-LIMIT.
     MOVE SPACES TO A-PRINT-LINE.
     PERFORM WY-WRITE THRU WYX-WRITE-X
         VARYING WX-SPACE-INDEX FROM 1 BY 1 UNTIL
         WX-SPACE-INDEX GREATER THAN WX-SPACE-LIMIT.
 WOX-PAGE-END-X.
     EXIT.
*
*
*
 WQ-NOTE.
     NOTE          LOOP, WRITING SPACES.
 WQ-TOP-PAGE.
     PERFORM WY-WRITE THRU WYX-WRITE-X.
 WQX-TOP-PAGE-X.
     EXIT.
*
*
*
 WR-NOTE.
     NOTE          MOVE EACH HEADER TO OUTPUT BUFFER
                   PERFORM WRITE AND EXIT.
 WR-HEAD-LOOP.
     MOVE P-HEAD-RECS (WX-HEADER-INDEX) TO A-PRINT-LINE.
     PERFORM WY-WRITE THRU WYX-WRITE-X.
 WRX-HEAD-LOOP-X.
     EXIT.
*
*
*
 WY-NOTE.
     NOTE          WRITE SIGNALING END OF PAGE AND EXIT.
 WY-WRITE.
     WRITE A-PRINT-LINE AFTER ADVANCING 1 LINES
         AT END-OF-PAGE
         MOVE 'Y' TO W-PAGE-END.
 WYX-WRITE-X.
     EXIT.
*
*
*
 ZA-NOTE.
```

```
    NOTE         CLOSE FILE.
ZA-CLOSE.
    CLOSE A-PRINT-LIST.
ZAX-CLOSE-X.
    EXIT.
```

INDEX